IMAGES
of America

LAKE COUNTY SCHOOLHOUSES

On the Cover: This is the Lakeport Grammar School, built around 1867. It served the students in and around Lakeport until 1880, when a new, larger school was built. (Courtesy of Historic Courthouse Museum.)

IMAGES
of America

LAKE COUNTY SCHOOLHOUSES

Antone R.E. Pierucci

ARCADIA
PUBLISHING

ISBN 978-1-4671-1621-3

Published by Arcadia Publishing
Charleston, South Carolina

Printed in the United States of America

Library of Congress Control Number: 2015952498

For all general information, please contact Arcadia Publishing:
Telephone 843-853-2070
Fax 843-853-0044
E-mail sales@arcadiapublishing.com
For customer service and orders:
Toll-Free 1-888-313-2665

Visit us on the Internet at www.arcadiapublishing.com

To my parents, for instilling in me my love for history.
Having old parents isn't such a bad thing after all.

Contents

ACKNOWLEDGMENTS

Many people assisted me in the research and writing of this book—too many to thank individually. To my longtime friend and sounding board Sydney Taylor, thank you for reading the manuscript of this book. Special thanks also go to Anita Crabtree, who has herself researched the history of schools in Lake County in her role as a genealogist and provided me with information and insight. Thanks also go to Jan Cook of the Lake County Library, whose keen editing eye helped me avoid silly errors. (Any errors that remain are my own.) And of course, thanks are due to Jane and John Weaver, Les Parker, and Tom Malley and all the other hardworking volunteers who helped preserve the Lower Lake Historic Schoolhouse, which served as the inspiration for this book. Unless otherwise stated, the photographs in this book are courtesy of the Historic Courthouse Museum in Lakeport, which was first established as the Lake County Museum in 1934 and has been collecting Lake County history ever since.

INTRODUCTION

Whether sitting in a plowed field out in the countryside or tucked between modern cement buildings in the heart of a downtown, these rustic clapboard-sided structures strike a chord within most viewers. In many cases, rural schoolhouses—especially one-room schoolhouses—evoke a sense of nostalgia, a word derived from the Greek *nostos* (return home) and *algia* (longing). Nostalgia, in a literal sense, means homesick. As education historian Johnathan Zimmerman points out, one-room schools appropriately evoke this sense of homesickness because they were at once schools and homes. Far from the large, modern consolidated schools of several hundred students, the rural schools of yesteryear were more intimate in size. This duality of home and school was especially prominent in rural, isolated areas where they served as the backdrop to some of the most important moments in a young child's life. From the first meeting of life-long friends to learning how to read and write, schools held a special place in the lives of rural Americans.

If nothing else, even to this day, life in Lake County is characteristically rural.

Well into the 20th century, the most direct way to reach the county seat of Lakeport, a visitor had to travel on the line of the Northwestern Pacific Railroad from San Francisco to Pieta, which took four hours by a combination of ferry and train. From there, the visitor could travel by automobile to Highland Springs and then on to Lakeport, but only in the summer since the roads over the mountains were treacherous at the best of times. In the winter, a stagecoach was marginally safer.

This isolation was two-sided; after all, what keeps people out also keeps people in. When asked why his school never had an organized sports team, Lower Lake resident John Jago asked, "Who would we have played? A round-trip to Burns Valley [the closest school to the one in Lower Lake] took several hours." It is no doubt because of this isolation that schoolhouses themselves played such important roles in the communities they served. Remembering her time in a one-room school in 1890s Lake County, Helen Rocca remarked that "the two most important buildings in town were the dance hall and the schoolhouse." Sometimes they were one and the same, as Mary Jean Sullivan remembered of the Lower Lake Schoolhouse: "I remember public dances held at the school that our parents would take us to and us kids would fall asleep on the benches while the parents danced."

It might be true that these rural schoolhouses are now largely viewed through the rose-tinted glasses of nostalgia, but this is not always the case. In truth, schoolhouses embody the same vices and prejudices as those who built them. Until the early 1930s, Lake County schoolhouses were segregated, and the Native American children in the area either received no education, were shipped to boarding schools out of the county, or were placed in federal, all-Indian day schools within the county. Even for those Anglo-American children who were allowed to attend public school, the experience of spending days locked away in cramped quarters with upwards of several dozen other students left a dark memory in some people's minds.

When historic preservation efforts kicked off in Lake County in the 1970s, these rural schools were some of the earliest structures flagged as historically significant. True, the sheer ubiquity of the buildings might have something to do with this early interest; at the turn of the 20th century, there were upwards of 44 schoolhouses in the county. However, the importance of these iconic buildings in the lives of those striving to preserve them was more of a factor than simple numbers. This was certainly the sentiment when four septuagenarians rallied to raise funds to save the Lower Lake Schoolhouse in the late 1980s. Now, nearly 30 years later, thousands of visitors—including students on tours—visit the Lower Lake Historic Schoolhouse Museum each year. Alternatively coming because they were simply passing through, they read about the place in the newspaper or their teacher made them go, each visitor is confronted with the history of the building and the community it served.

This book is an attempt to compile a similar history, one that uses historical photographs to chronicle the lives of rural Californians in Lake County. In writing this book, a few primary sources were especially valuable, including the Lake County Board of Supervisors minutes, which detail the opening and closing of each school district. These minutes are housed in the Lake County Board of Supervisors' Office in Lakeport, California. Another useful source was the annual reports submitted to the state by the Lake County superintendent of common schools, which are housed in the California State Archives. When using a primary source that is not listed here or in the select bibliography at the end of the book, the author cites it within the caption itself.

Lake County is lucky enough to have a significant collection of photographs of early schoolhouses that act as windows into the past. Granted, many of these photographs are staged, with the outfits, posture, and gaze of those pictured carefully arranged by either the photographer, the photographed, or both. However, some pictures within this book seem to actually capture an authentic moment in time; the viewer is dropped into the middle of things, no longer a historical voyeur but an active participant in the scene itself. When thought of as simple buildings of wood, lead paint, and iron nails, schoolhouses themselves are closed windows to the past, providing a very narrow view of history. However, when understood as the backdrop for innumerable social activities, the history of schools can be used as a means to better understand the people whom they served or did not serve. Whether readers are looking at the following photographs with a feeling of homesickness or critical judgement, the author invites them to jump in and explore the history of Lake County via its rural schools.

One

History of Lake County 1856–1900

As the first wagon trains of American settlers struggled down the grade from Napa into the Clear Lake Basin in the early 1850s, public education had not yet been established in California. In fact, it was a contentious topic being argued in local newspapers and on the floor of legislative houses across the United States. The massive expansion westward at the time only served to magnify the issue as new communities arose out of what were once empty prairies and isolated mountain ranges. After securing food and shelter, the next concern for pioneers of the American west increasingly became education. These communities and the states they formed were, in effect, tabulae rassae—free to incorporate the new ideas of education into their very constitutions.

Informed by the varying circumstances of the communities they served, rural schools in California developed in uniquely local ways. To understand the history of schools and schooling in Lake County is to discover the true character of the communities that have called this land home. And so, this story must start at the beginning, with a brief history of early Lake County.

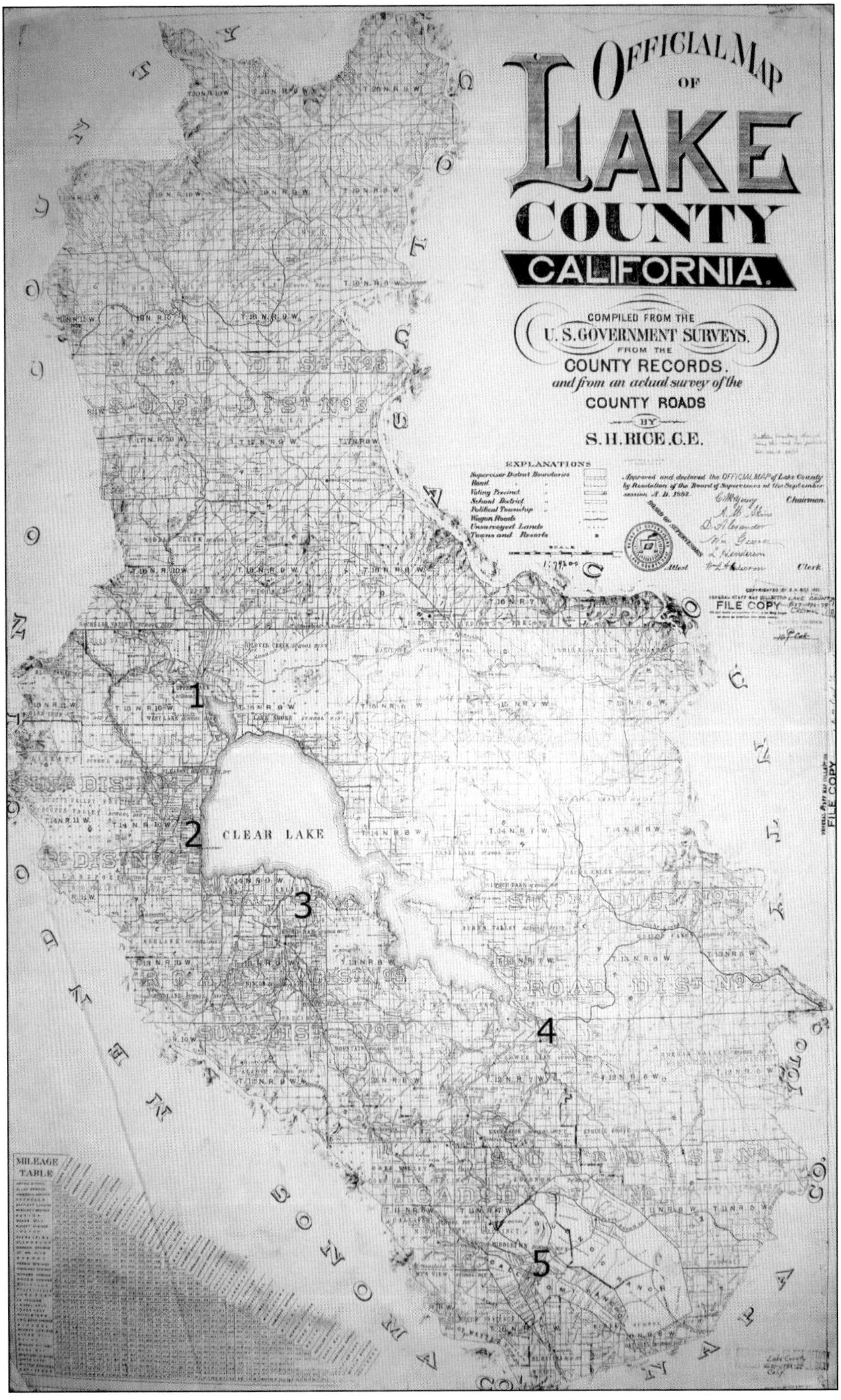

Official Map of
Lake County
California.
Compiled from the
U. S. Government Surveys.
from the
County Records.
and from an actual survey of the
County Roads
by
S. H. Rice. C.E.
Explanations
Clear Lake
Mileage Table
Sonoma
Napa
Yolo Co.
1
2
3
4
5

Lake County is a land of mountains and valleys, a dramatic result of violent, albeit slow, tectonic movement. Girding in the Clear Lake basin to the west are the Mayacamas, a series of mountains that include Mount St. Helena and Cobb Mountain. To the east are the no-name mountains of the Coastal Range, and to the north is Mendocino National Forest. Most of the good farming land is situated in valleys along the western and southern shores of Clear Lake, to which settlers quickly flocked. Within a very short time, towns arose: Upper Lake on the northern shores of Clear Lake (1), Lakeport (2) and Kelseyville (3) on the western shore, and Lower Lake to the south (4). There was also the small town of Middletown (5), so named because it was halfway between Calistoga to the south and Lower Lake to the northeast. The eastern shore of the lake lacked the same flat topography that attracted farmers to the west, so the population to the east never grew beyond the occasional sprawling ranch.

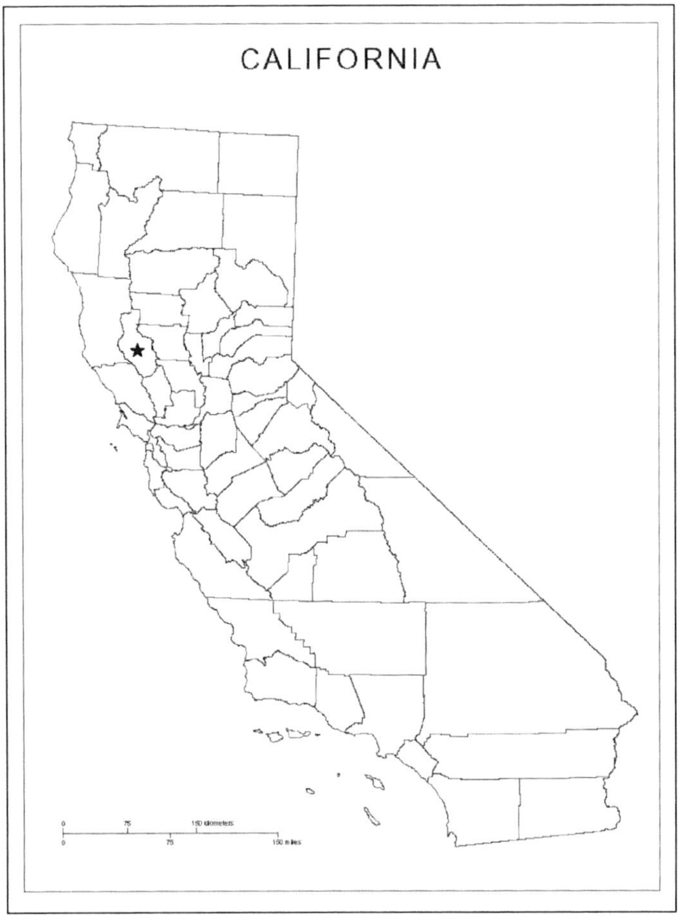

Lake County is bounded to the west by Mendocino County, to the south by Sonoma and Napa Counties, and to the east by Yolo, Colusa, and Glen Counties. Although well positioned, the county's rough terrain prevented it from ever fully realizing its potential as a crossroads of trade between the California coast and the Central Valley.

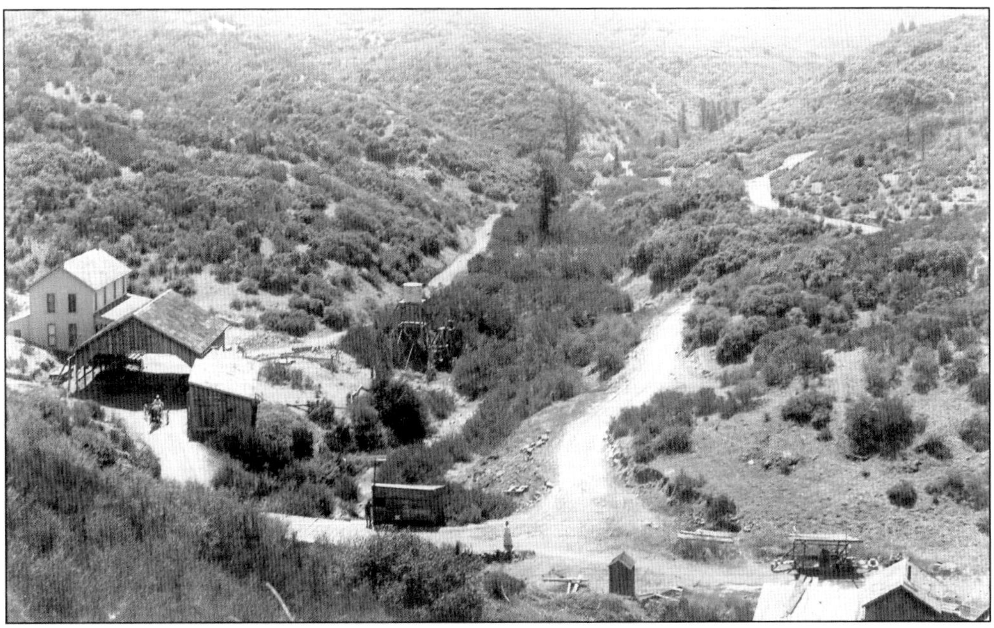

From the 1850s until the 1910s, only stagecoaches could make the trek into Lake County. Developed from of age-old Native American hunting trails, these routes proved treacherous to passenger coaches and nearly impassible for freight wagons. Pictured here is the Hopland toll road, which wound a treacherous path into Lake County from the west.

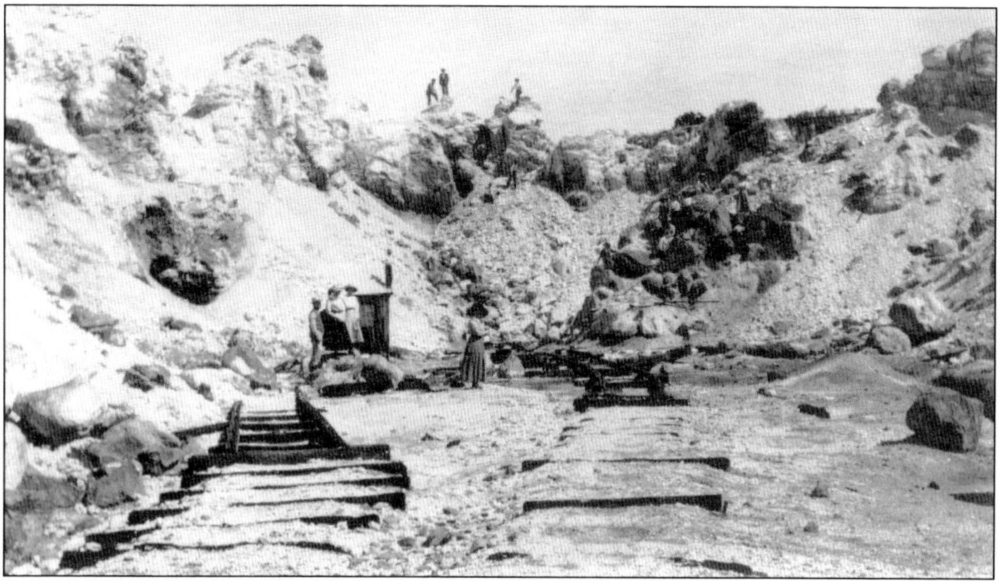

These same mountains and valleys that made travel difficult provided wealth to those hardy settlers who made the trek into the Clear Lake basin. From mercury to borax and everything in between, riches were hidden beneath the land for those with the resources and drive to retrieve them. Located along the southeastern shores of Clear Lake, the Sulphur Bank Mine operated throughout the 19th century. The image below shows the remains of one of the mine's brick furnaces, which were used to process the sulfur. Small communities grew up around these mines, and schools were built for the children of the miners.

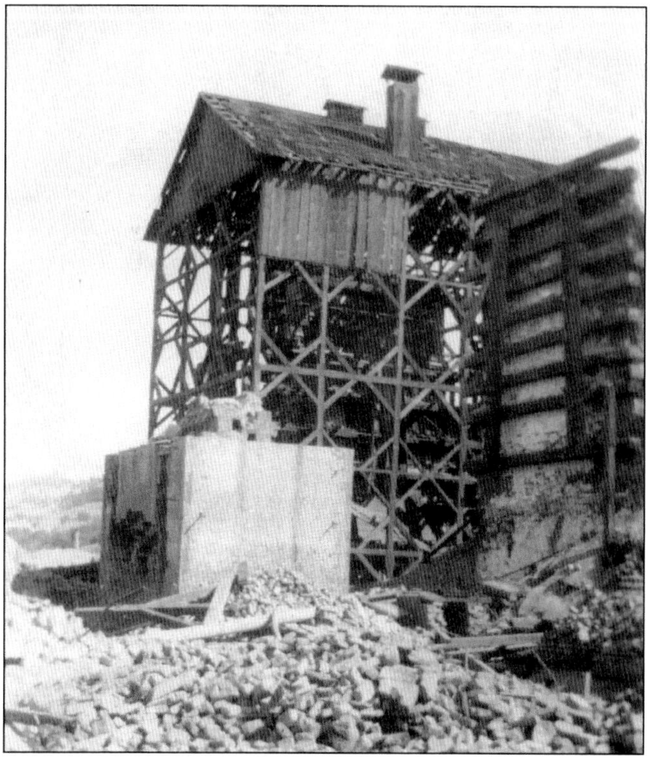

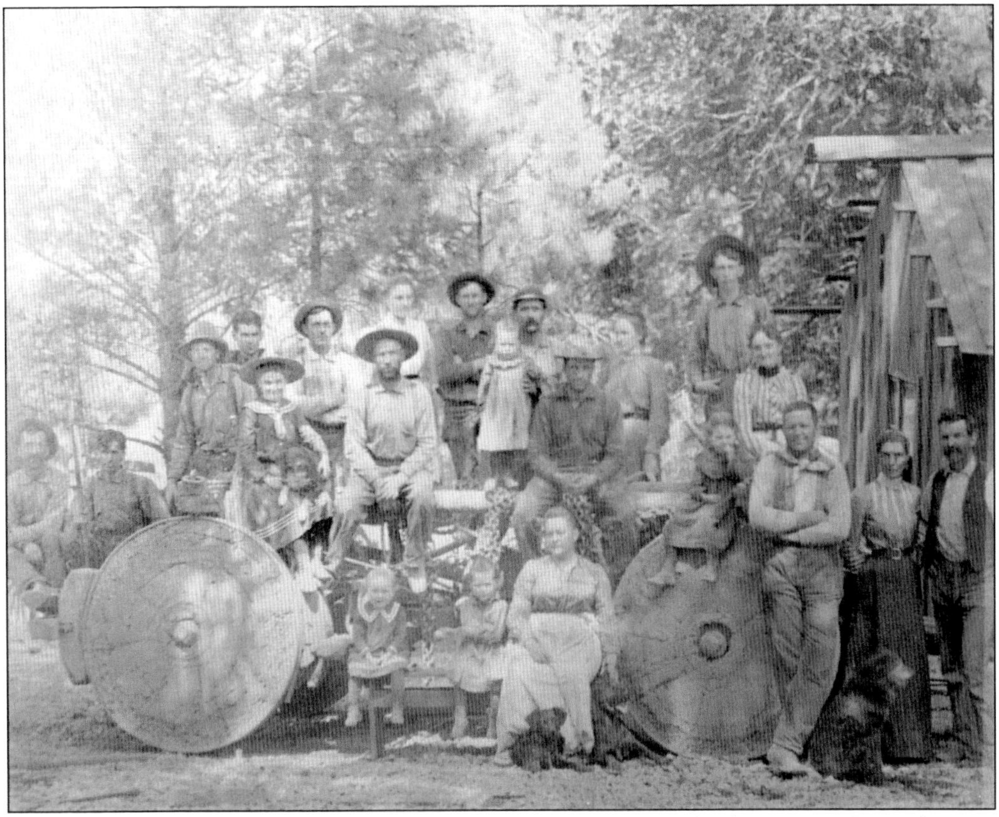

Minerals and precious metals were not the only natural bounties of Lake County. From the very beginning, logging was a major industry along the fir- and pine-crested mountains surrounding the lake. One of the earliest schools in the county was constructed in the 1860s to serve the children of a logging camp near modern-day Lucerne. In the picture above, the Akers family poses around one of their homemade carts for hauling felled trees out of the forest. Below, M.B. Elliot poses in front of a tractor at the Buckridge sawmill at the end of the 19th century.

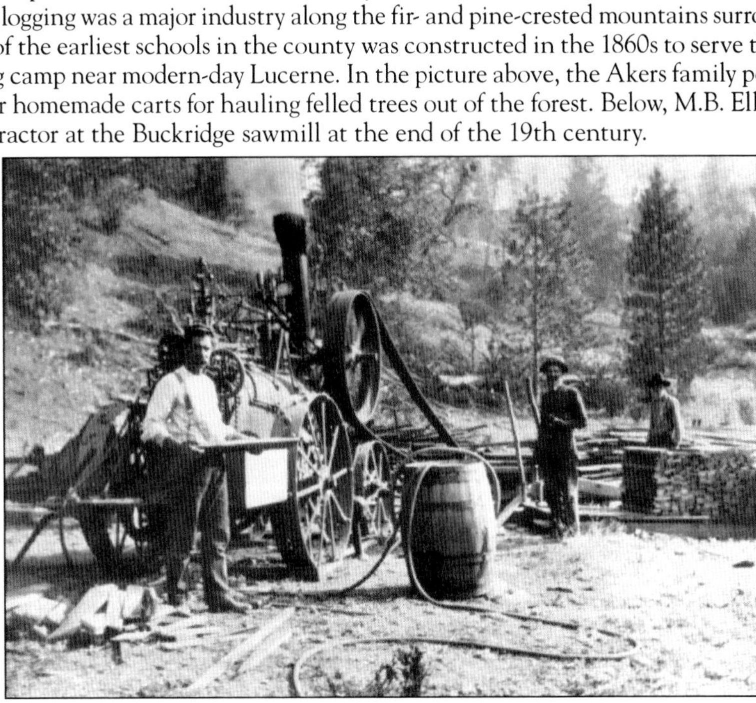

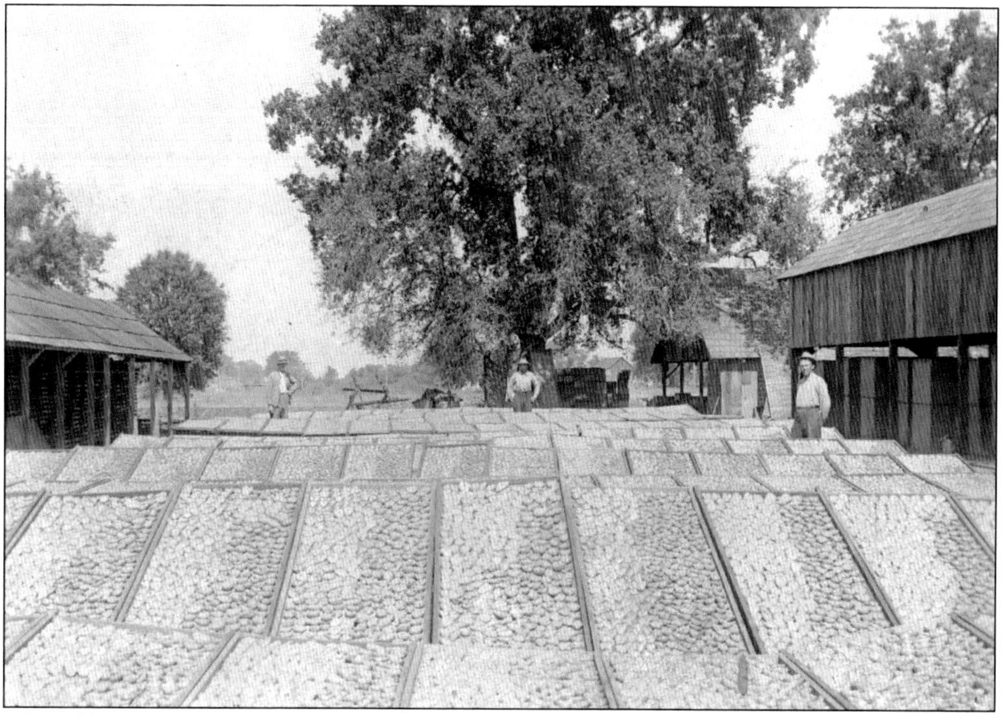

The valleys to the west and north of Clear Lake made for fine farming land. Although cattle ranching proved most popular early on, settlers soon found that the land was especially fertile for wheat and other grains. When gristmills were built in the 1860s and 1870s, Lake County's wheat no longer had to be shipped out of county to be processed into flour. Pictured below, farmers in Big Valley work in their wheat field. Toward the end of the 19th century, people started planting fruit trees, which yielded crops that exploded in the 20th century to place Lake County on the map. Pictured above, pears sit out to dry on a Lake County farm.

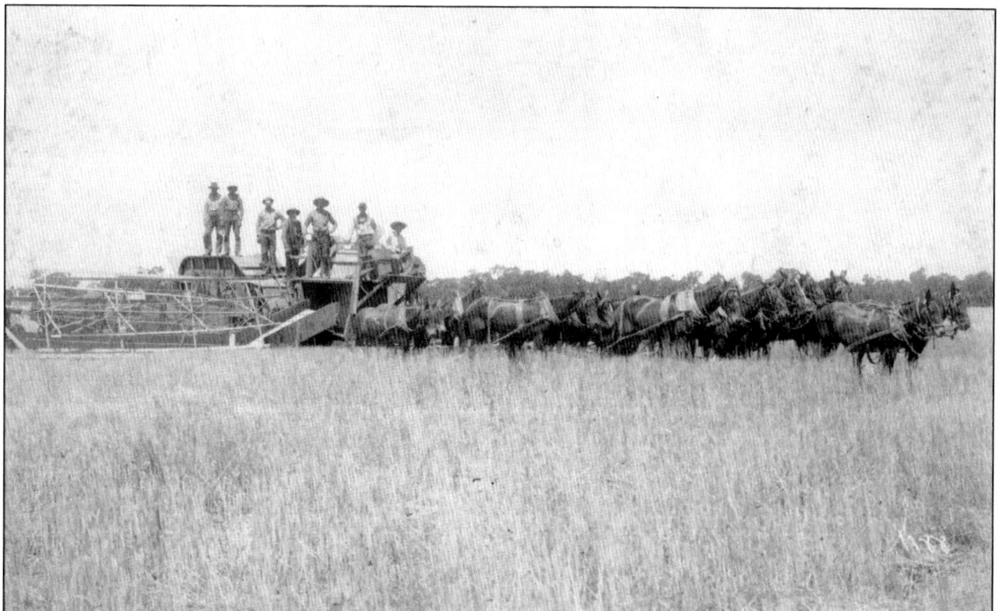

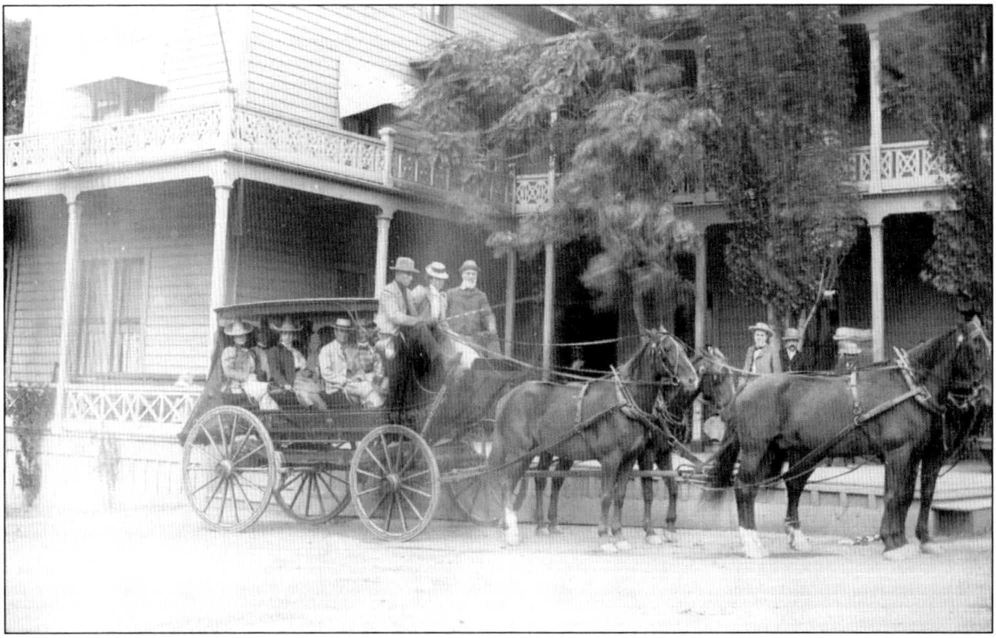

The same volcanic activity that created sulfur and borax deposits also created unique mineral springs, which became sites of luxury spas and resorts. These resorts catered to a wealthy elite that came from around the world to enjoy the curative powers of the springs. In this picture, visitors have piled into a stagecoach to be taken to Bartlett Springs.

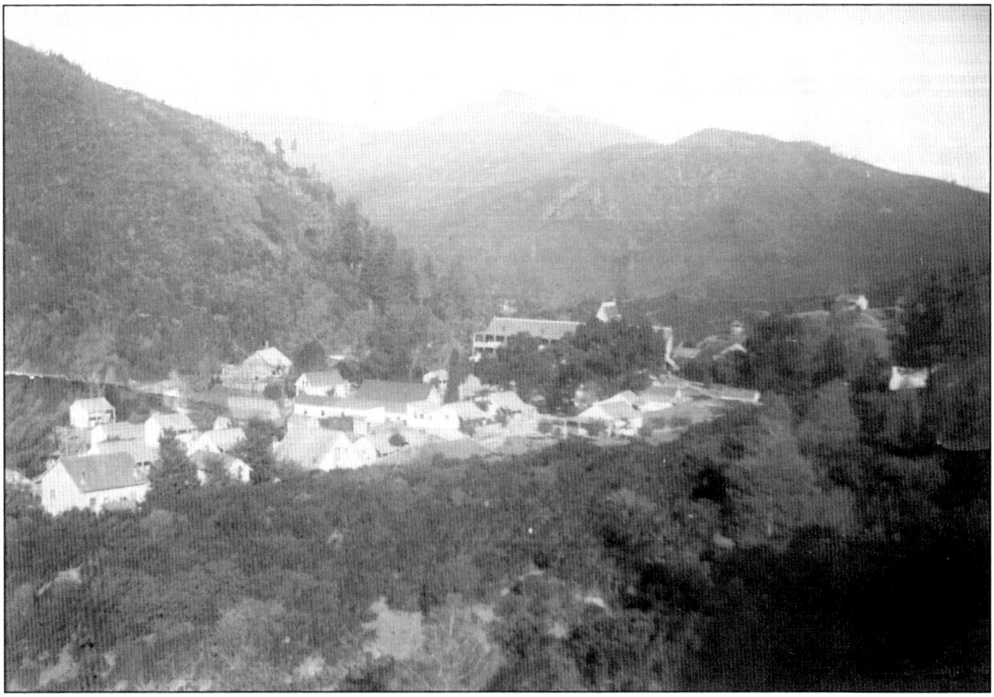

Pictured here is the sprawling resort of Bartlett Springs, one of the most popular springs of the 19th century. By the end of the 19th century, Lake County was being touted as the "Switzerland of America," and the resorts only added to the allure of this picturesque destination.

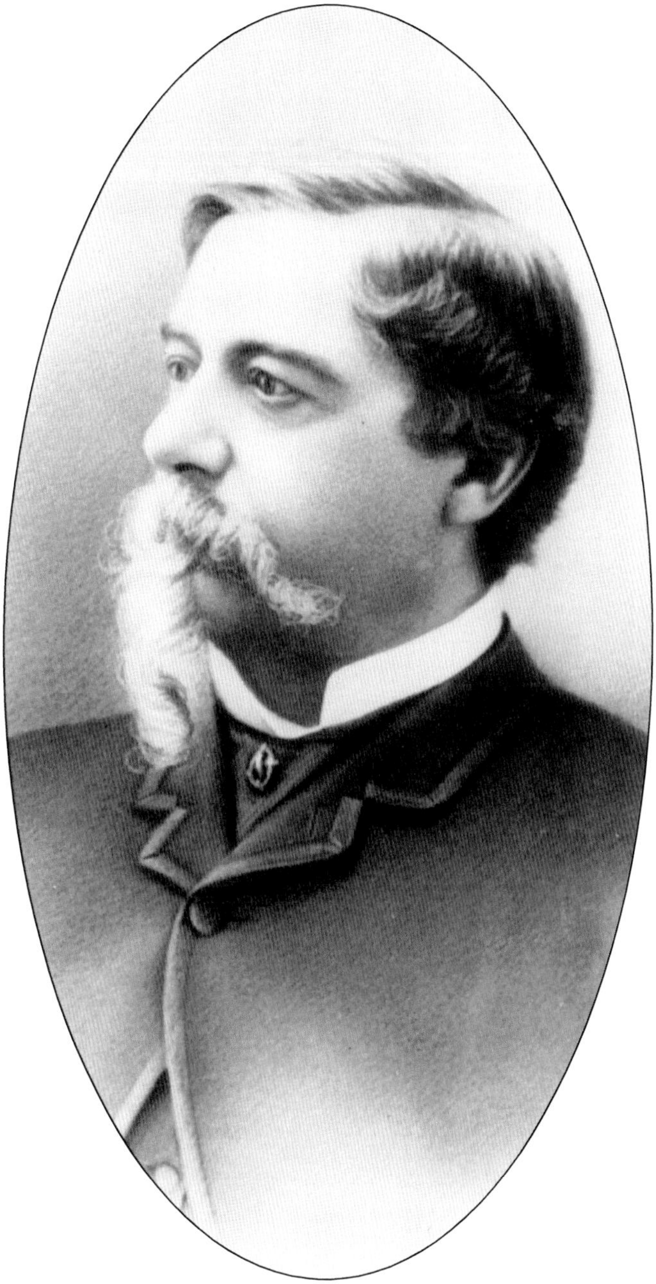

The last quarter of the 19th century saw Lake County's star on the rise. The resorts were bustling with activity, and the shores of Clear Lake and the surrounding mountains echoed with the sound of industry. In the middle of it all, a wealthy elite class began to call Lake County home. In the following years, some of these citizens put their considerable resources toward civic improvements like libraries and schools. One of the more colorful characters of this class was Capt. Richard Floyd, a wealthy transplant from Georgia. Floyd first moved to Lake County in the early 1870s and purchased the Mounds Cottages and Hotel. Being a seafarer, Captain Floyd built the first pier on Clear Lake and in the following decades was responsible for bringing steamships and other boats to the lake.

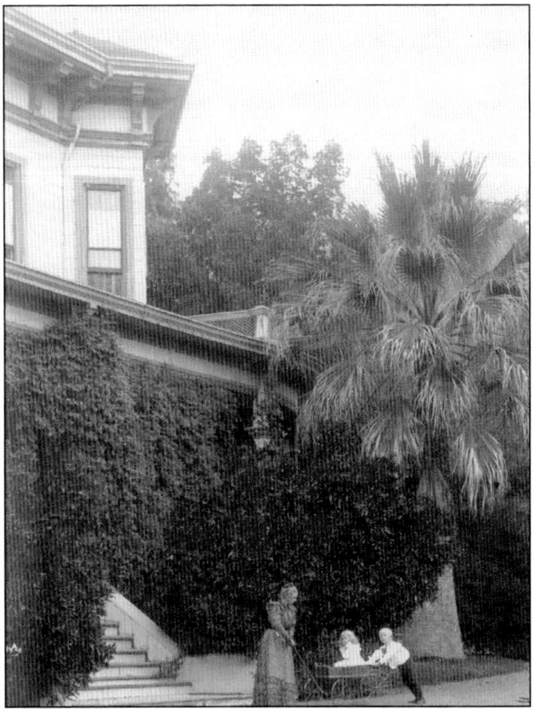

In 1874, several years after arriving in Lake County, Captain Floyd began construction on a large estate, located on a 300-acre peninsula on the eastern shores of Clear Lake. This estate became known as Kono Tayee (Mountain Point) and on it, Captain Floyd played host to many of the upper crust of Lake County. At left is one of the few surviving images of the sprawling house constructed on the property, and below, visitors lounge in the shade of the estate's sculpted gardens. Naturally, Floyd built several piers on his property so that he could easily travel across the lake to his business interests in Lakeport and beyond.

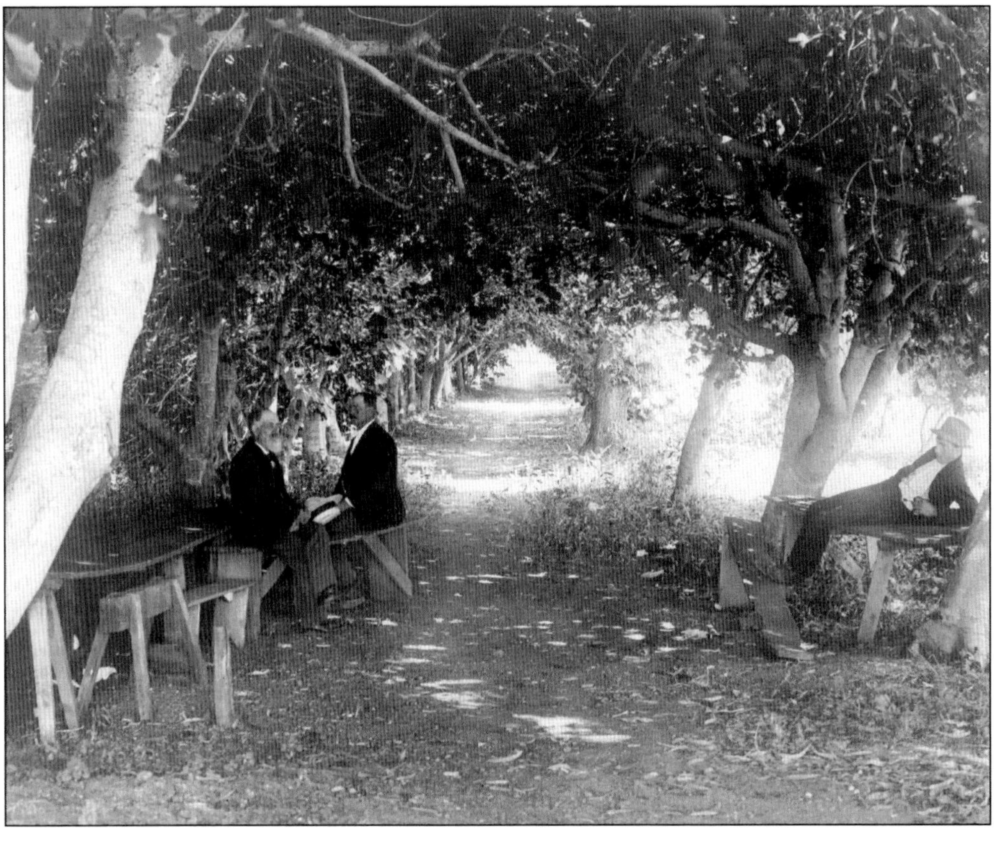

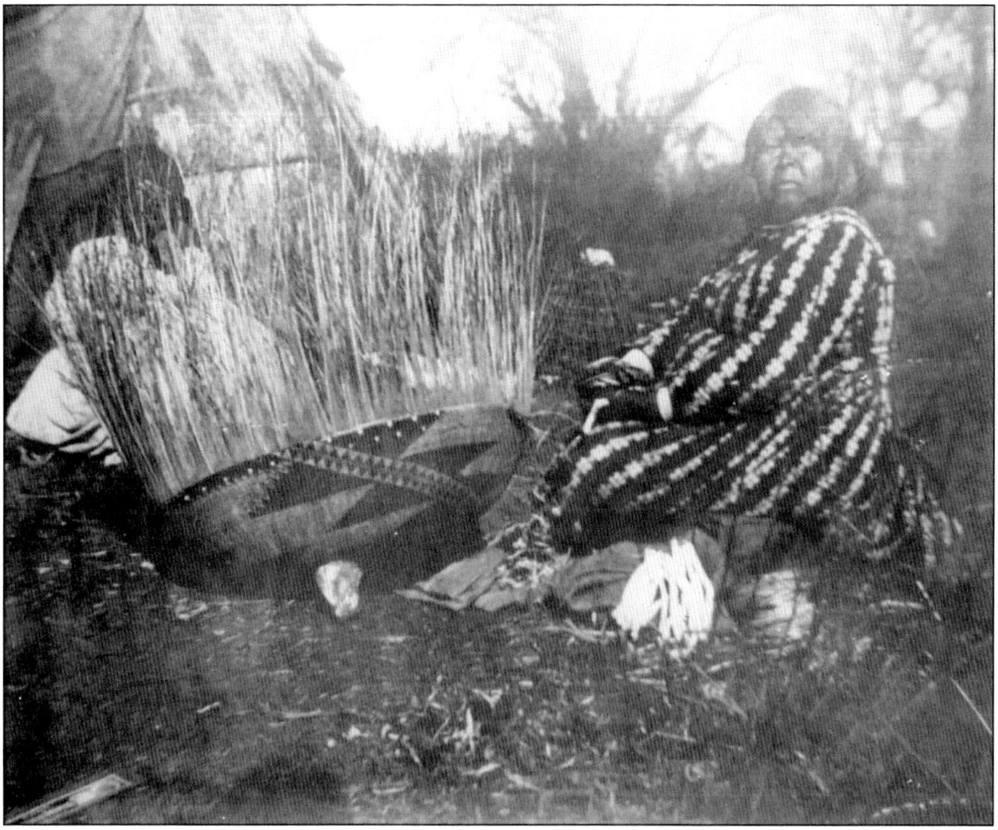

Lake County was traditionally home to four major groups of Native Americans—the Pomo, Lake Miwok, Wintun, and Wappo. In 1851, the tribes of the Clear Lake region signed a treaty with a representative of the United States that stipulated much of the Clear Lake Basin would be reserved for them and the rest would be ceded to the newly arrived settlers. The treaty was never ratified. The result of these duplicitous actions was that by the middle of the 1850s, just a few short years after the first American settlers arrived, the Native groups of Lake County were deprived of their homeland. For the next 60 years, these people lived a seminomadic existence as a labor force for the mines, logging camps, and farms that had begun to sprout up where once virgin land spread.

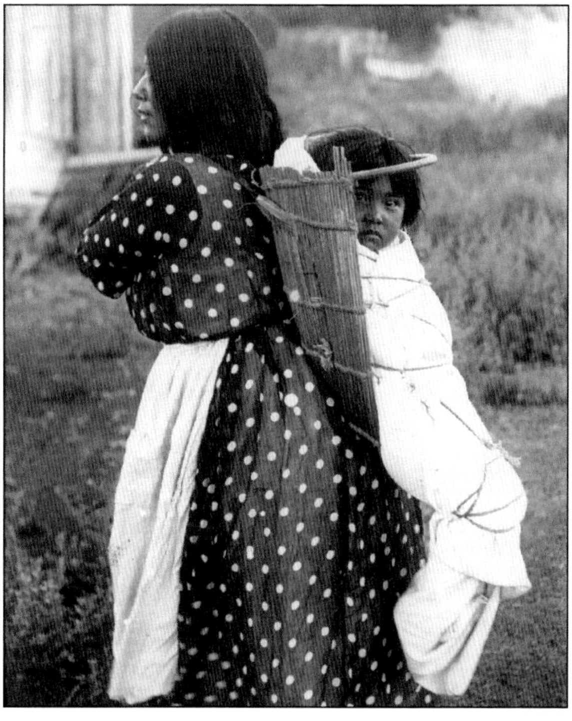

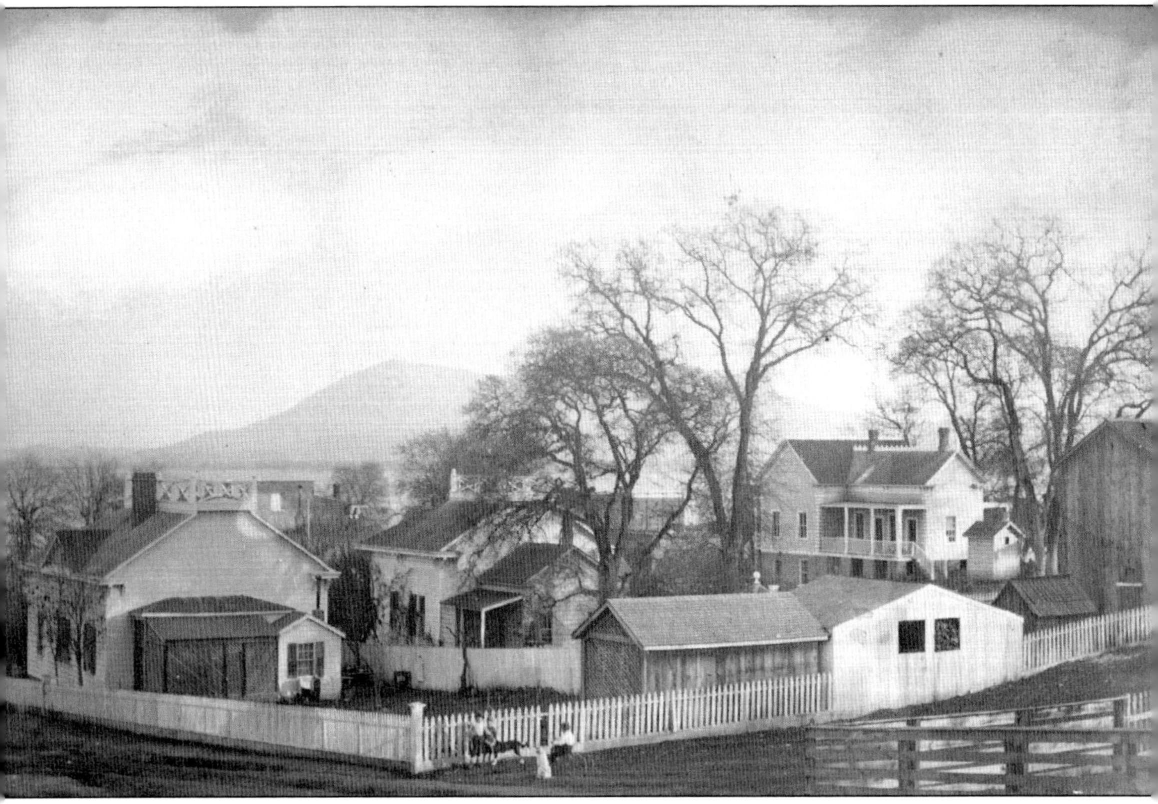

By the end of the 1870s, the major towns of the county had been established, primarily centering on Clear Lake. Lakeport, pictured here in 1882, served as the center of the judicial, administrative, and financial worlds of the county. The other towns of Upper Lake, Kelseyville, and Lower Lake naturally developed along similar lines. But at its heart, Lake County remained a rural county centered on farming, mining, and logging. The few towns developed only to serve the needs of these industries, providing central places where goods could be sent to markets outside of the county proper. Even the wealthy disdained the confines of the city, choosing instead to build estates outside of the limits of town, like Kono Tayee. Like the rest of the county, the schools that arose in the 19th century embodied the isolated, rural character that gave Lake County the title "the Switzerland of America."

Two

EARLY SCHOOLS 1856–1900

The unique social and economic landscape of 19th-century Lake County determined, in some fashion, the character of its schools. But just as no person is an island, the schools of Lake County did not develop in complete isolation from those in the rest of the state. The newly created state of California found itself at the forefront of a wave of groundbreaking legislation and, for the next half century, struggled to create a patchwork of laws that would eventually become the public education system of today.

The first decade of public school legislation in California established the framework that would eventually allow for incorporated cities and counties to build and fund schools. But legislation takes time, and for most of the 1850s, the paltry tax of 3¢, 5¢, and then finally 10¢ on every $100 the state allowed counties to levy for schools barely covered the cost of construction. The law was kinder on urban centers, with incorporated cities able to levy 25¢ on every $100, but Lake County was no urban center.

Starting in the early 1860s, the new California state superintendent of public instruction, John Swett, wrote and lobbied for the passing of legislation that created a state school tax and required counties to levy sufficient taxes to raise at least $2 per census child between four and eighteen years of age. With this patchwork of monies, all counties in California were required to maintain free public schools for at least five months out of the year.

Washed along by the ebb and flow of the legislative process, California communities like Lake County tried to stay above the tide. The shifting populations of a growing community only added to the confusion. Between state laws on one side and the local changes in demographics on the other, the school districts of Lake County, like drops of quicksilver, were ever shifting, moving together one minute only to split apart the next.

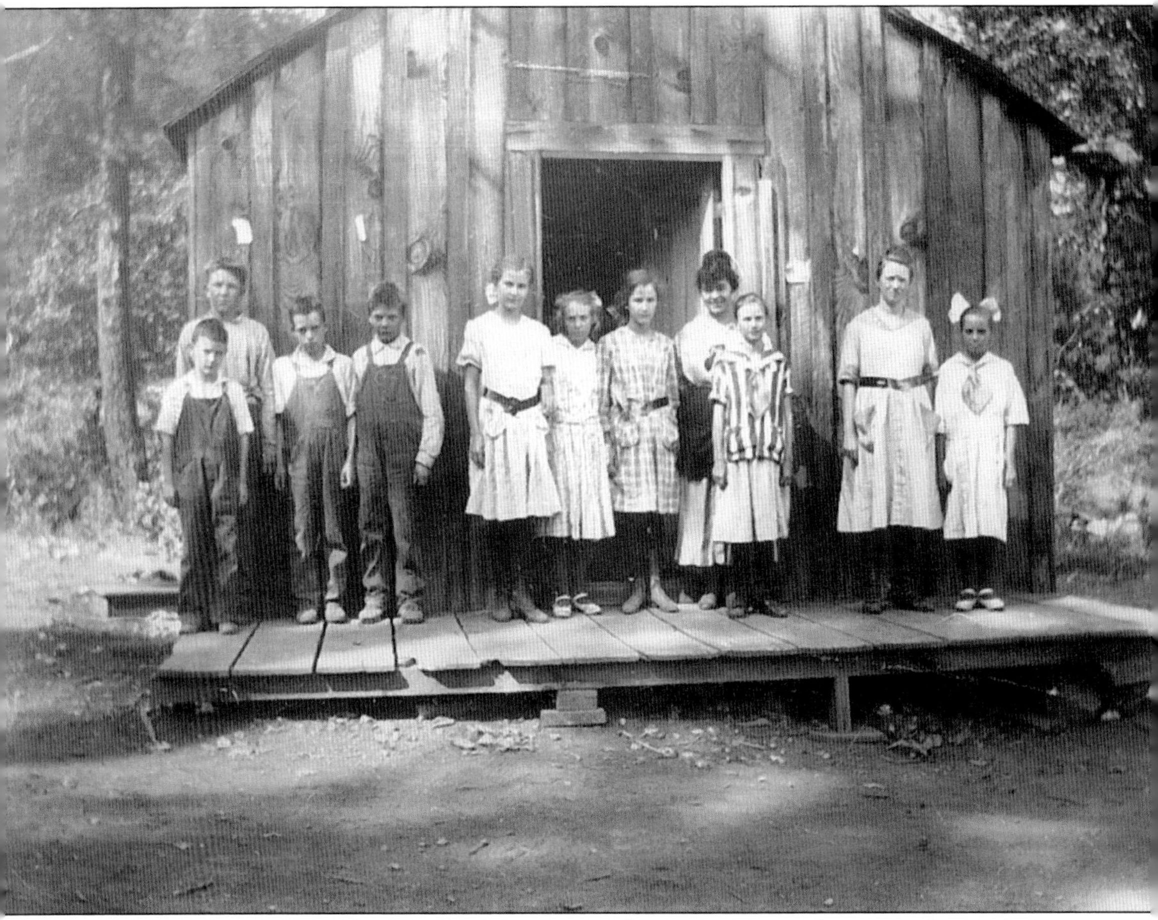

The first step in establishing a school district in Lake County was to determine the need. County policy seemed to change over the years, but as a general rule, a proposed school district needed to have at least 10 pupils living in the area in order to justify the existence of a school. The "area" varied throughout the county. In the more remote regions, like on Cobb Mountain, students were expected to travel five miles or more to get to school—compared to towns like Lakeport, where students lived right around the block from their school. If the number of school-age children dropped below 10, then a school district lapsed and district lines were redrawn. Cobb Valley School District formed in 1871, and a small one-room schoolhouse was built to serve the small community, as pictured here. Throughout the 19th century, this little school was plagued by lack of attendance, with only 13 pupils in 1881.

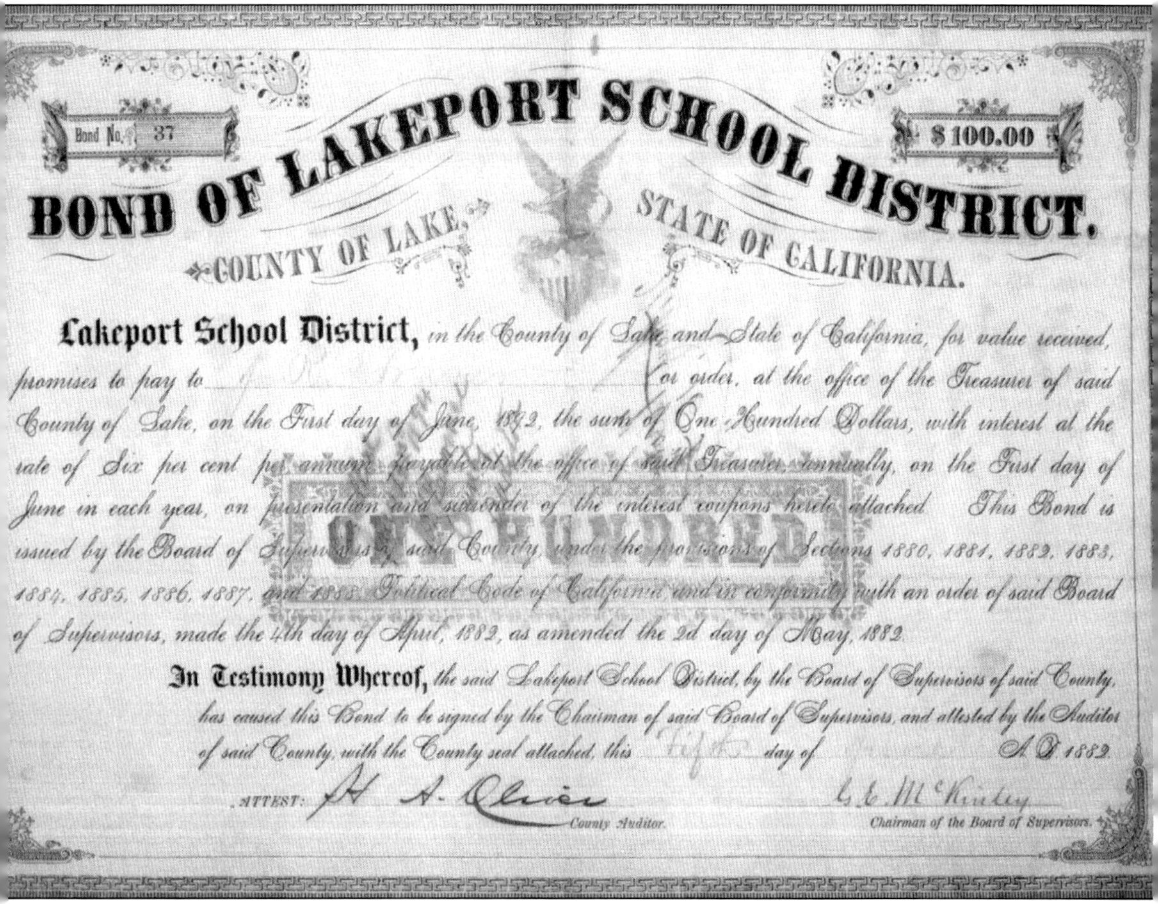
Bond No. 37

$100.00

BOND OF LAKEPORT SCHOOL DISTRICT.

COUNTY OF LAKE, STATE OF CALIFORNIA.

Lakeport School District, in the County of Lake and State of California, for value received, promises to pay to [illegible] or order, at the office of the Treasurer of said County of Lake, on the First day of June, 1892, the sum of One Hundred Dollars, with interest at the rate of Six per cent per annum payable at the office of said Treasurer annually, on the First day of June in each year, on presentation and surrender of the interest coupons hereto attached. This Bond is issued by the Board of Supervisors of said County, under the provisions of Sections 1880, 1881, 1882, 1883, 1884, 1885, 1886, 1887, and 1888, Political Code of California, and in conformity with an order of said Board of Supervisors, made the 4th day of April, 1882, as amended the 2d day of May, 1882.

ONE HUNDRED

In Testimony Whereof, the said Lakeport School District, by the Board of Supervisors of said County, has caused this Bond to be signed by the Chairman of said Board of Supervisors, and attested by the Auditor of said County, with the County seal attached, this Fifth day of [illegible] A.D. 1882.

ATTEST: County Auditor. Chairman of the Board of Supervisors.

Once enough children were found to be living within a proposed school district, lines were drawn and money was raised. By 1862, one year after becoming its own county, Lake County boasted five school districts, which it funded by levying a small tax on the growing population. In 1862, this tax amounted to only $639.53, but only two years later, it had nearly tripled to $1,805.30. This set the stage for more schools to be built in the growing Lake County as more money was brought to bear. By the end of the decade, upwards of 14 schools were in operation. Issuing bonds was another way school districts could pay for capital projects like building new schoolhouses or renovating old ones. Residents of the Lakeport School District voted for bonds like the one shown here for the construction of a new schoolhouse.

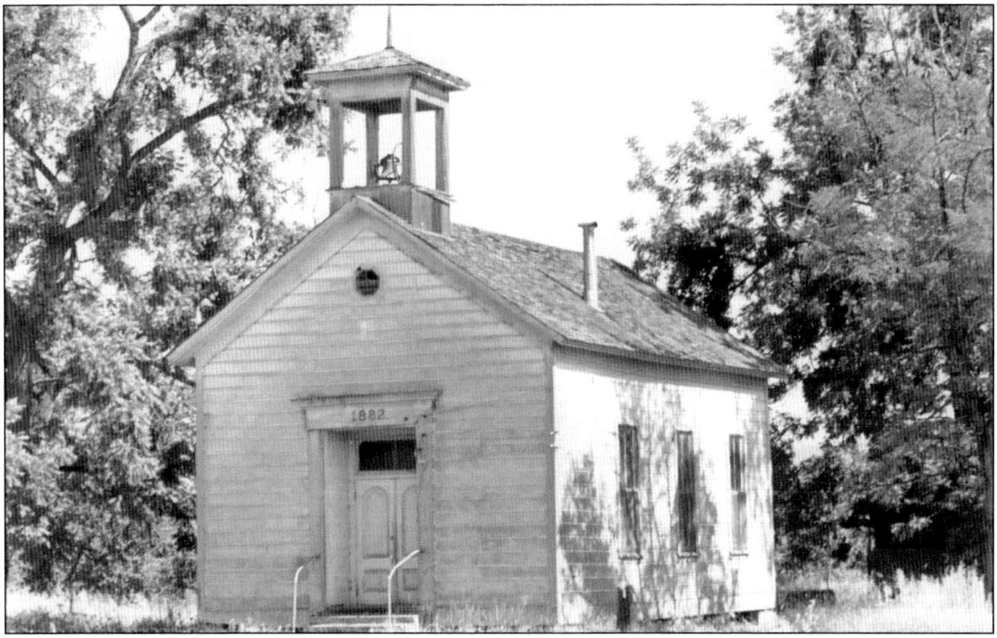

After the county raised enough money to construct a new schoolhouse, it then looked for a preferably free place to build it. Rarely were donations of land offered by locals out of a sense of philanthropy. The first Morgan Valley Schoolhouse, pictured below, was built on an acre of land donated by homesteader Joe Butege, who offered the plot so that the county would not build the schoolhouse where it originally intended to—right in front of his own house. The Kelsey Creek Schoolhouse, pictured above, was moved several times during its life. Each time, land was donated by local farmers who wanted it nearby so their children did not have to walk miles to attend. (Above, courtesy of Lake County Historical Society.)

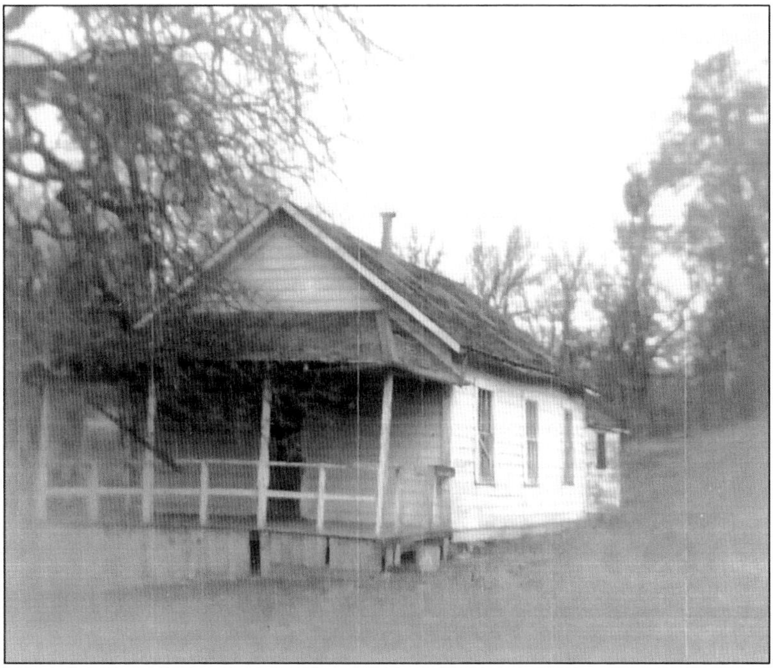

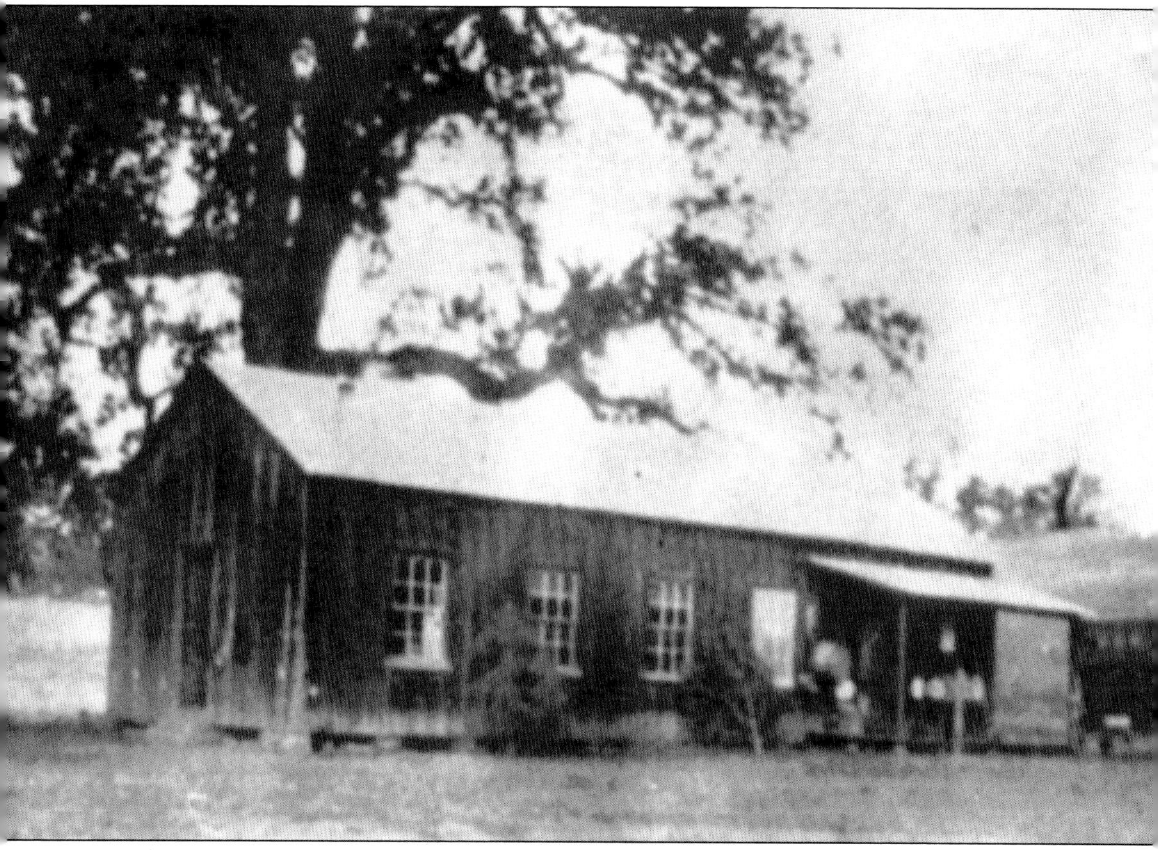

Pioneers living in the remote stretches of Lake County wilderness went to great lengths to ensure their children received education. In the Long Valley School District in eastern Lake County, the John family lived so far away from the school (pictured) that the children were not able to attend each day. So, the father dropped his kids off at school at the beginning of the week, where they lived with their teacher, Bertha Woodward, until week's end. In what would become emblematic of rural schools of Lake County, the Long Valley School District (also known as Arabella) underwent several phases of closing and reopening due to the shifting populations in the remote hillsides. With rural schools only serving 10 to 20 children, it sometimes only took one family moving away for that school's attendance to fall below the 10-child minimum and therefore risk closure of the school.

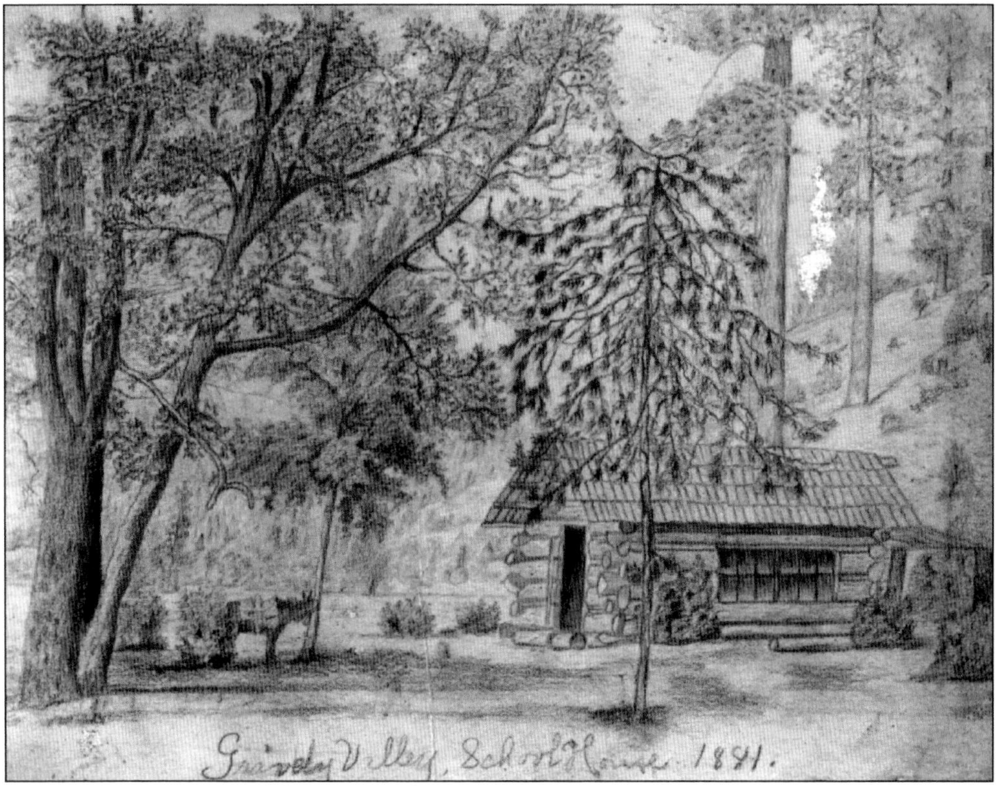

The northernmost school district in Lake County was the Gravelly Valley School District. The district was formed in 1871, and the log cabin depicted above was built in 1879 to serve as a one-room schoolhouse. Within a few decades, the log schoolhouse burned down and the simple clapboard building pictured below was erected. In order for the county to be able to levy a school tax on a particular district, that district had to serve at least 25 pupils and have an assessed property value of at least $75,000. In 1872, the assessed value of the Gravelly Valley School District only amounted to $11,673 and attendance was between 15 and 20 pupils. For rural districts like these, the county instead relied on the state school tax and issued bonds in order to fund them.

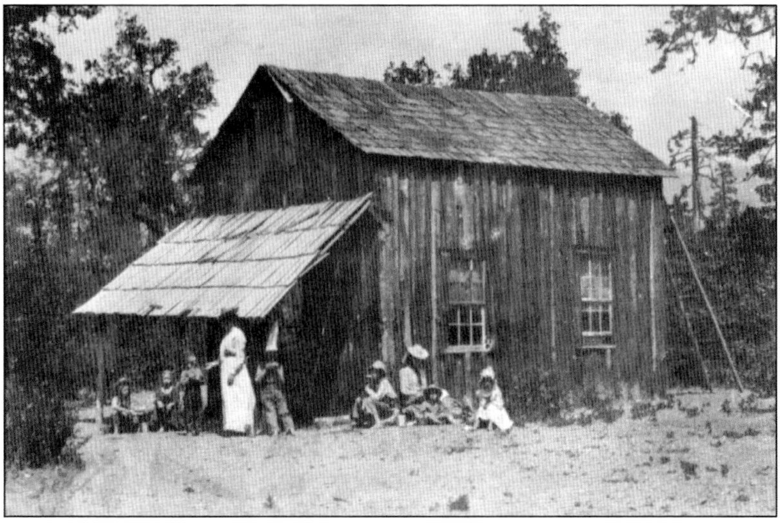

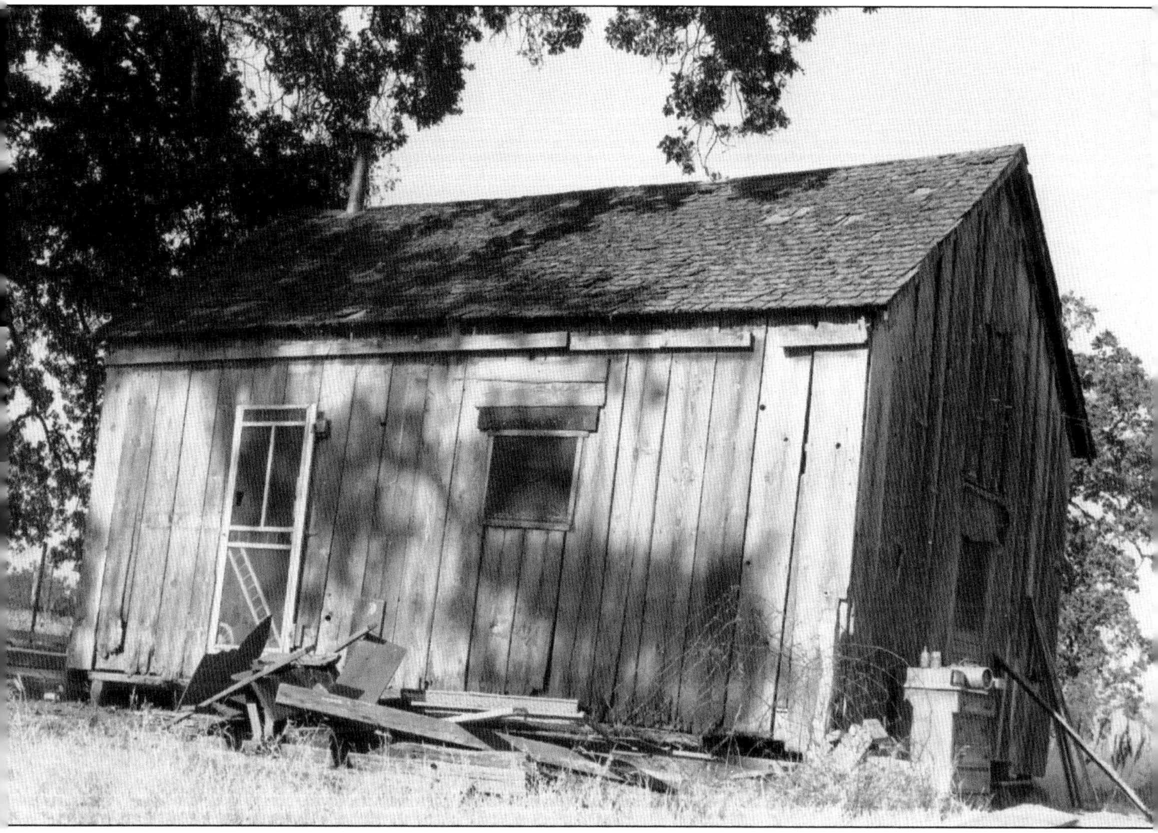

Occasionally, people's passions over schools exploded into fiascos like the one resulting in the burning of the first schoolhouse of the Big Valley School District in 1868. Being relatively large public buildings with open floor plans meant that early schoolhouses in Lake County often served a variety of functions from churches and dance halls to community centers. The citizens of the Big Valley School District near Kelseyville were debating whether the schoolhouse could be used for extracurricular activities when the building in question burned to the ground. Each side blamed the other for starting the fire. A nearby shed on the property of the Argonaut Ranch was commandeered and used as a school for several years. The Argonaut Schoolhouse, pictured here, stood for about a century in the same location until it was destroyed by the owner. (Courtesy of Lake County Historical Society.)

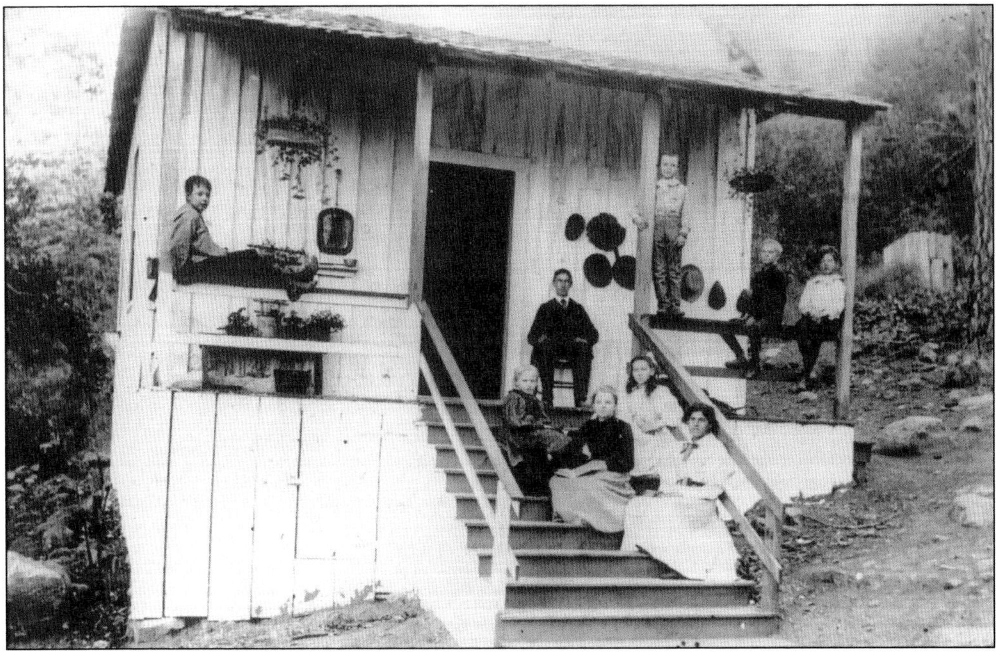

Many of these remote, rural schools served the various industries that sprouted up in the mountains and vales of Lake County. The Seigler Springs (pictured above) and Highland Springs (pictured below) School Districts were established in the 1870s and 1880s to service the children of those working in and around the resorts. The Highland Springs Schoolhouse is particularly interesting for its style of architecture. Built in 1885, this white clapboard building with a small bell tower atop resembles the design of the larger schoolhouses of Upper Lake, Lakeport, and Middletown. It is as if the relatively small school district aspired to be just as civically conscious as its urban neighbors by building an equally urban-style schoolhouse.

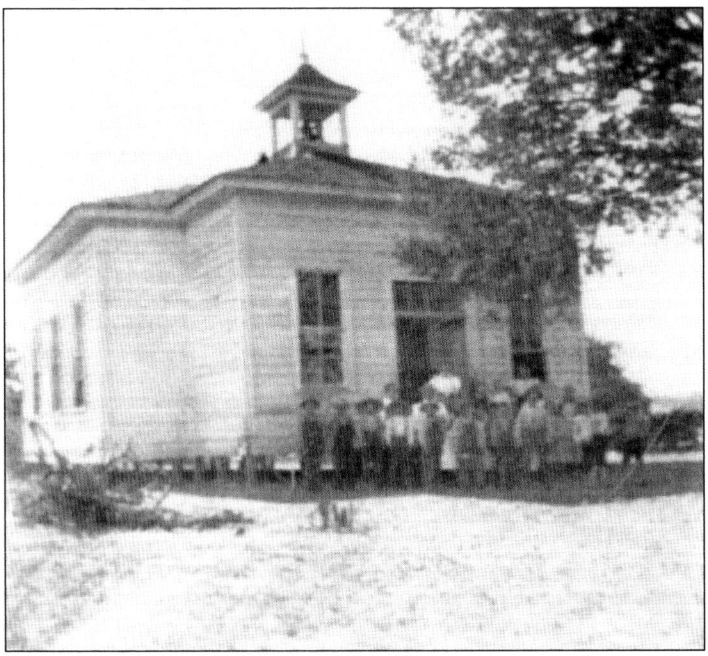

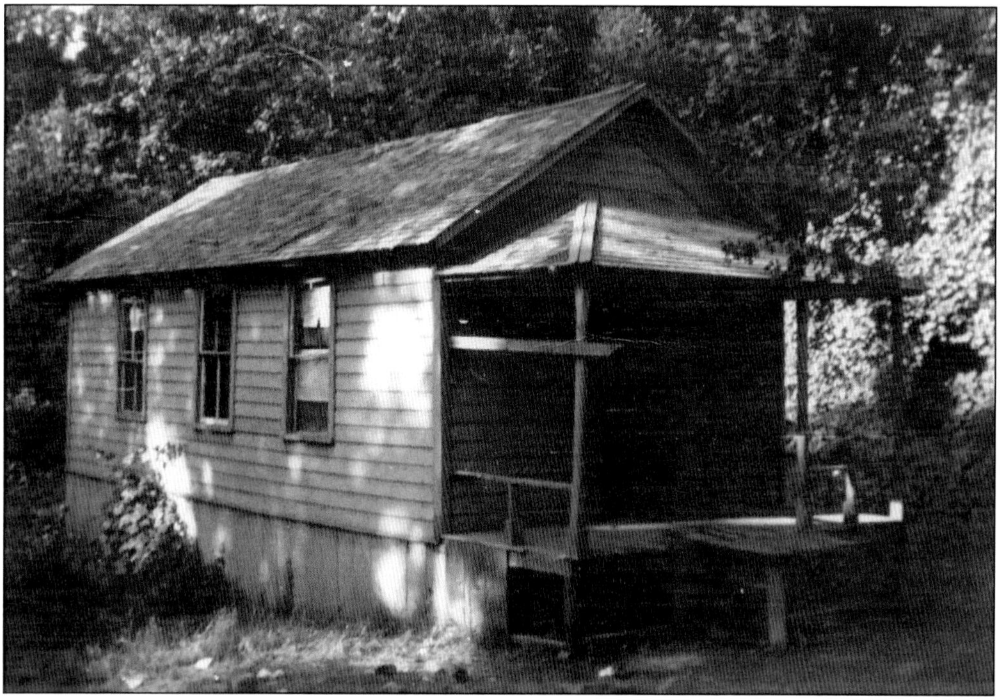

As the Seigler Springs and Highland Springs School Districts served those workers associated with the resorts, the Callayomi School District was established for the growing population of miners and loggers in southern Lake County. It was established in 1875; by 1881, there were already 34 children who attended the school.

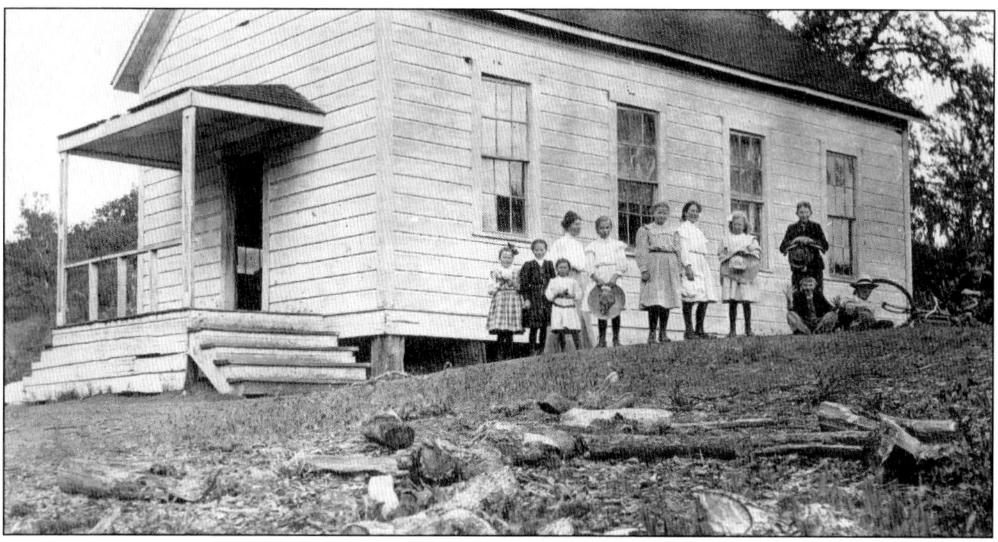

Establishing and maintaining a school district in rural Lake County was not always easy. With the population nearly tripling during the 1870s, the county could not always keep up with the demand. The Liberty Schoolhouse, for instance, was built in 1870, but a school district was not actually formed until 1874.

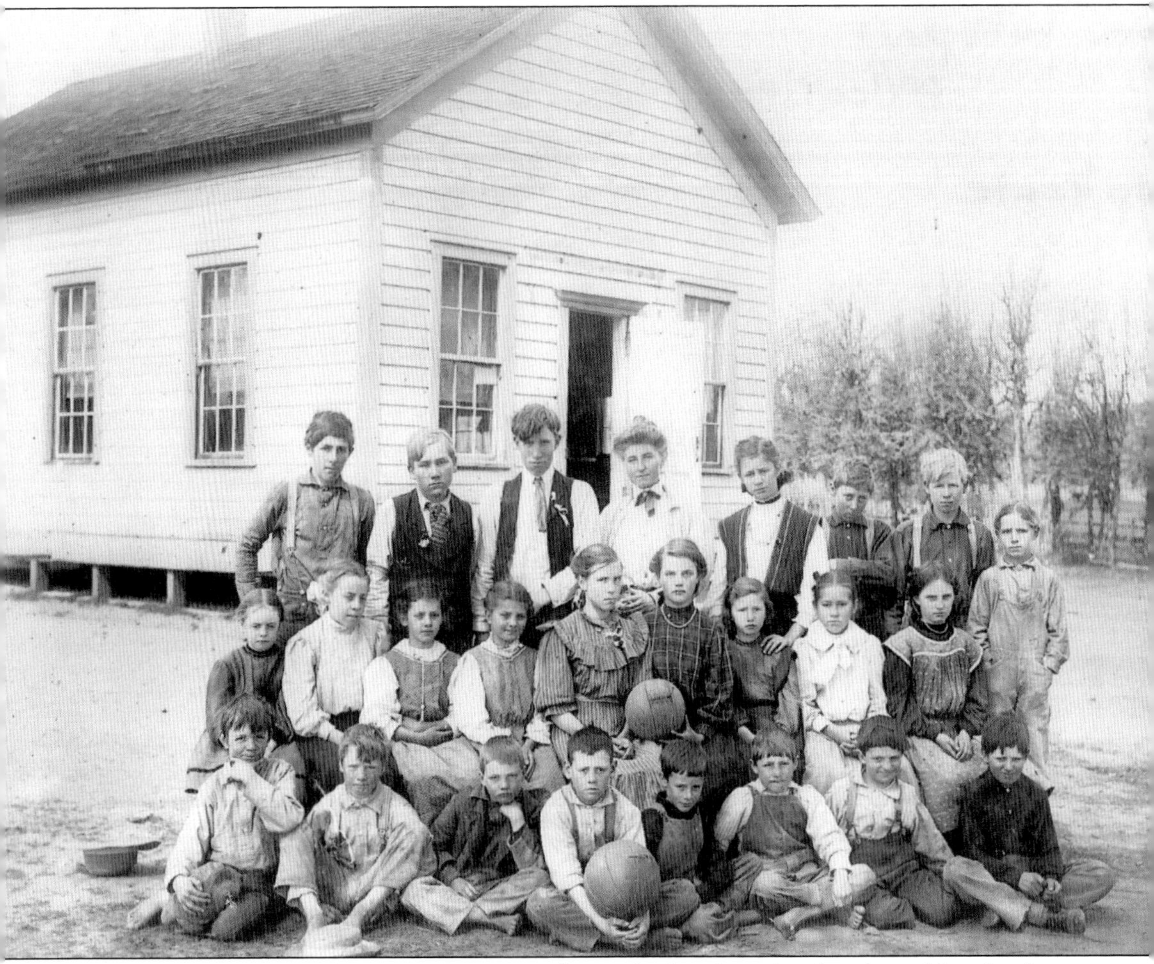

The rapid rise in population in Lake County during the first three decades of its public school system resulted in an equally rapid growth in the number of schoolhouses being built. Pleasant Grove School District is a good example of this phenomenon. The first schoolhouse was constructed in 1869, and 72 children attended during that year, making it one of the most populated schools in Lake County at the time. There were so many children that sheds were constructed to either side of the old building to serve as additional classrooms; however, by the beginning of the 1880s, the areas around the school district had become more and more populated, necessitating the creation of other school districts. Every time district lines were redrawn, Pleasant Grove got smaller and smaller so that by 1884, a smaller schoolhouse was constructed to reflect the school's decreased attendance. This smaller schoolhouse is pictured here.

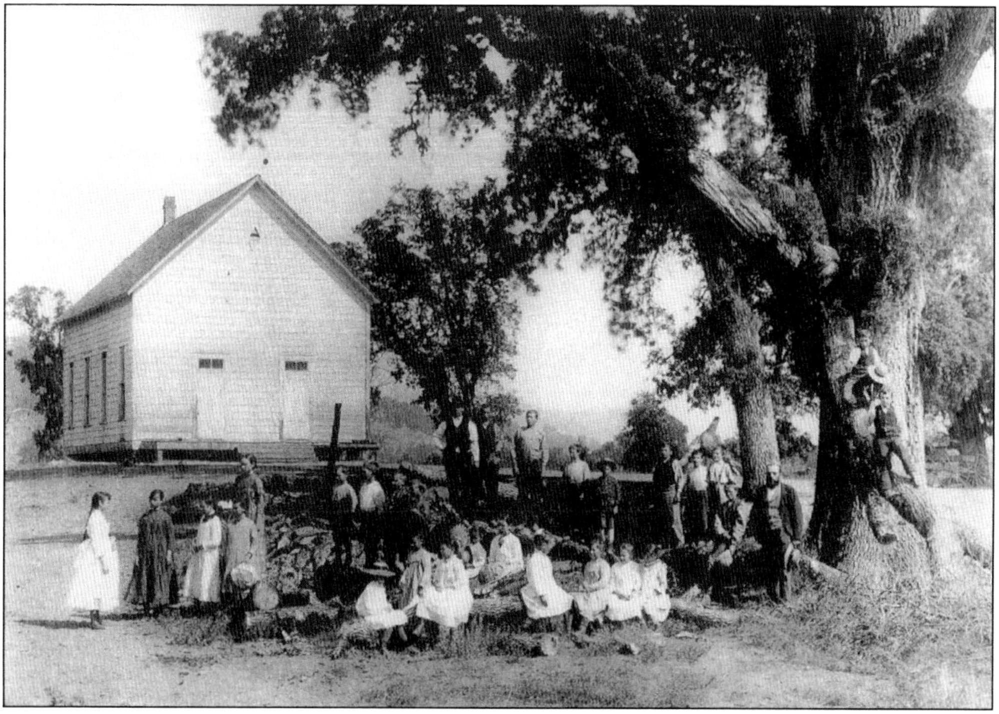

The rural districts were not the only ones to suffer the effects of rapid population shifts in 19th-century Lake County. Whereas rural districts lost students, those closer to the urban centers of the county experienced the opposite problem. The county established the Middle Creek School District in 1882 and built a small schoolhouse shortly thereafter (pictured above). Around the turn of the century, however, the little schoolhouse proved too small, and the district was split, with some students going to the Upper Lake Grammar School (pictured below) and the rest going to a newly constructed Middle Creek Schoolhouse.

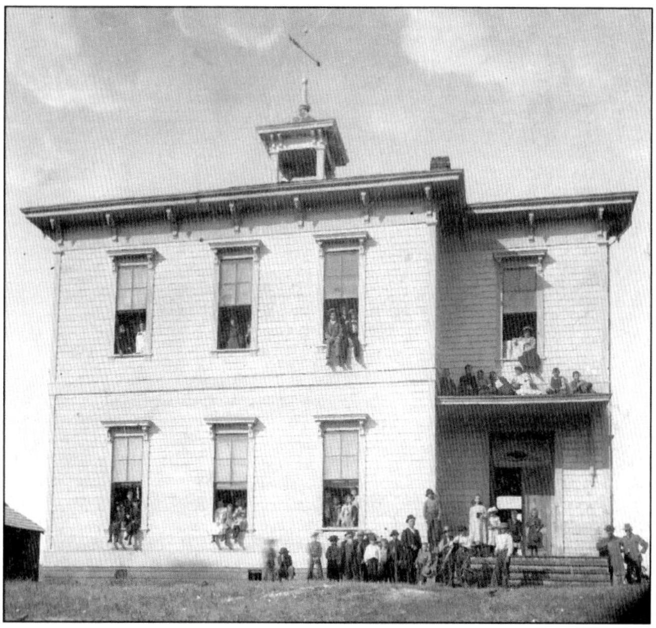

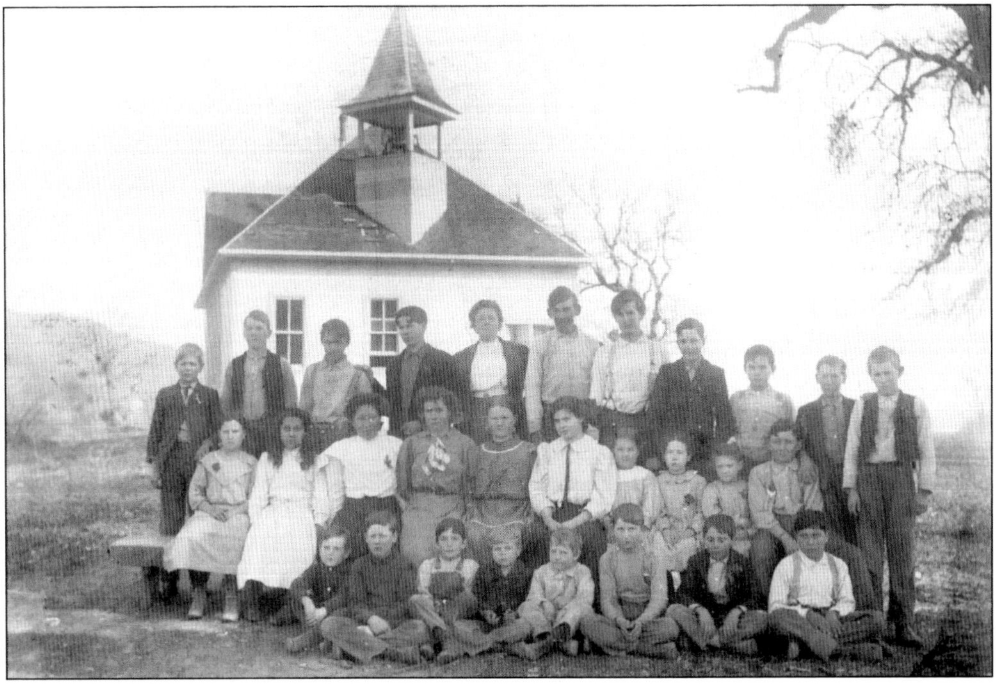

The Bachelor Valley School District was formed out of the Upper Lake School District in 1870. Like the Middle Creek schools, Bachelor Valley School had too many students and insufficient room, so a new schoolhouse was constructed (pictured above). While these one- and two-room schools served the children living around the town of Upper Lake, those within its bounds benefited from the construction of a large schoolhouse in 1884: the Upper Lake Grammar School. The style of this two-story white clapboard school, with the entrance offset at one corner, was the favored design of 1880s urban schoolhouses in Lake County. Initially, this schoolhouse consisted of two large classrooms, which were divided into four smaller classrooms in later years.

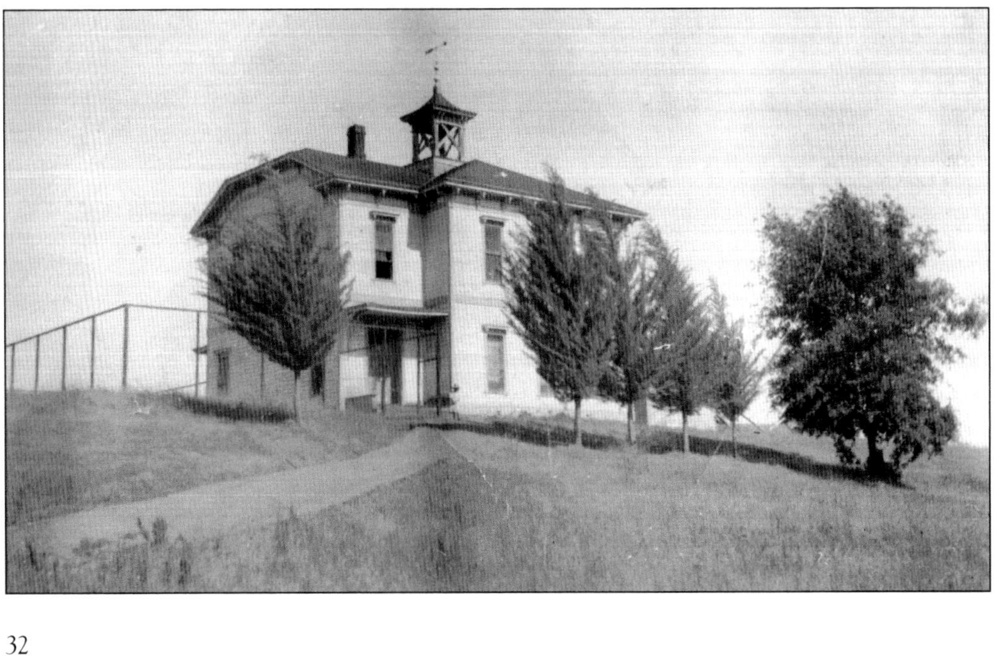

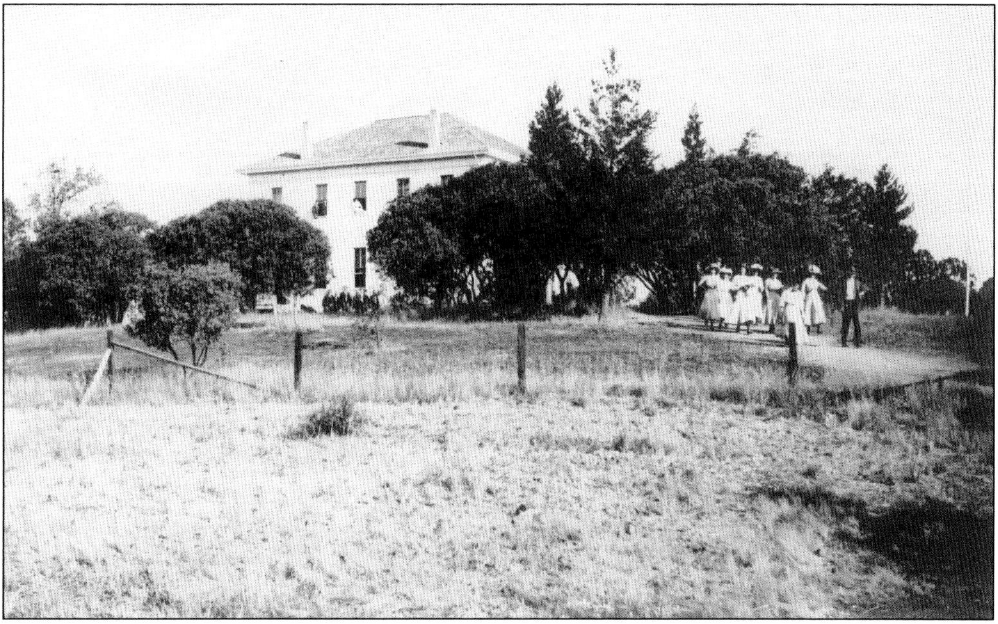

As the county seat, Lakeport was the administrative and judicial center of the county. It is no wonder, then, that it was also an educational center. Up to this point, all the schools illustrated in this book have been public schools—not because there were not any private schools, but because these were often short-lived affairs, with even more problems with attendance than rural public schools. But one particular private school operated for two decades in Lakeport: the Lakeport Academy. Throughout the 19th century, Lake County only guaranteed public education from first through eighth grades. Beginning in 1884, the Lakeport Academy provided one of the only means of post-eighth-grade education for youth in the county.

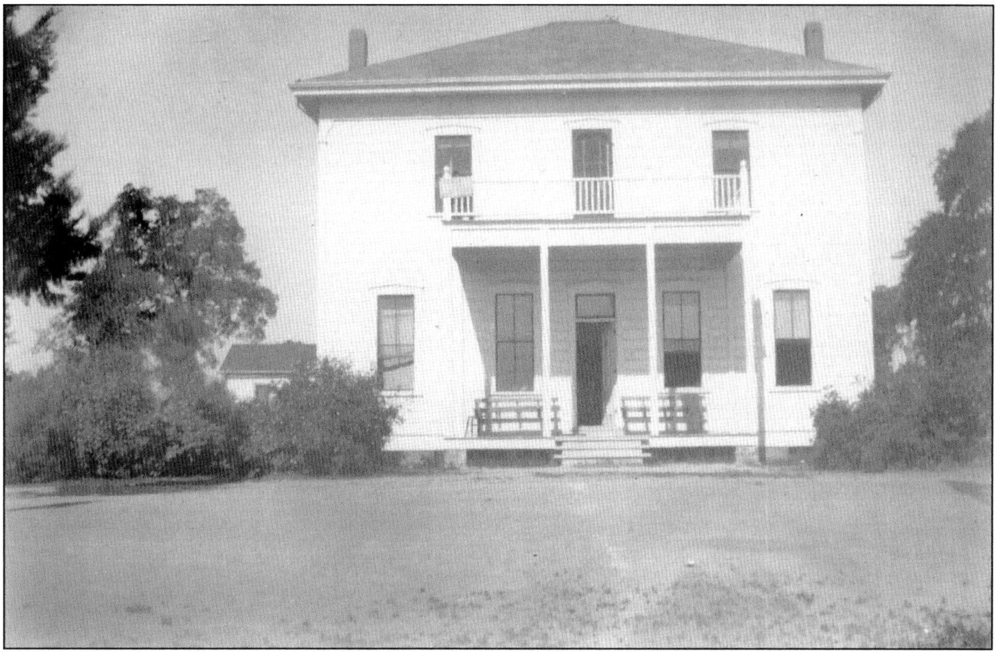

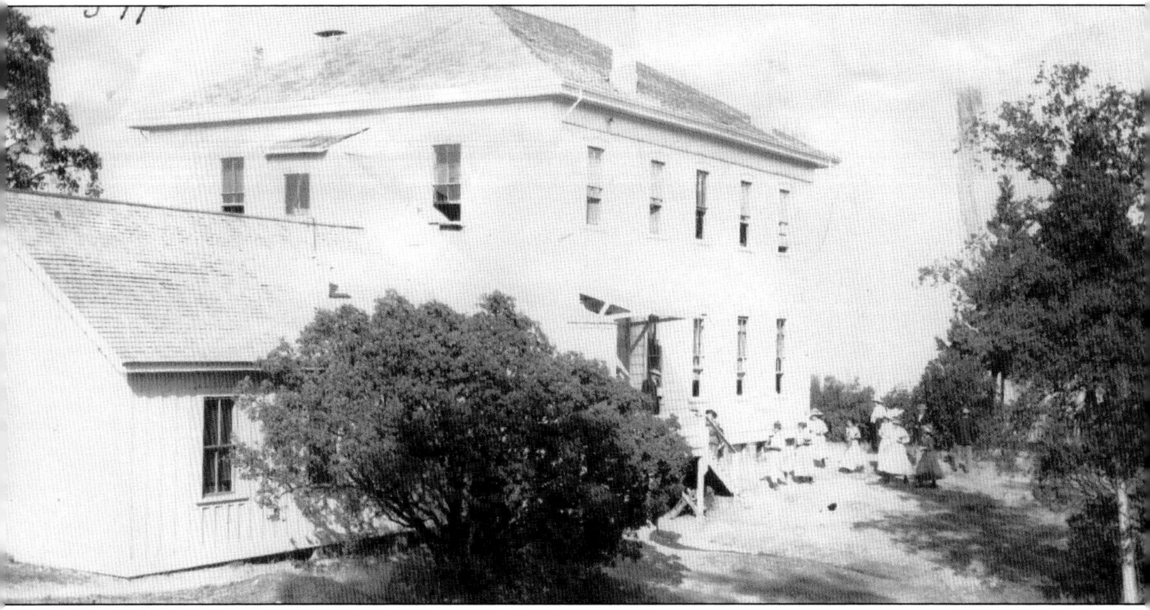

Instead of taking a job as a teacher at the nearby Kelseyville Academy, recent immigrant John Overholser decided to start his own academy in the county seat, and so Lakeport Academy was born. At the beginning of that school year, only four students were in attendance, but by the end of the year, 16 sat in class. In 1890, Overholser incorporated Lakeport Academy and used the $2,000 of subscribed stock to build a much more spacious building (40 by 50 feet), with two stories and a boardinghouse attached to the back (seen in this picture). The first floor consisted of three classrooms, a large assembly hall, and a library. The second floor contained more classrooms and a large chemistry lab. The building was rounded out by bathrooms for boys and girls and several service closets. All in all, the new Lakeport Academy was one of the finest schoolhouses in Lake County at the time.

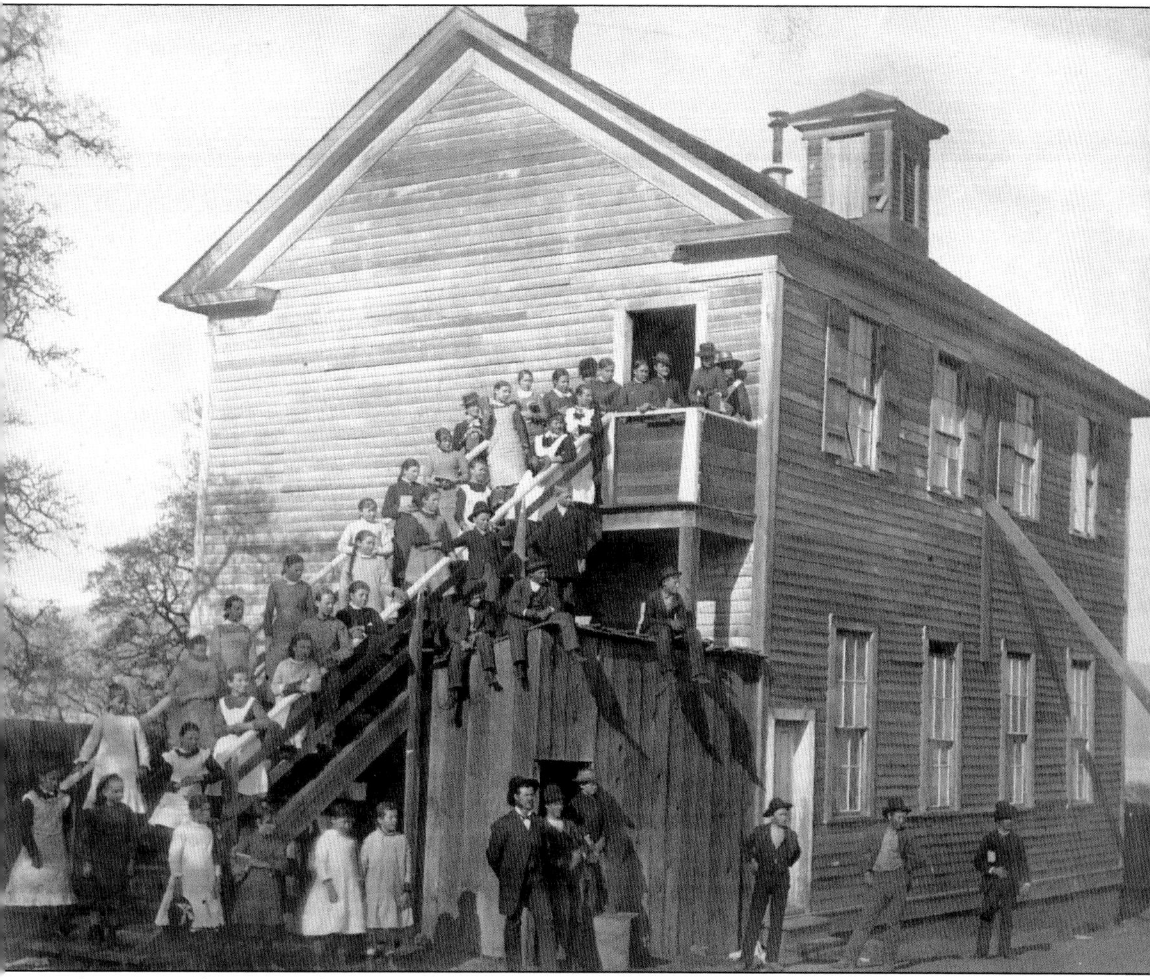

Lakeport Academy served all children of roughly high school age who could afford the modest tuition fees. But the majority of school-age kids in Lakeport matriculated through public school. This picture depicts the first Lakeport Grammar School, which was erected around 1867 and operated until 1880 when the city sold bonds for a larger schoolhouse to be built. When the new school was constructed, the second floor was rented to Prof. John Overholser for his newly established Lakeport Academy. In 1877, the county superintendent of common schools reported to the state that 11 schools at the time had outhouses and 14 did not (there were 28 schools in the county at that time, so presumably three schools had not given the superintendent information to pass on). In the foreground of this photograph is the outhouse of the Lakeport Grammar School.

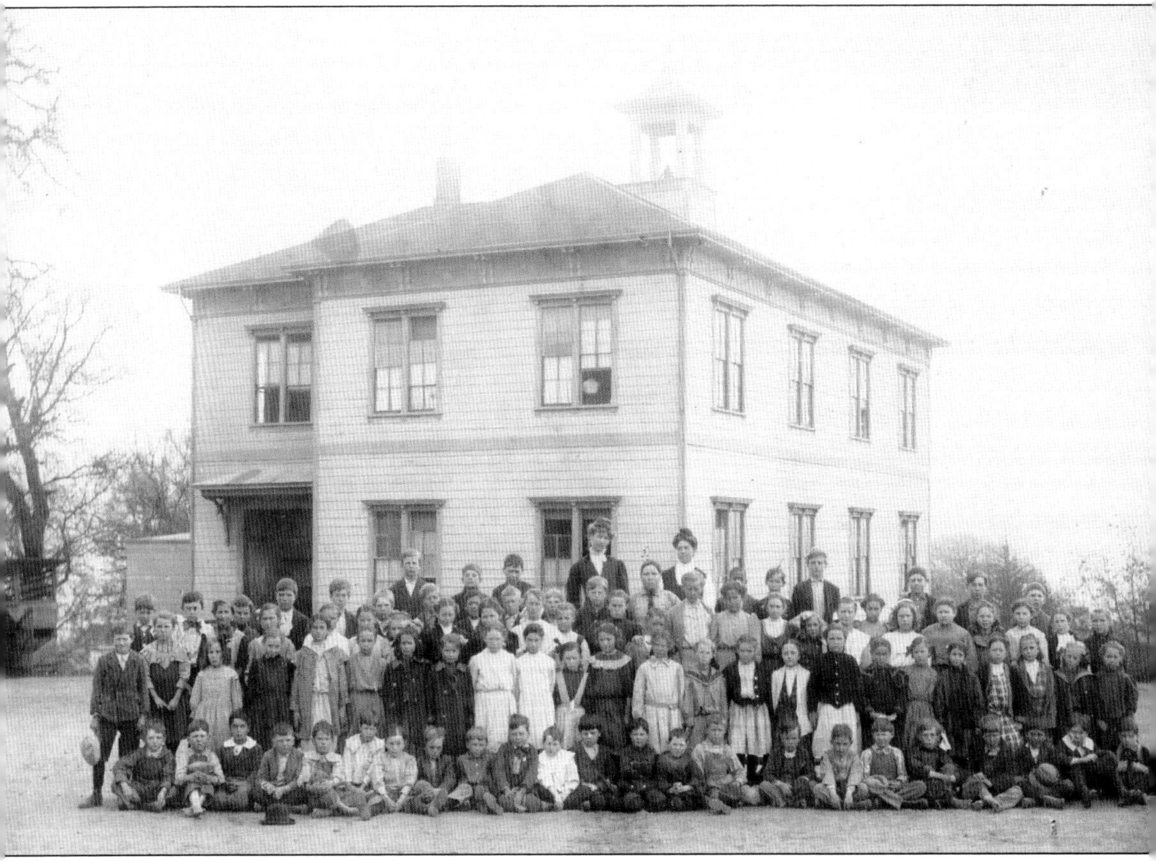

Built in 1880, the new Lakeport Grammar School became the first of the two-story, clapboard urban schoolhouses of Lake County. Even though the other towns in the area tried to imitate it in the years to come, Lakeport's grammar school remained the largest. Unlike the Upper Lake Grammar School, built in 1884, this schoolhouse featured space for six, not two, classrooms. The recessed entranceway created an L-shaped building, rather than a square. Two large classrooms and two smaller ones made up each floor of the long arm, while one additional small classroom was situated on each floor of the smaller arm. Topping the building, a small bell tower with a conical roof dominated the landscape, even more so since the schoolhouse was built on a hill. Decorative wood trim above the windows and along the gutter gave this building a stately appearance without appearing too gaudy.

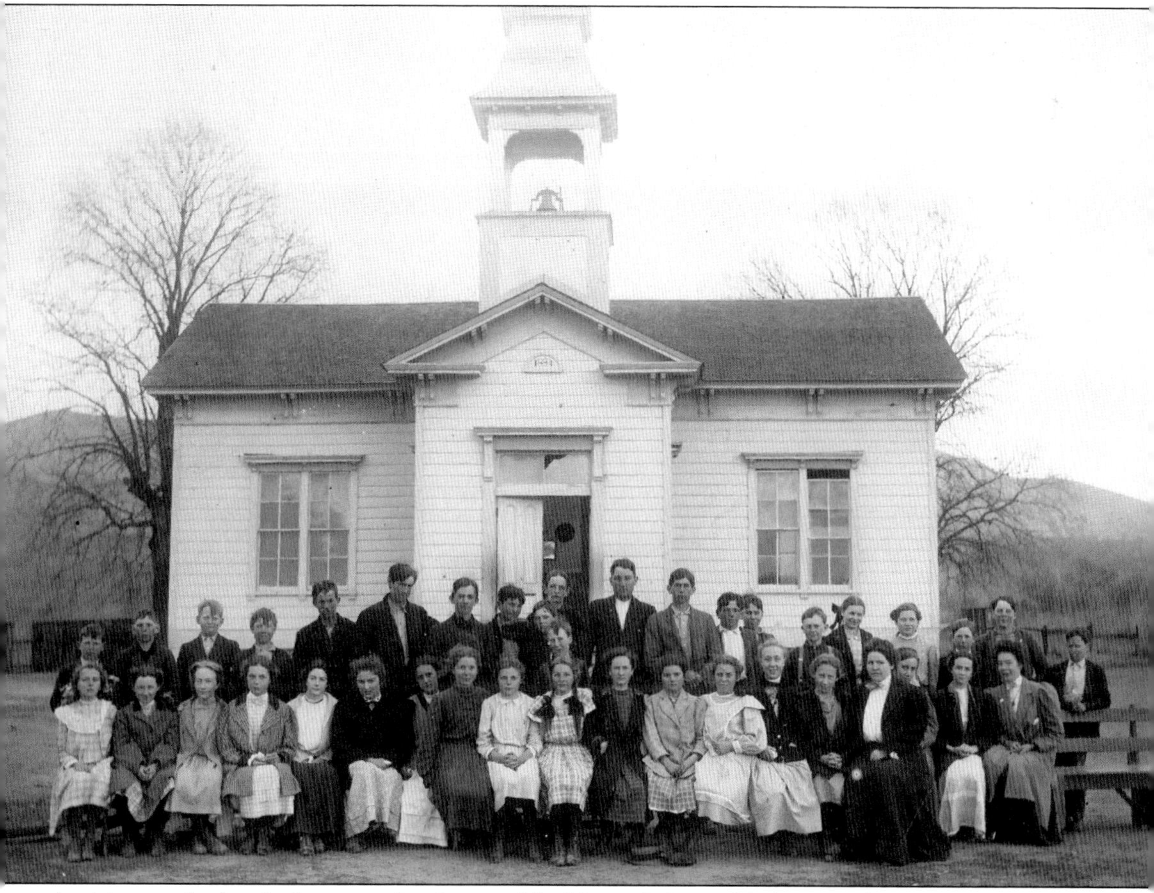

Aspiring to the level of civic pride of towns like Upper Lake and Lakeport, the small farming town of Kelseyville (called Uncle Sam at the time) would not be outdone. In 1884, it too built a white clapboard schoolhouse, complete with a decorative broken pediment on the front and decorative brackets lining the roof. Of course, the number of pupils did not justify a two-story building, so the new school was a single-story structure. But what it lacked in capacity, it made up for in sheer uniqueness. Instead of its entrance at one of the ends of the rectangular floor plan (like the Pleasant Grove Schoolhouse), Kelseyville had a small entrance and vestibule attached along the length of the building. The French-style roof for the bell tower mimics the roof of the Lower Lake Grammar School, built several years earlier in nearby Lower Lake.

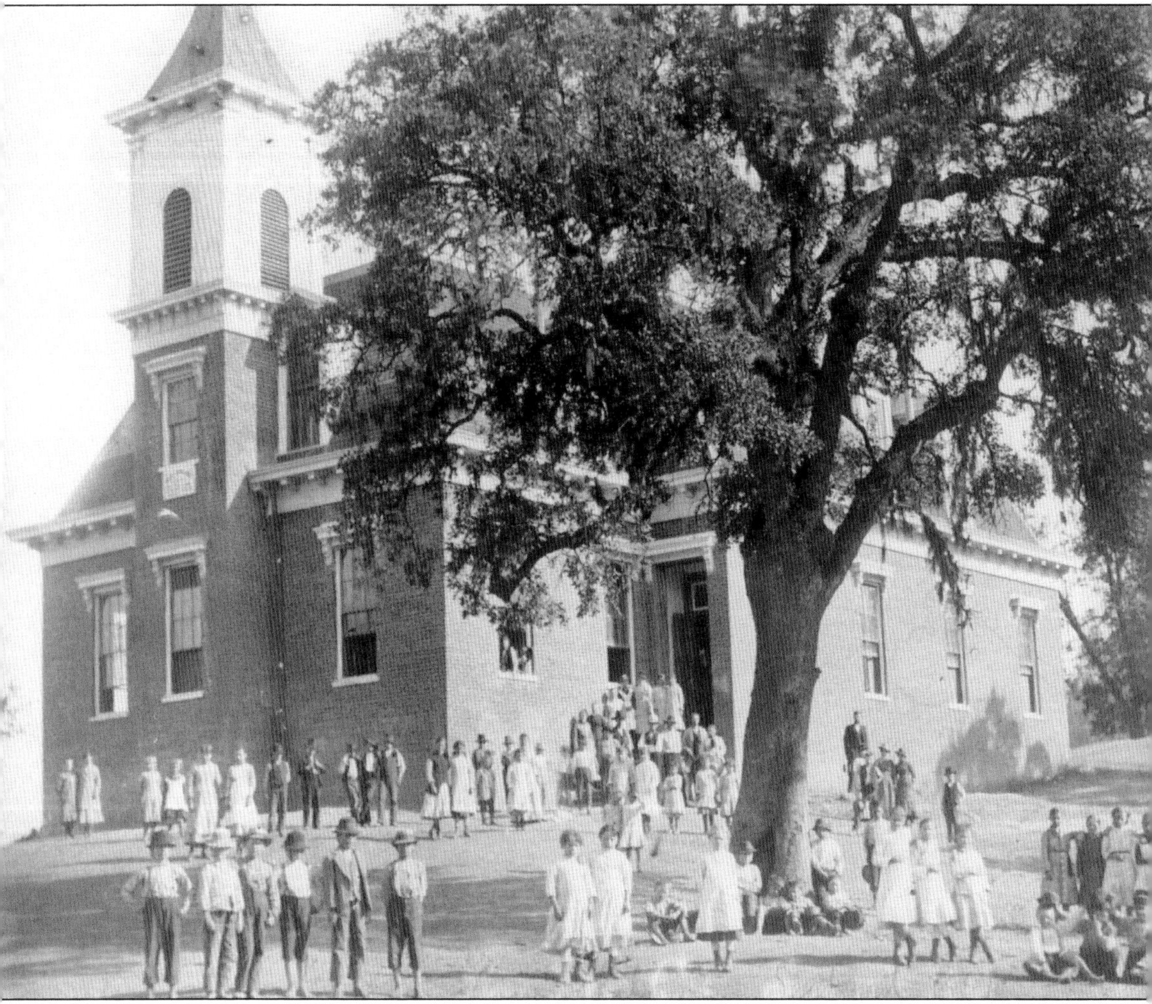

Farther south of Kelseyville, the people of Lower Lake had already had a boom in population and had built a larger schoolhouse accordingly. In fact, by 1870, the population of Lower Lake had risen to 1,000, but it was not until 1877 that the new L.P. Nichols Schoolhouse was unveiled. By far the most unique schoolhouse in all of Lake County, the Nichols Schoolhouse (later called the Lower Lake Grammar School and the Lower Lake Schoolhouse) was the only school in Lake County made of a material other than wood. Locally kilned brick walls supported a French-style roof with ornately carved wood brackets. The tall roof allowed for an entire second story. The school itself consisted of three classrooms—two large ones in the south and a single classroom positioned centrally in the north with a large bell tower mounted to the front. (Courtesy of the Lower Lake Historic Schoolhouse Museum.)

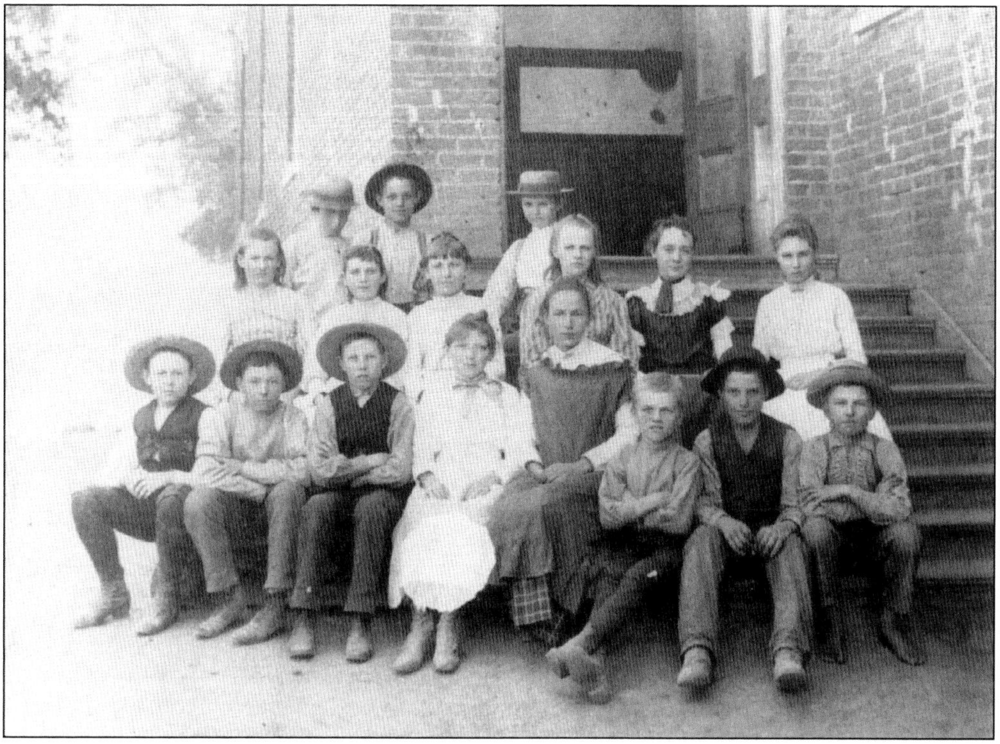

Positioned on either side of the smaller classroom were two separate entryways with vestibules inside where students could hang their hats and coats (as seen here). The school also had a wooden staircase at the back, which led to the large auditorium that made up the second story. This large space had a seating capacity of well over 100. (Courtesy of the Lower Lake Historic Schoolhouse Museum.)

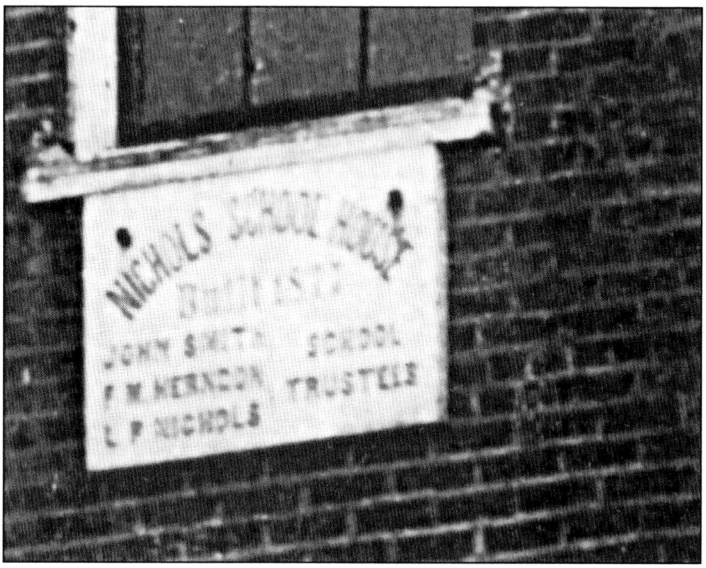

Leslie Phineas Nichols was a longtime resident of Lower Lake who first arrived in Lake County as an agent for the Clear Lake Water Works Company. In 1876, he was commissioned to design and build the unique structure that would soon bear his name. After the schoolhouse opened in 1877, Nichols served as one of the first school trustees. (Courtesy of the Lower Lake Historic Schoolhouse Museum.)

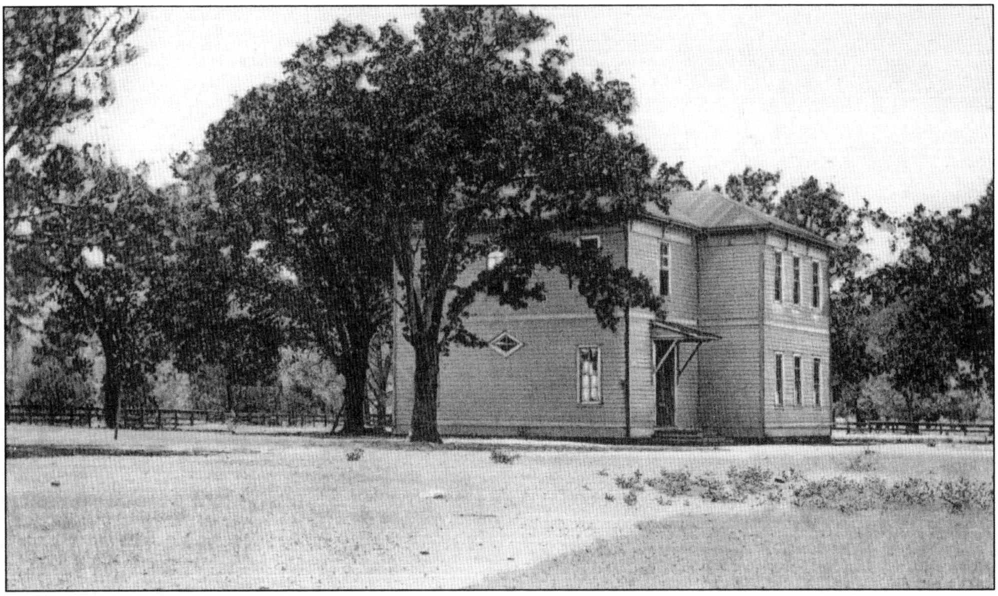

Sometime in the late 1880s or early 1890s, the Middletown School District built a new school for its growing student population. Almost identical to the 1884 Upper Lake Grammar School and a smaller version of the 1880 Lakeport Grammar School, this building served the students of the Middletown area until the 1920s. Not wanting to simply reproduce these other schoolhouses, though, the builders of this schoolhouse added a decorative diamond-shaped window on one side of the first floor (seen in the picture above). As in the other schoolhouses of the period, a single woodstove in each classroom warmed the students during winter months and the tall windows could be opened in summer to cool them in turn.

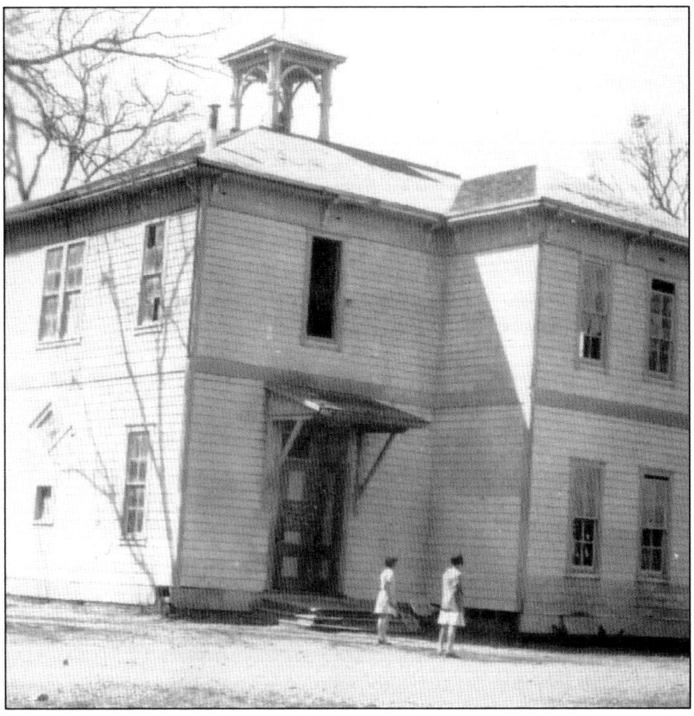

Three

Teaching and Learning in Lake County 1856–1900

Rural farming, mining, and lumber communities characterized Lake County society at the time. Not just buildings where students went to school, the schoolhouses constructed in 19th-century Lake County became gathering places for their communities. Trying to reconstruct the actual classroom experience of Lake County students is challenging, not least because they differed from one school to the next and even from one student to the next.

In the earliest years, when schoolhouses were only just starting to appear, parents had teachers board with them at night and teach their children during the day. Susannah Roberts Townsend, who had immigrated to Lake County in late 1859 after first living in the goldfields during the Gold Rush, relates to a relative back east that the woman on whose property she lived "made it a condition . . . that either I or Emory [her husband] teach her children," which Susannah agreed to do. Word quickly got around, and other nearby families sent their children so that Susannah was soon teaching nine children. But, as was customary in such rural areas of that time, she took her payment in potatoes or "a sack of cabbage or beets or some eggs." In the end, Susannah worked three months as a teacher, in which time she earned $60—only $1 of which was cash, the rest being goods in kind.

The massive population boom in the 1870s, which saw Lake County's population nearly triple, coupled with a maturing education system in the rest of California, created the foundation for a modern school system in the county. Teachers became better trained and better paid, and the curriculum they taught was well thought out.

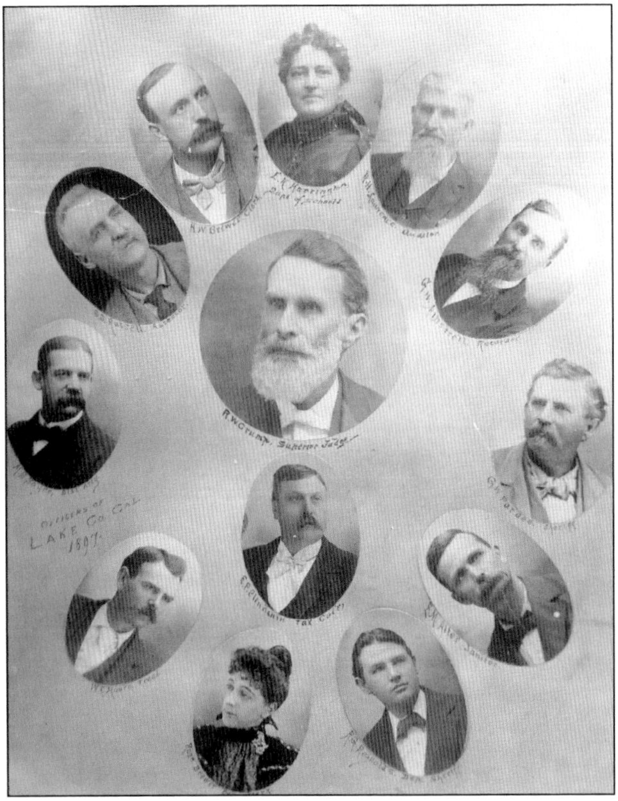

The picture at left depicts all the elected county officials for the year 1897. As one can see, there is a noted lack of women. In fact, other than the county clerk, the only other female official is Etta K. Harrington, the superintendent of schools. As the first female to hold that position in Lake County, Harrington represented a larger statewide trend in 1890s California—women educators were rising to positions of prominence within their communities. Among her many responsibilities as superintendent, Harrington ensured that all teachers and schools in Lake County operated according to state laws, and each year, she compiled a written report on their status, which she sent to the state superintendent. Harrington held her position from 1890 to 1898.

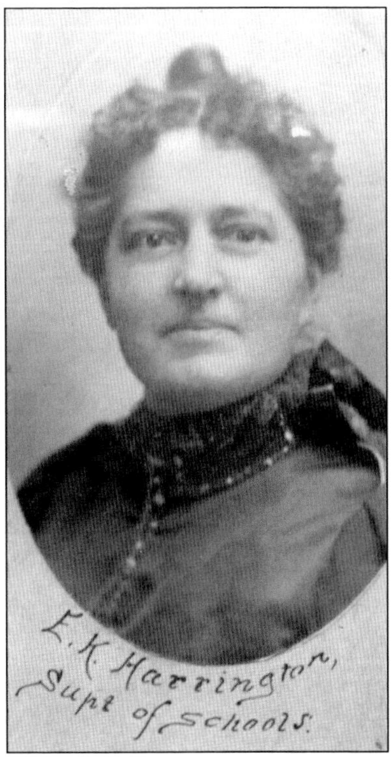

According to the 1877 annual report of the county superintendent of common schools, 33 teachers taught at 28 different schools in Lake County. Albert Morrell, a longtime teacher at the Lower Lake Grammar School (where often more than one teacher taught at any given time) is depicted here. (Courtesy of the Lower Lake Historic Schoolhouse Museum.)

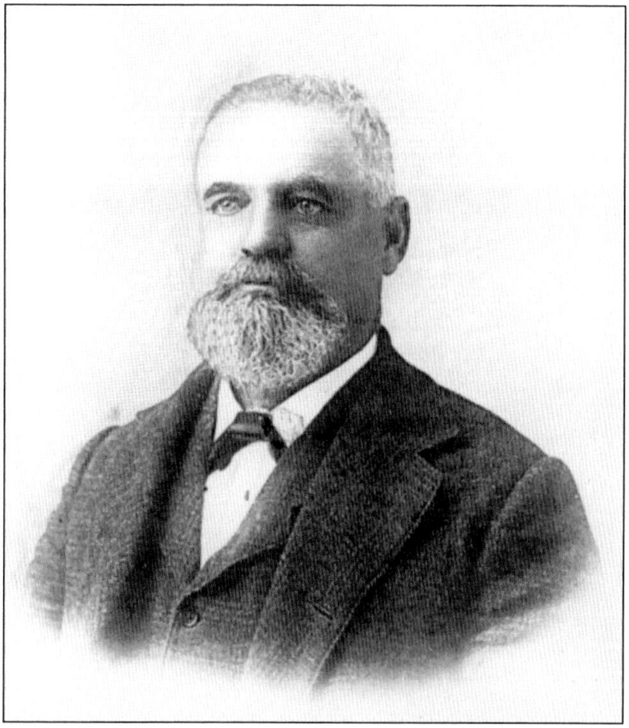

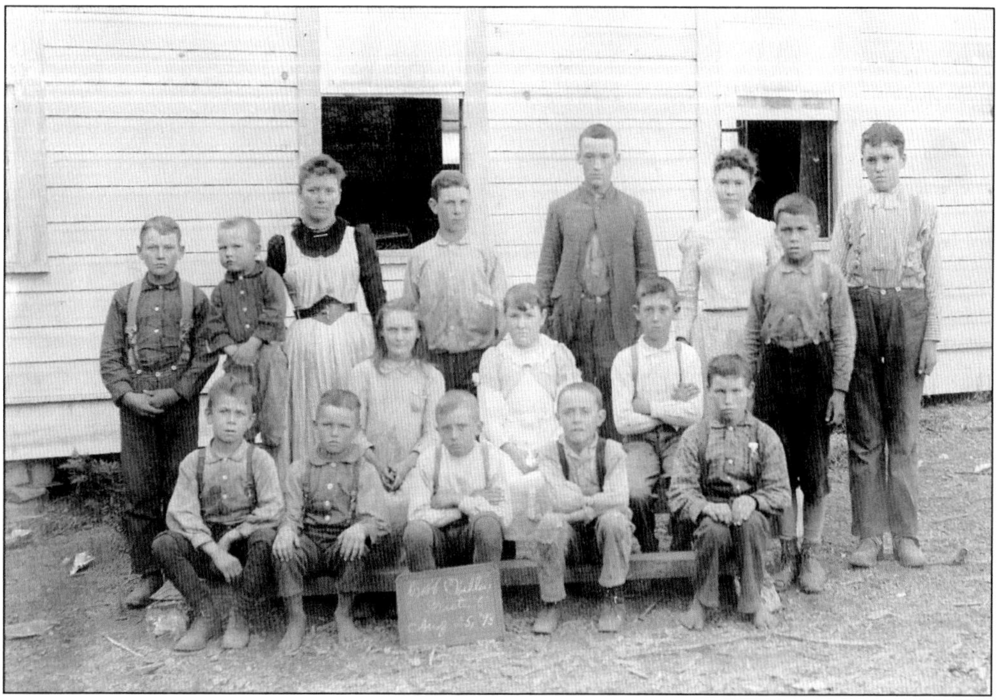

Like in the rest of California, women quickly took to the profession of teaching in Lake County. In 1870, only 4 of the 13 teachers in the county were women. But by 1877, female teachers outnumbered their male counterparts, with 17 women and 16 men teaching. Pictured here, a young teacher poses with her students at the Cobb Valley School in 1893.

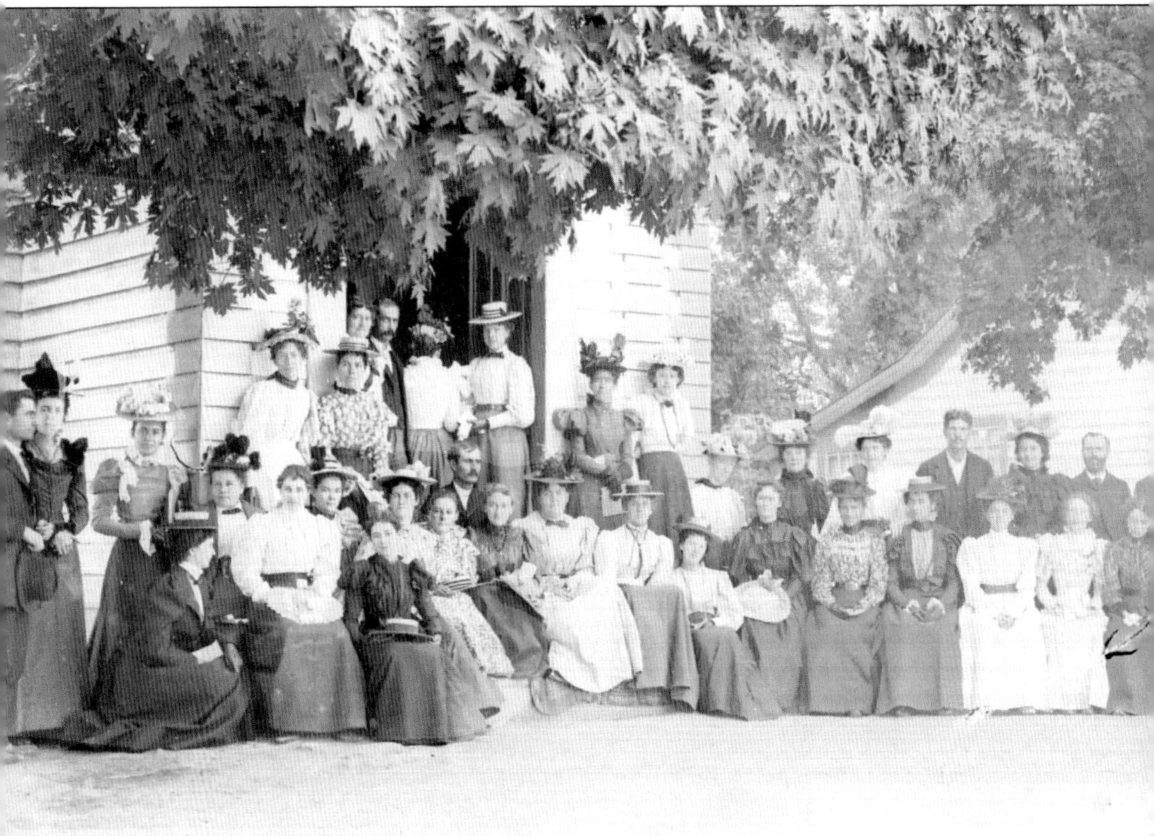

From the very beginning, the state laid out detailed requirements for becoming a teacher. Since the 1850s, modest attempts to develop teacher certification exams were pursued, although they did not fully gain ground until the 1860s. One of the earliest methods of ongoing education for teachers came in the form of teachers' institutes, which were days-long workshops for teachers featuring lectures on pedagogical issues. In 1863–1864, the state passed a law that provided funds for county teachers' institutes, and by 1879, all counties with 20 or more schools were required to hold one. The December 6, 1877, issue of the *Lake Democrat* newspaper reports on such an institute in Lake County, but only 6 of the reported 33 teachers in the county attended. By the middle of the 1880s, attendance was mandatory. Shown here is the earliest known picture of the Lake County Teachers' Institute, dated 1895.

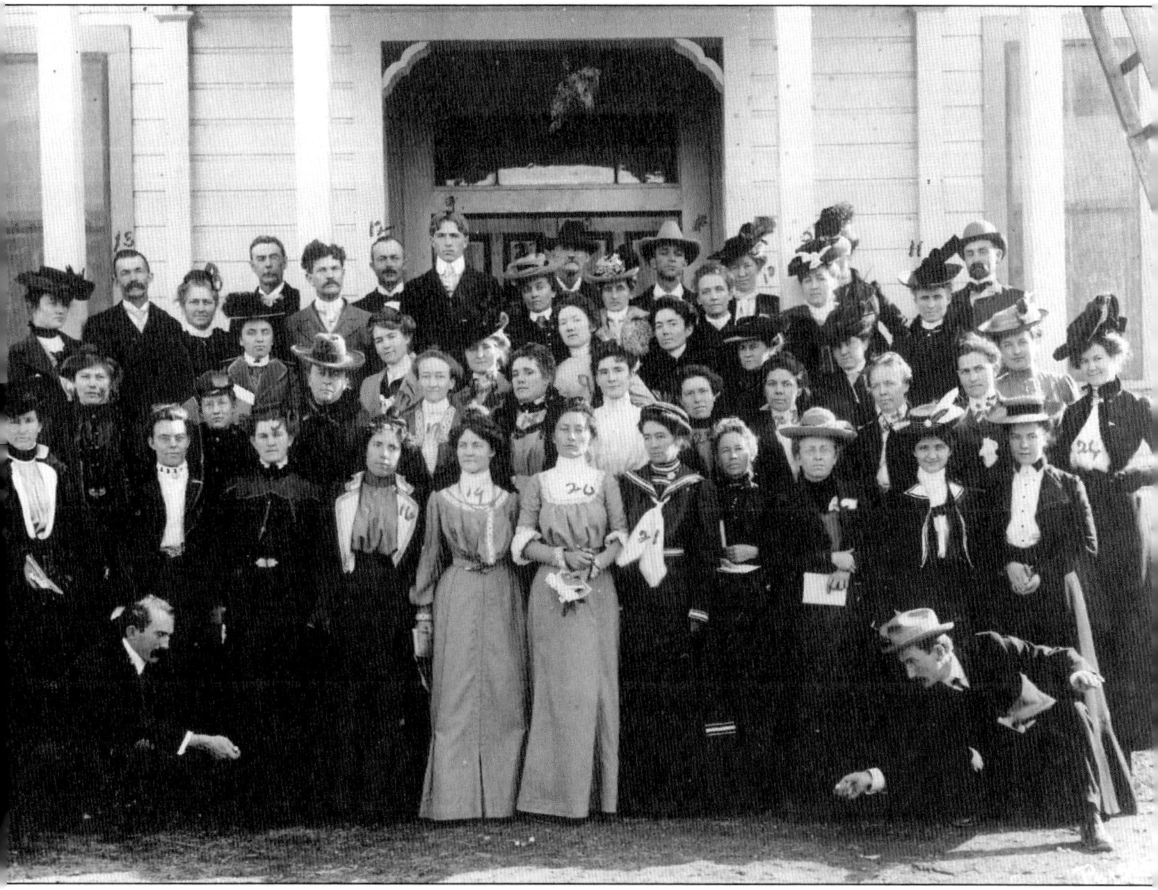

It is somewhat challenging to determine how much teachers were paid in Lake County at any given time. In an editorial in the *Lake Democrat* on December 22, 1877, a certain N. Smith was said to be receiving $120 a month, which, according to the newspaper, was $20 more a month than any other teacher in the county. This account is probably exaggerated, since the county superintendent of common schools reported to the state that the average wages for male teachers in 1877 was $75.14 a month and female teachers only $71 a month. Interestingly, a series of receipts for checks written by the county treasurer in 1877 survives in the Historic Courthouse Museum that lists the monthly salary of the county superintendent of common schools as only $54.17. Pictured is the 1899 Lake County Teachers' Institute (notice the two teachers at the front "playing" marbles).

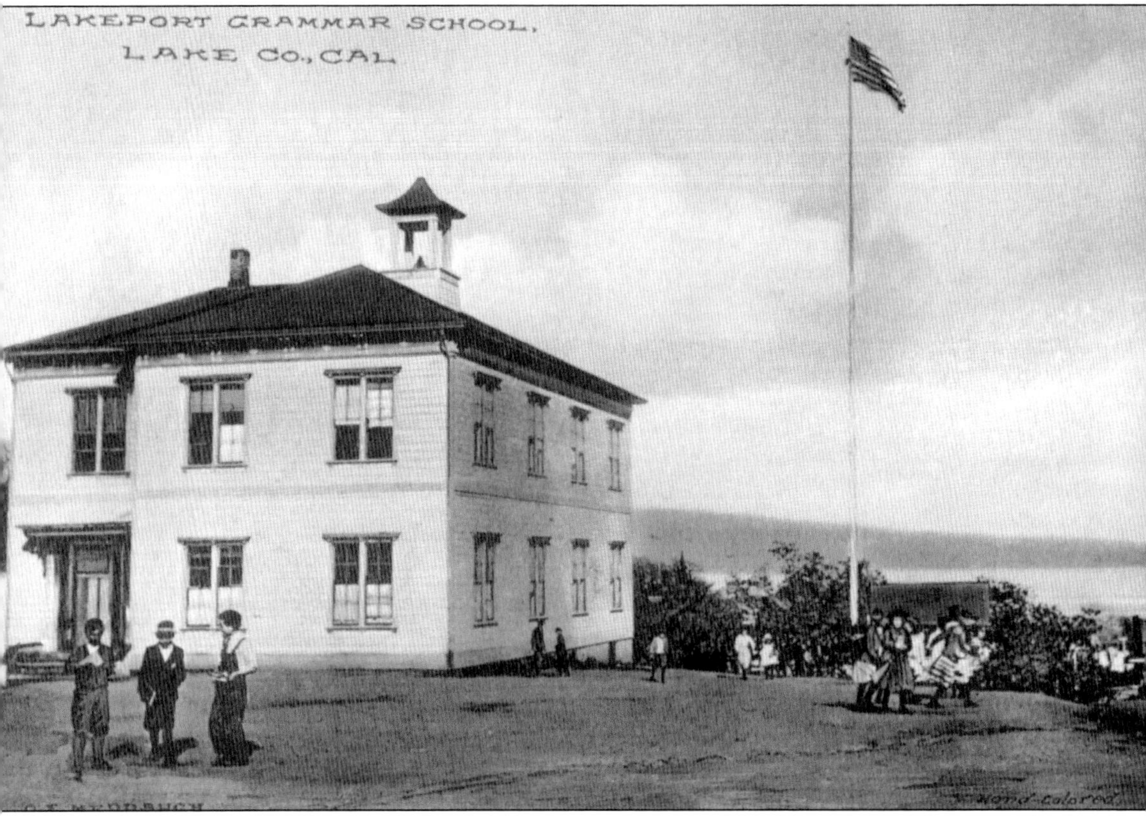

As today, not all teachers were made the same in 19th-century Lake County. Former student of Lakeport Grammar School and later state assemblyman (in 1888) C.M. Crawford remembers in his autobiography that his grammar school teacher "was the laziest man I ever saw in my life." This man, A.P. McCarty, would regularly lie down for a nap in the middle of the school day, using a *Webster's Unabridged Dictionary* as a pillow. One day, Crawford and some of his pals took it upon themselves to teach their teacher a lesson. Sneaking up to the bench on which the instructor slumbered, Crawford and friends gave a mighty push, and down the hill tumbled the now-awake McCarty. As seen in this image, it would have been quite a fall down the hill from the schoolhouse. (Courtesy of the Lake County Historical Society.)

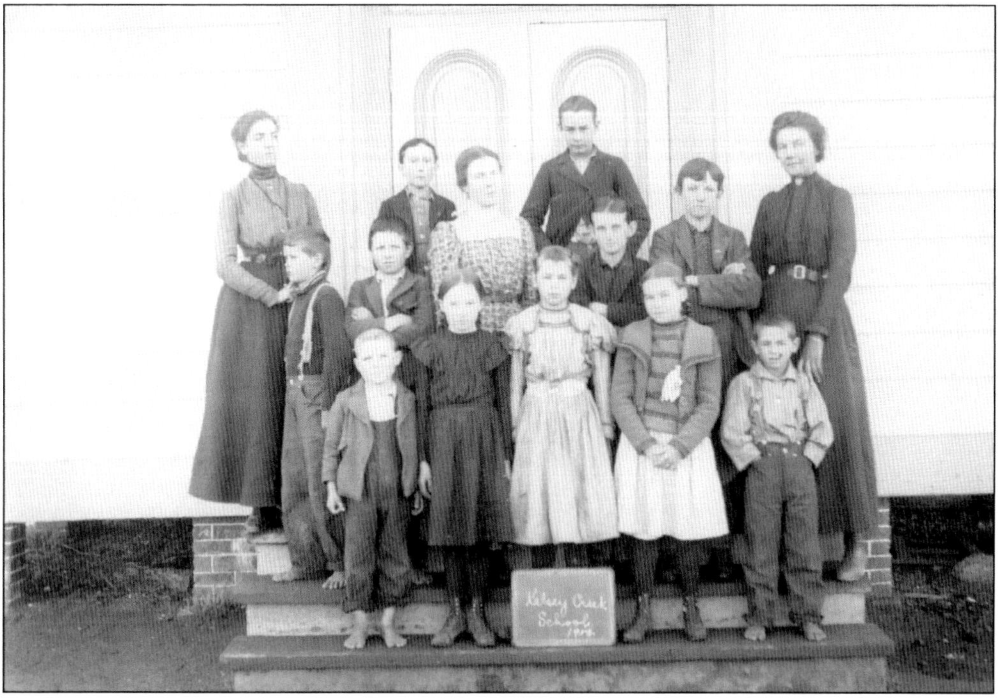

Other than for those living in Lakeport, Upper Lake, Lower Lake, or Middletown, the one-room schoolhouse characterized the educational experience for most Lake County children. Although they came in slightly different sizes, these schools shared a similar layout that had a single rectangular-like classroom broken only by the presence of desks or benches for the students, an elevated platform and desk for the teacher, and a wood-burning stove in a corner. The pictures here illustrate the age range of students who attended these schools. The picture above shows the class of 1900 at the Kelsey Creek Schoolhouse near Kelseyville, and the one below shows the 1892 class at the Middle Creek Schoolhouse near Upper Lake.

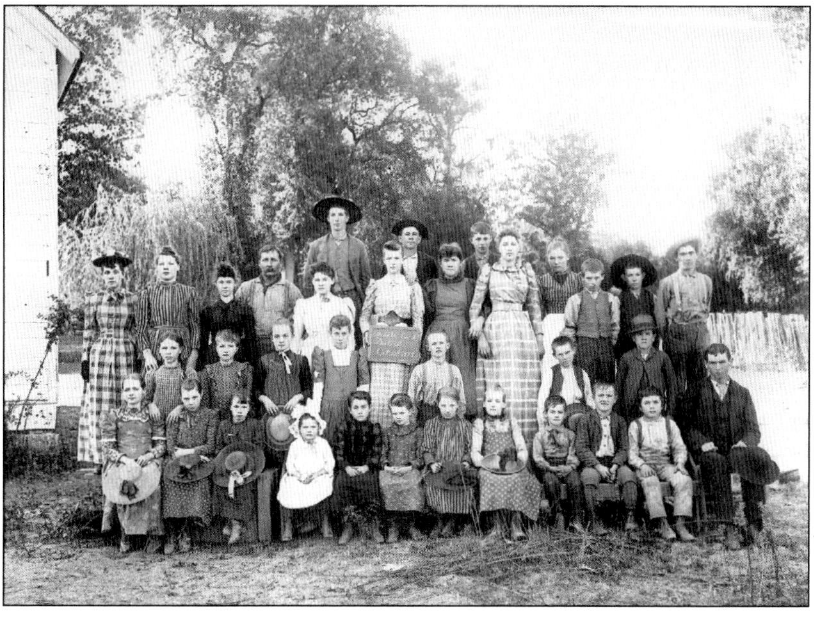

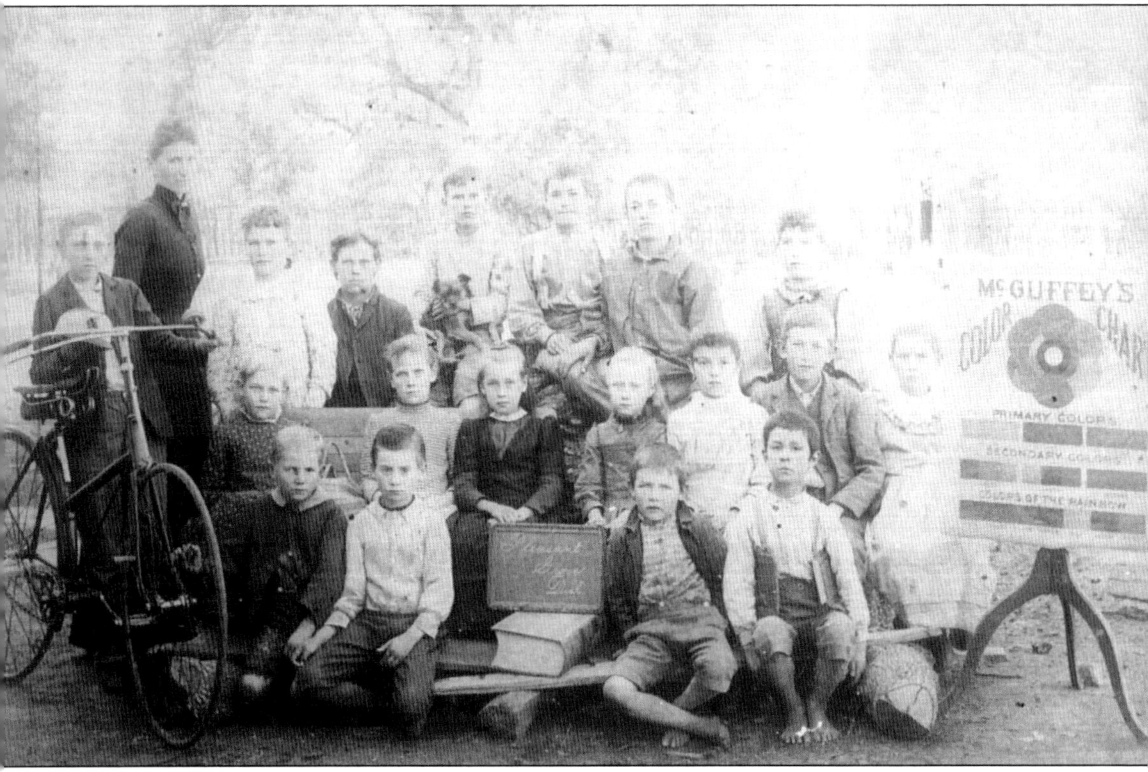

Early on, most of the burden for purchasing books for Lake County classrooms fell to the individual school districts. The result was a wide discrepancy in the quality of educational aids between urban and rural schools. *Eclectic Reader* by William McGuffey—popularly called *McGuffey*—was the most popular teaching book of the time. However, the rise of public education and shifting pedagogies saw an increase in the need for teaching aids beyond these simple instructional books. And so, charts, maps, and posters began to fill classrooms in school districts that could afford such extravagancies. Amid the rustic atmosphere of this class portrait of the Pleasant Valley School District is one of these state-of-the-art tools, a McGuffey's Color Chart. The school district was so proud of its teaching aid that it was given a place of honor in the annual class picture.

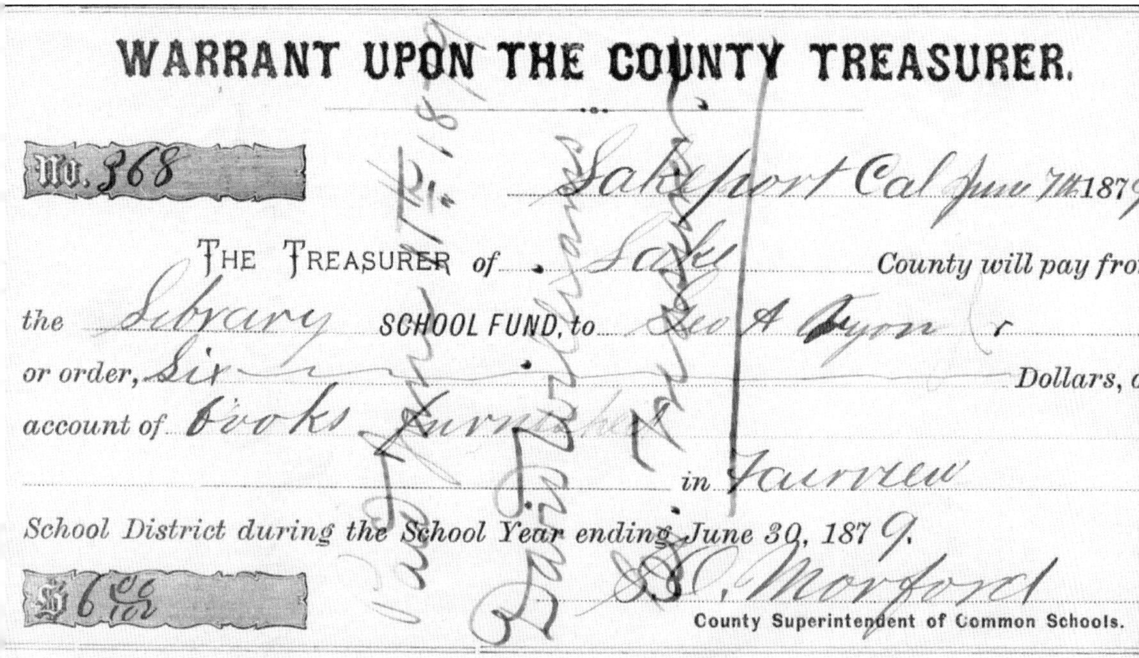

WARRANT UPON THE COUNTY TREASURER.

No. 368 Lakeport Cal June 7th 1879

THE TREASURER of Lake County will pay from the Library SCHOOL FUND, to [illegible] or order, Six Dollars, on account of Books furnished in Fairview School District during the School Year ending June 30, 1879.

$6 00/100

[illegible] Morford
County Superintendent of Common Schools.

The types and number of books available in the classroom also differed from one school to the next. In records compiled at the state level for the year 1865, only one of the then seven schools in Lake County was using the full series of state-suggested textbooks. By the 1890s, however, even the smallest of schoolhouses appear to have been supplied with enough books to constitute small libraries. A state-issued "Librarian's Record Book" from 1890, used in the Burns Valley School District now resides in the Lower Lake Historic Schoolhouse Museum. In it are meticulous records noting which pupils checked out what books. In total, the school district (serving a single schoolhouse) owned 101 books. Topics ranged from *Longfellow's Selected Poems* to *Origin of Civilization and the Primitive Condition of Man*. A collection of receipts for checks issued by the county in 1877–1878 also shows that the county had a library fund from which the different school districts could draw money to buy books. Pictured is one of these receipts.

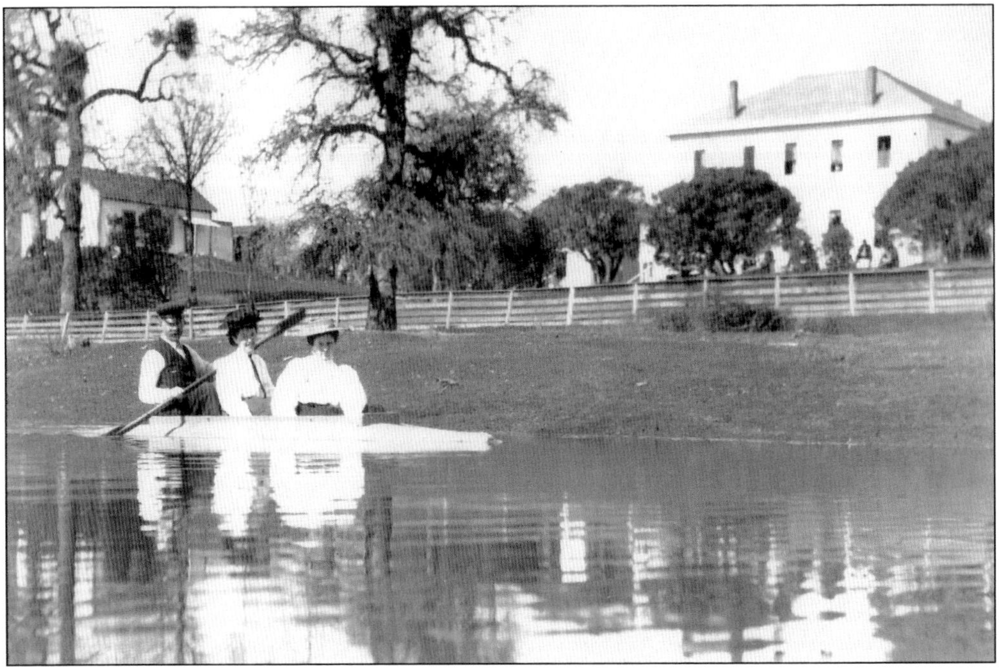

In a time when the only means of leaving Lake County required an arduous stage trip over mountains and across streams, many people lived their entire lives within sight of Clear Lake. The individual communities in which they lived became that much more important because of this. With a school year lasting anywhere between three and six months (and sometimes eight, depending on the district), these schoolhouses became important points of community contact, where children made friendships that lasted their entire lives. For this reason, the activities that happened outside the classroom were just as, if not more, important than those within. It is also these activities that were most often photographed. Pictured here is Professor Overholser of the Lakeport Academy taking some of his students out on Clear Lake around 1900.

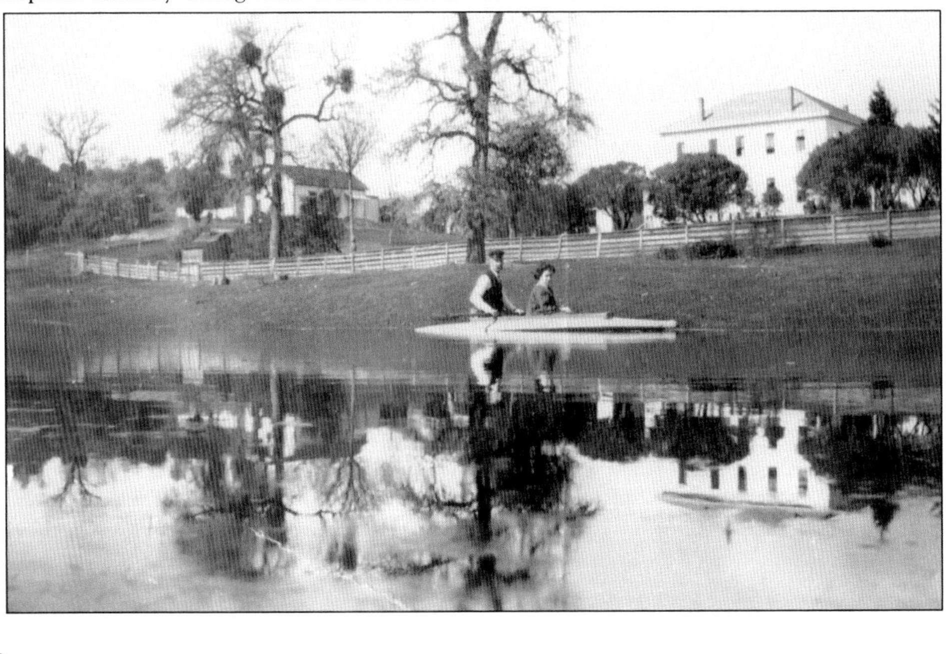

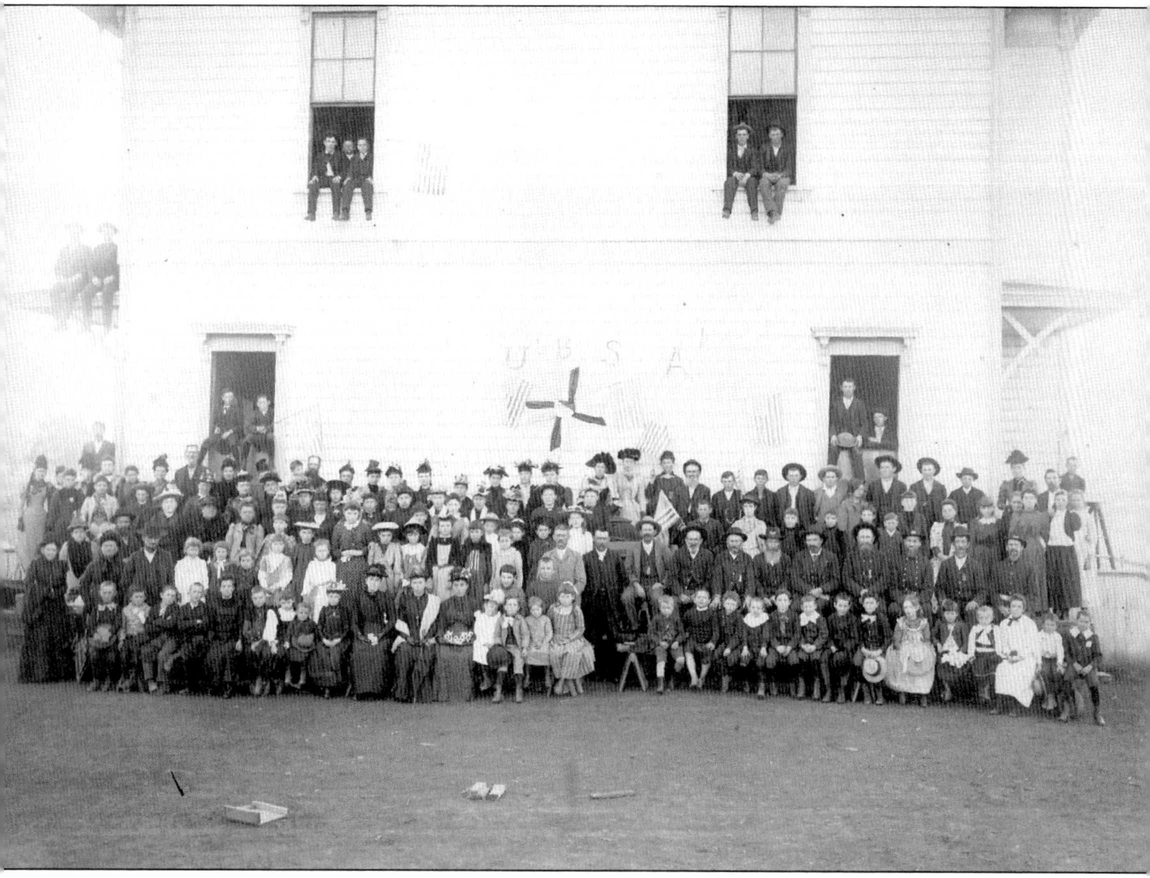

Schools were not only the purview of teachers and children, either. Pictured here is a large crowd of students and their parents and the teachers at Upper Lake Grammar School in the late 1880s. Remembering her time in a one-room school at the Great Western Mine in rural south Lake County, Helen Rocca Goss recalled that her mother got on the school board and quickly immersed herself in matters of the school. Because they lived in such a rural community, she remembered that her mother frequently dealt with trying to find a new teacher. Between 1891 and 1895, six different teachers taught at the Great Western school. Not only her mother, but her father too got involved. Helen remembered that, as he was the chief school trustee, her father's "decision was the controlling one in all important school matters." Such detailed involvement like Helen recalls was at a small school of only a dozen or so students. Imagine the anguish teachers at larger schools experienced dealing with several times that number of parents.

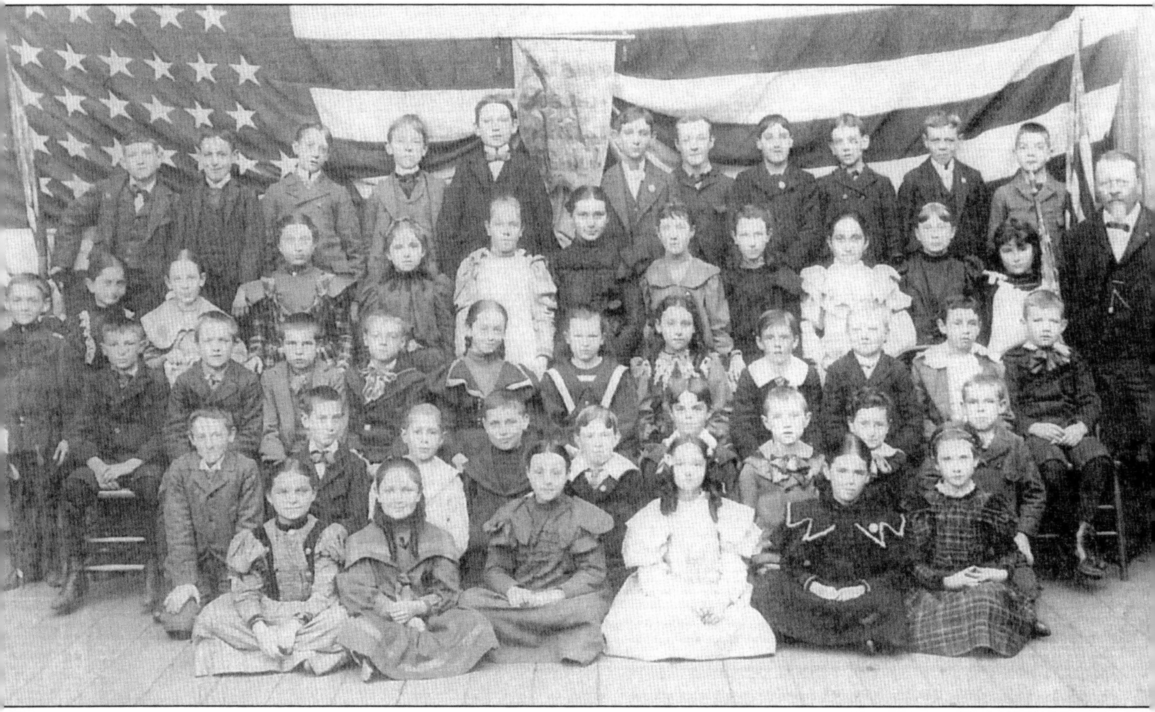

Towards the end of the 19th century, advocates for public education argued that public schools served a vital role in the development of a moral and patriotic populace. At the end of his annual report to the state, Lake County's superintendent of common schools in 1880 took some time to wax poetic on the role of public schools. In a solemn manner, he prophesied that "not till the American public realize the fact that the industry, morality and intelligence of our nation depend upon the Public Schools, will our star of progress rise high in the heavens and the perpetuity of our American institutions become fixed and certain." Pictured here, the young students at the Lower Lake Grammar School pose for a class picture in front of a large American flag. Patriotic scenes like these became more common, and more people subscribed to the same belief that education created a more industrious populace.

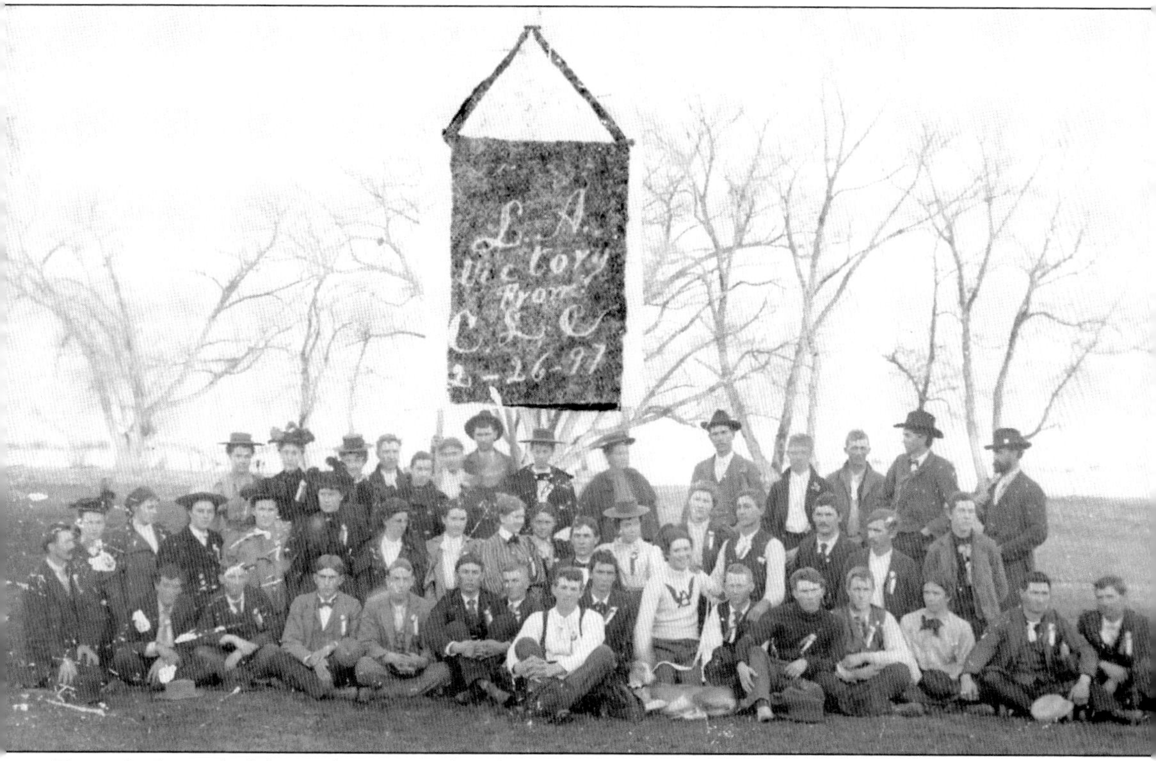

Towards the end of the 19th century, the idea of education began to include nourishment of the body as well as the mind. Organized sports teams at schools began to gain prominence. Here, students from the Lakeport Academy pose for a picture. Professor Overholser kept meticulous official notes on Lakeport Academy, which survive to this day. His journal entry for February 26, 1897, the date written on the flag in the photograph, tells the background to this picture: "In the afternoon the Academy boys competed with the Kelseyvilles [Clear Lake College, another private school at the time] in athletic field sports. They won in everything except the standing high jump. The Academy students wore badges [which are seen in the photograph], boys and girls, and the girls cheered every success with the Academy Yell: 'Wahoo, wahoo, wahoo wah, Lakeport Academy zip boom bah!'"

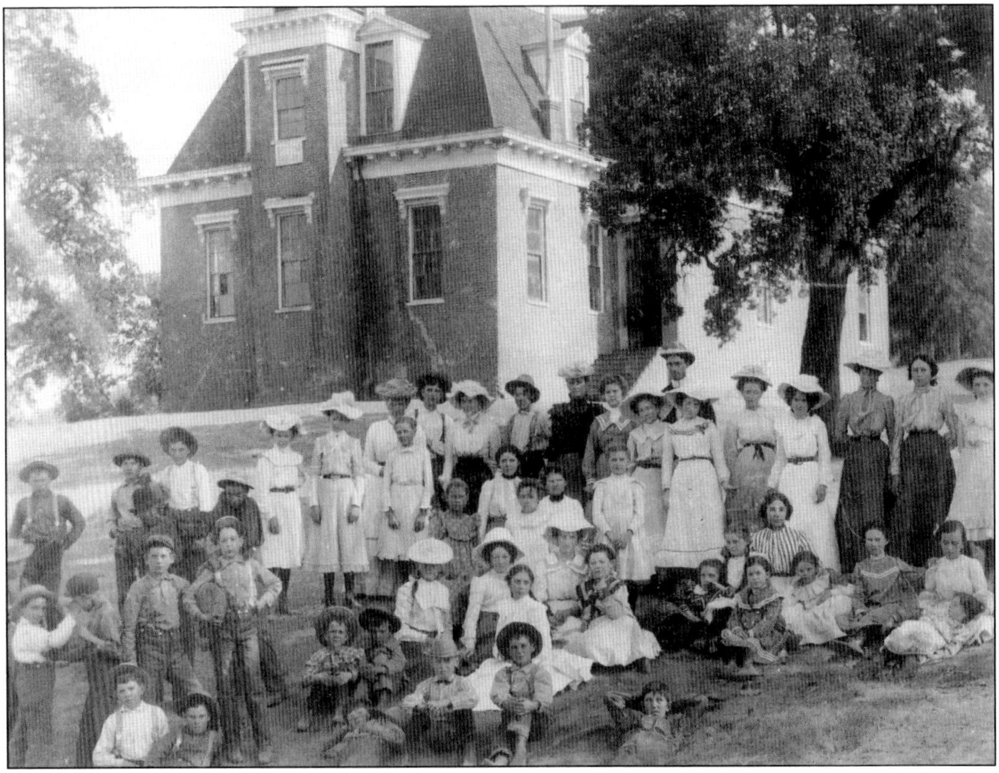

Of course, even before they were formally organized into teams, Lake County students enjoyed playing sports at school. Above is an 1898 photograph taken in front of the Lower Lake Grammar School. Notice the boys goofing off in the lower left corner of the picture; one of them is holding a football. Kids will be kids, and sometimes, all they want to do is run around during recess or ride around on their bikes. In the picture below, two boys pose proudly with their bicycles in front of the Liberty Schoolhouse.

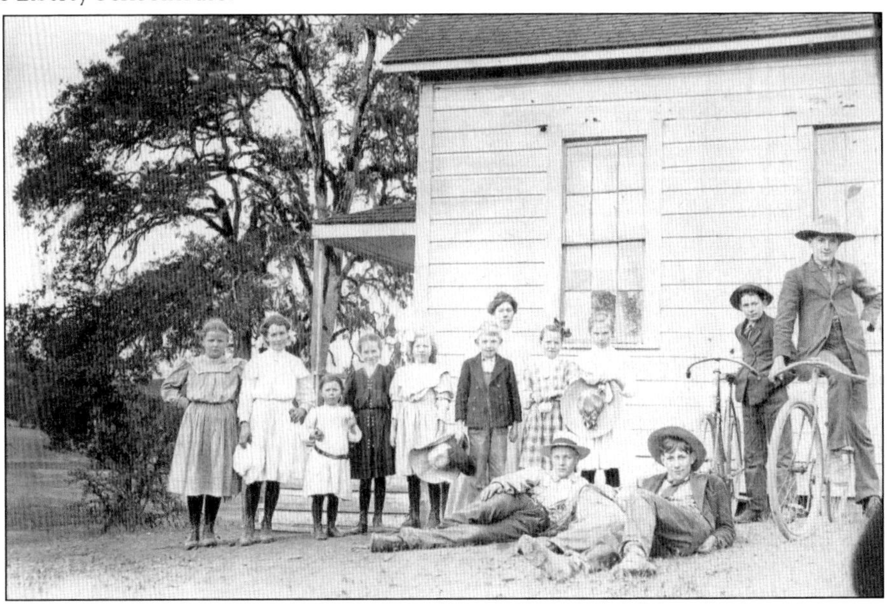

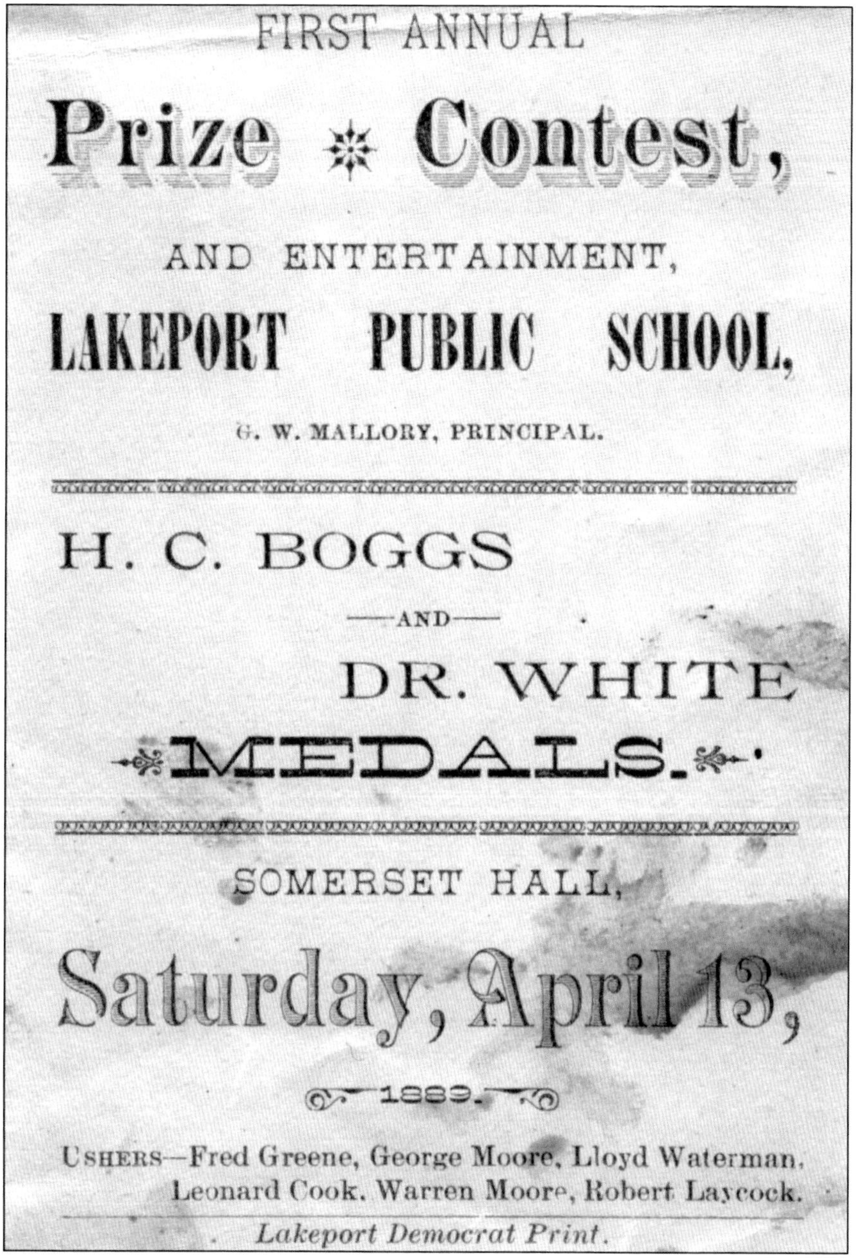
FIRST ANNUAL

Prize * Contest,

AND ENTERTAINMENT,

LAKEPORT PUBLIC SCHOOL,

G. W. MALLORY, PRINCIPAL.

H. C. BOGGS

—AND—

DR. WHITE

MEDALS.

SOMERSET HALL,

Saturday, April 13,

1889.

USHERS—Fred Greene, George Moore, Lloyd Waterman, Leonard Cook, Warren Moore, Robert Laycock.

Lakeport Democrat Print.

Not all extracurricular activities in 19th-century Lake County schools involved sports. Just as physical education began to be seen as an important element to a well-rounded education, so too were skills that have since been eclipsed in modern education: elocution and public speaking. Pictured is a playbill advertising a competition held in Lakeport between students from the local public schools. The night included two separate competitions: the first was a public forum debate and the second was an oratory contest. The subject of the debate was "Resolved: that a miser is more detrimental to society than a spendthrift" with two students on the affirmative side and two on the negative. The winners of the debate won the H.C. Boggs Medal, and the winner of the oration received the Dr. White Medal. (Courtesy of the Lower Lake Historic Schoolhouse Museum.)

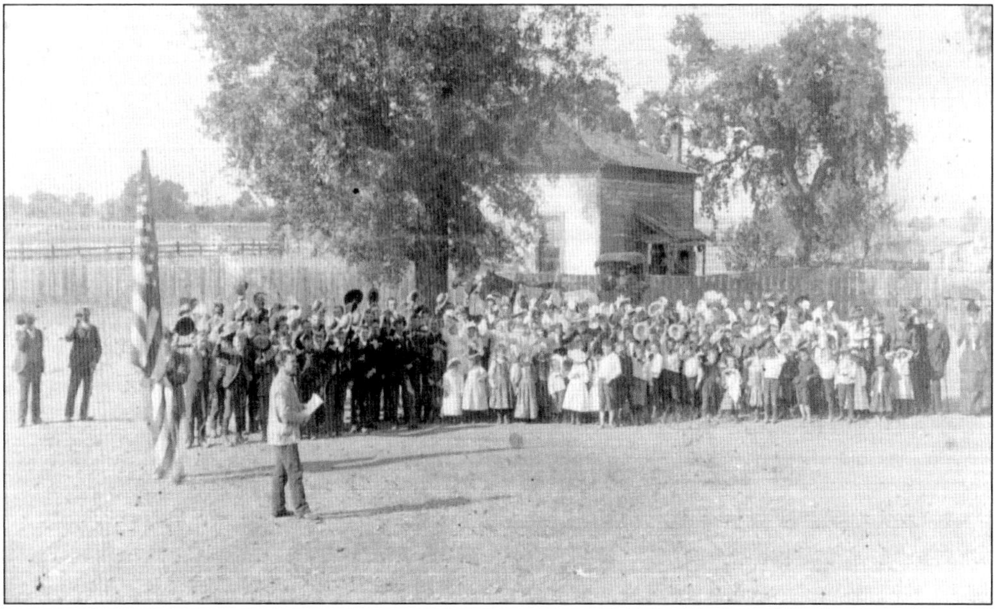

In a rural county like Lake County, public buildings were few and far between. The schoolhouses, often set in open fields, became natural locations for public gatherings. Pictured here is one of these gatherings, somewhere outside a Kelseyville school around the turn of the 20th century.

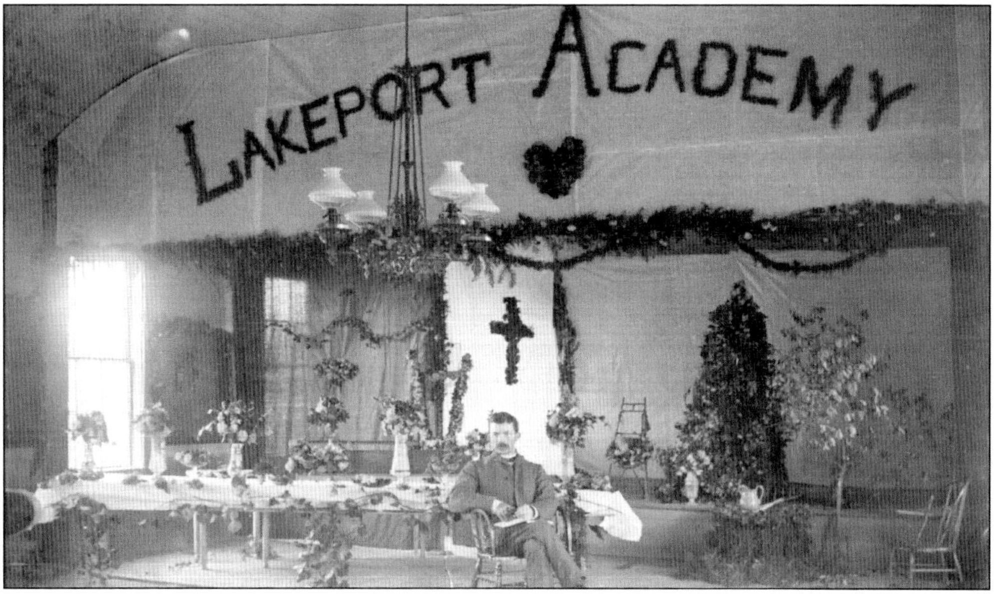

If the fields outside proved useful for gatherings, the open spaces of the large city schools like the Lakeport Academy were even handier for indoor public events. Here, Professor Overholser poses for a picture during a flower show held in the school in 1886.

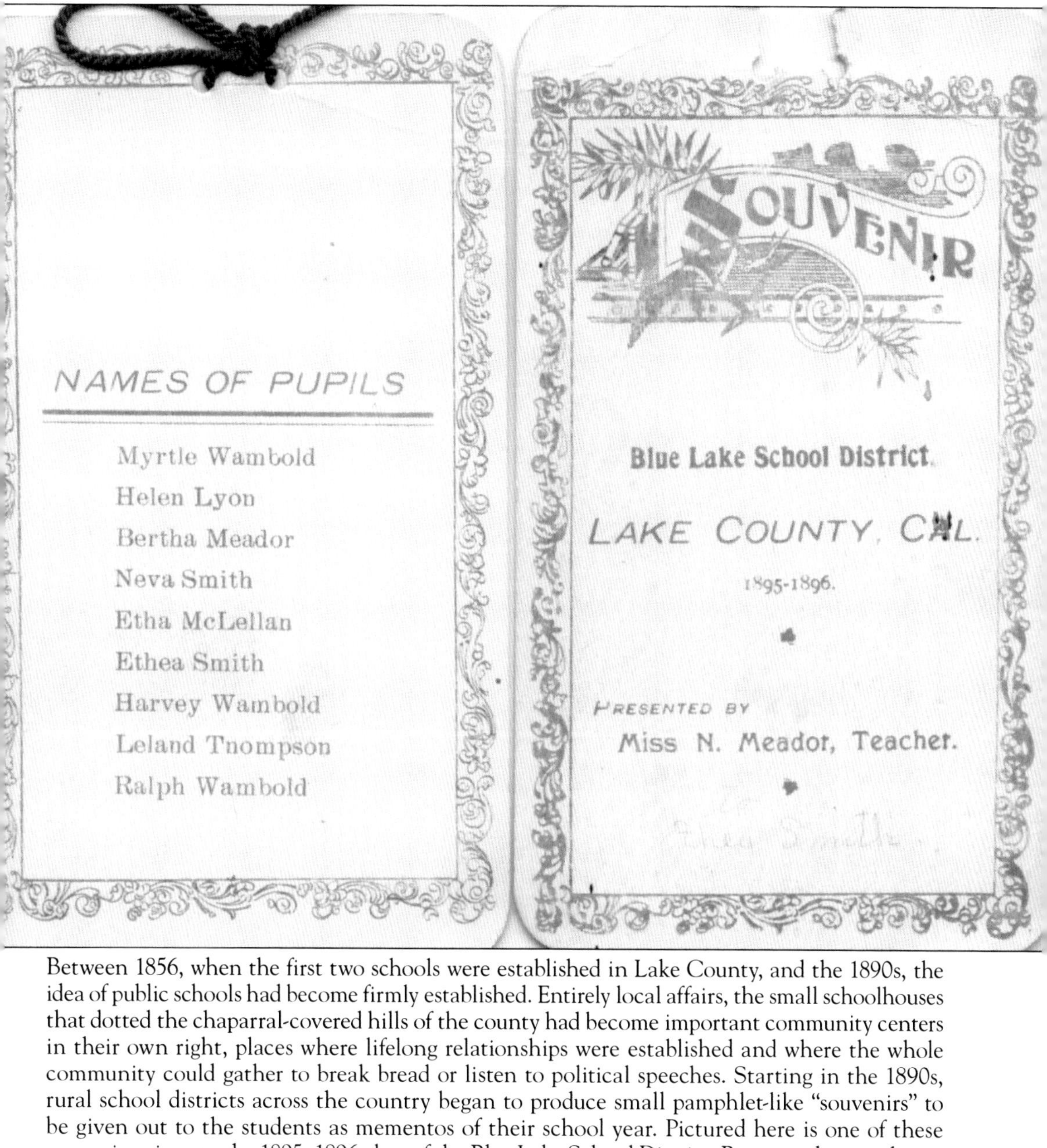

Between 1856, when the first two schools were established in Lake County, and the 1890s, the idea of public schools had become firmly established. Entirely local affairs, the small schoolhouses that dotted the chaparral-covered hills of the county had become important community centers in their own right, places where lifelong relationships were established and where the whole community could gather to break bread or listen to political speeches. Starting in the 1890s, rural school districts across the country began to produce small pamphlet-like "souvenirs" to be given out to the students as mementos of their school year. Pictured here is one of these souvenirs, given to the 1895–1896 class of the Blue Lake School District. Between the mandatory attendance laws passed in California and these souvenirs, school was beginning to be seen not simply as a public good, but a public necessity for the development of the American populace.

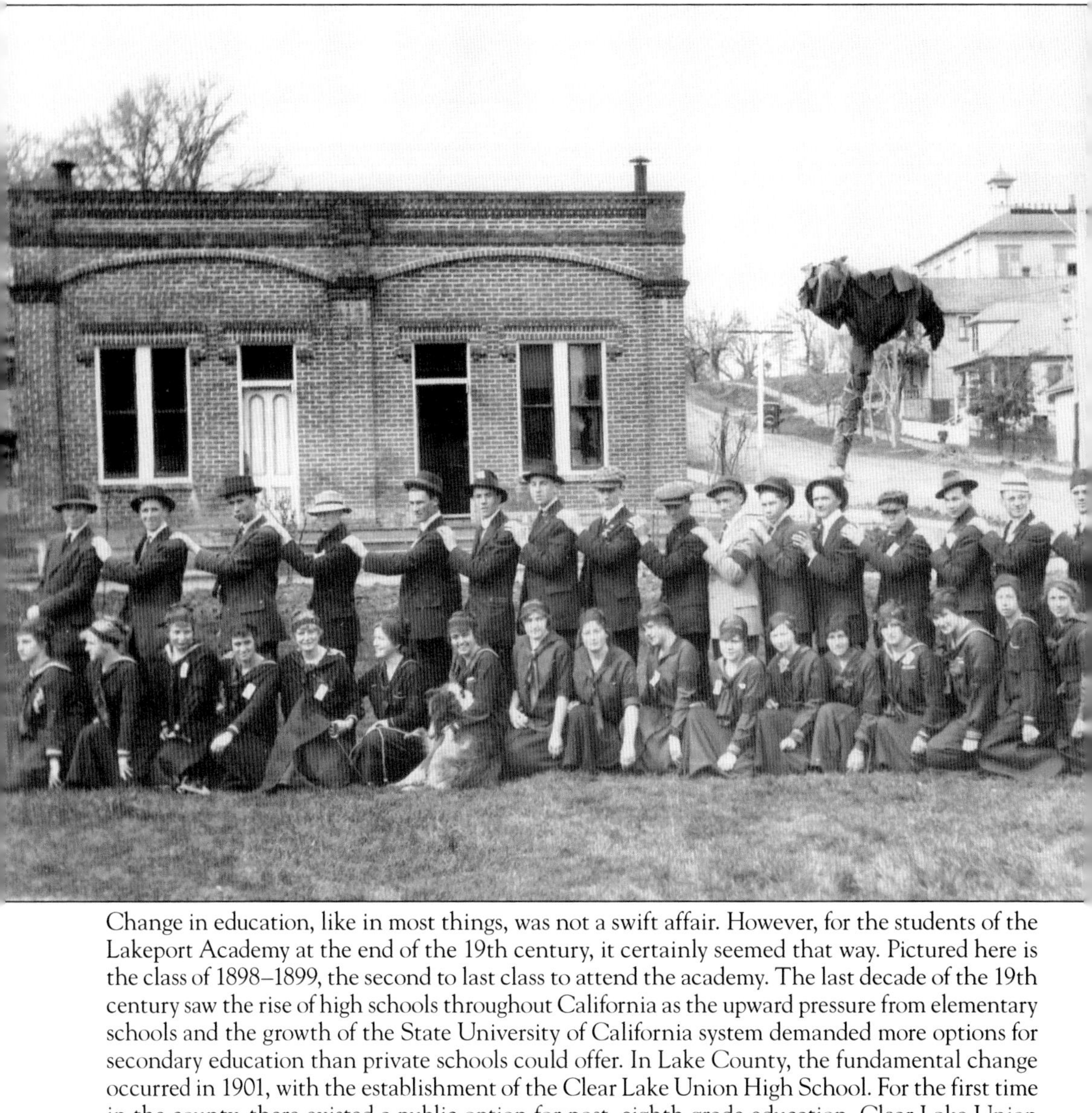

Change in education, like in most things, was not a swift affair. However, for the students of the Lakeport Academy at the end of the 19th century, it certainly seemed that way. Pictured here is the class of 1898–1899, the second to last class to attend the academy. The last decade of the 19th century saw the rise of high schools throughout California as the upward pressure from elementary schools and the growth of the State University of California system demanded more options for secondary education than private schools could offer. In Lake County, the fundamental change occurred in 1901, with the establishment of the Clear Lake Union High School. For the first time in the county, there existed a public option for post–eighth grade education. Clear Lake Union High was like a rock cast into a stream, as many developments in public education in the United States at the time got caught around this single high school (as they were implemented there) and forever altered the educational landscape of Lake County.

Four

History of Lake County 1901–1941

The decade of 1900 to 1910 saw the first drop in Lake County's population since Americans had immigrated to the area in the 1850s (from over 6,000 residents to just over 5,000). This depopulation might have something to do with the closing of several mines, including the large Sulphur Bank Mine in 1905. The population remained stagnant until the construction of roads into the county brought a new wave of families in the late 1920s.

These first three decades of the 20th century saw Lake County transition from a pioneer outpost of cattle wranglers, farmers, loggers, and miners into a modern California county—one still largely remote, but with its agricultural products traveling farther afield than ever before. By 1900, wheat farming had surpassed cattle ranching, which had been the county's first industry. But outpacing even that golden crop were pears—Bartlett pears to be exact. First planted in the 1880s, Lake County's pears—dried and canned then shipped via trucks out of the county—made their way around the world. With the close of World War I in 1918, the county's canned pears helped feed an impoverished Europe so that by 1925, Lake County had become the pear-canning capital of the United States. Largely focused in Big Valley, with Kelseyville as the primary hub, the pear industry set Lake County on the map.

Whether a result of this industrial growth or itself a product of it, the infrastructure in Lake County exploded. In a county once dominated by private toll roads, Lake County's board of supervisors started buying these back and opening public roads instead. By the early 1930s, State Highways 53, 20, and 175 connected Lake County to its neighbors.

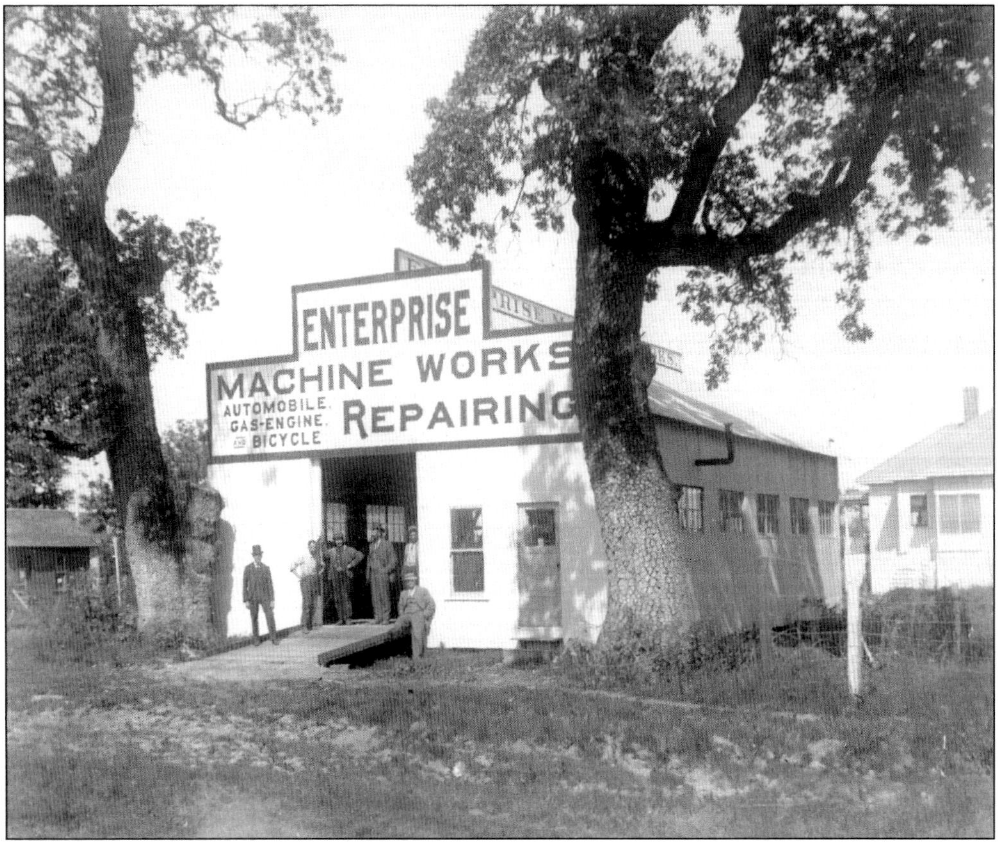

By 1900, the board of supervisors had created an ordinance prohibiting the operation of a motor vehicle within the borders of the county. This was soon revoked. Despite these early laws, Lake County quickly became the home of car enthusiasts. In the beginning only the purview of the wealthy, automobiles began to appear with more prominence by the mid-1910s, with the county itself purchasing its first—a five-passenger truck—in 1915. Pictured above is one of the earliest service stations for Lake County's growing auto population, located in Lakeport. Below is the first gas pump in Lakeport, serving its first customers in 1915.

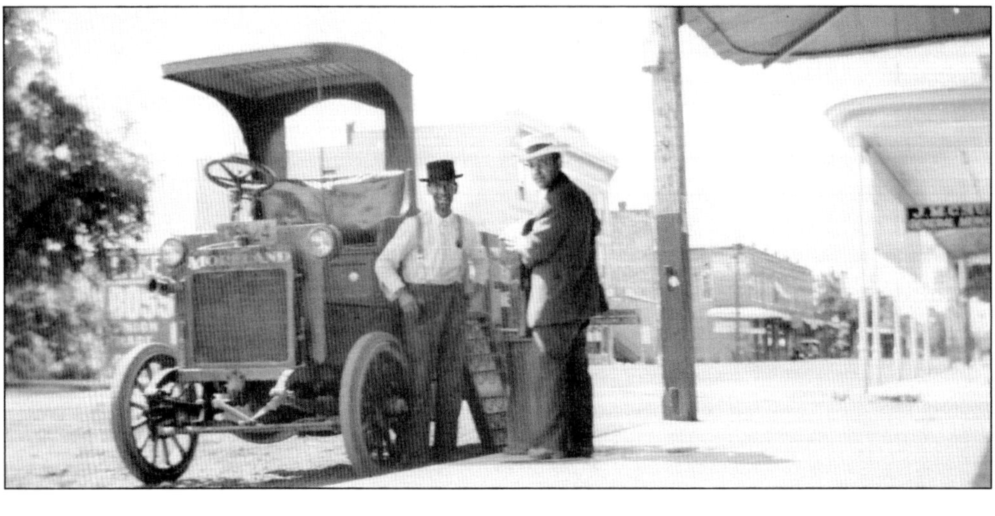

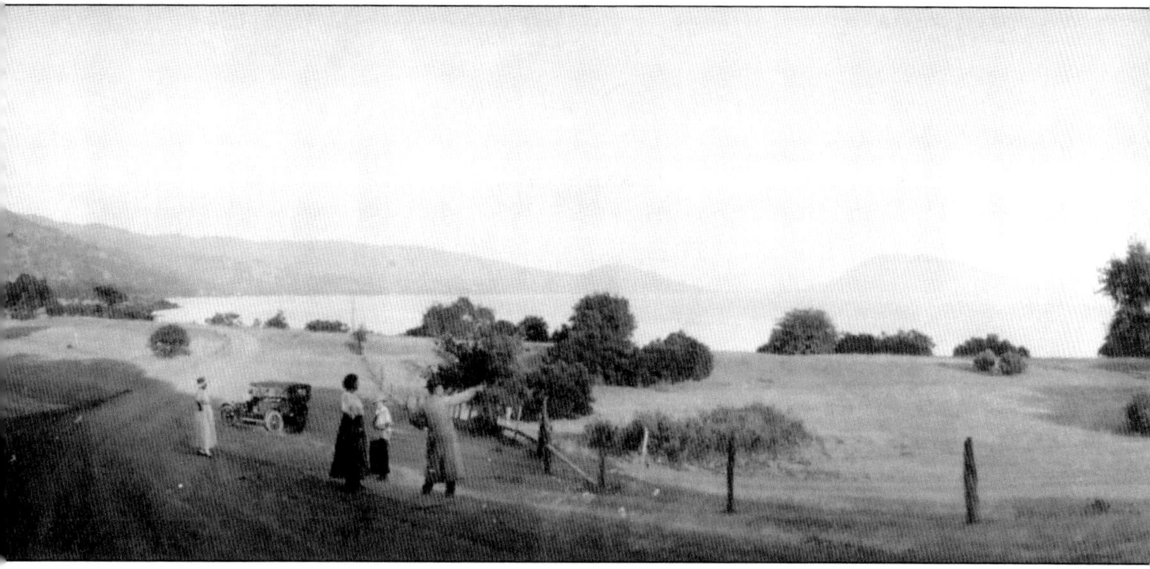

Simultaneously, the county began a campaign to rid itself of private toll roads in favor of public roads, which it soon started to construct on its own. In 1901, Lakeshore Boulevard, which runs between Lakeport and Upper Lake along the shore of Clear Lake, was authorized and declared a main thoroughfare of the county. As early as 1914, the State of California began talks with the Lake County Board of Supervisors to construct highways. Pictured here is one of these early county roads along the northeastern shores of Clear Lake. This road would become Highway 20, which would eventually run from Fort Bragg in Mendocino County to the Sierra Nevada.

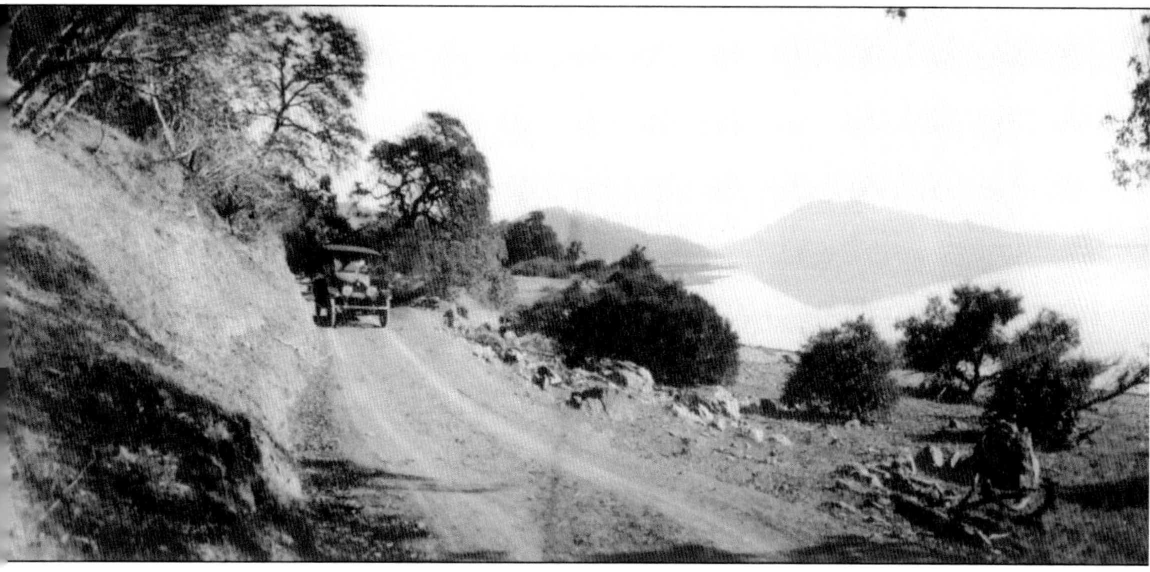

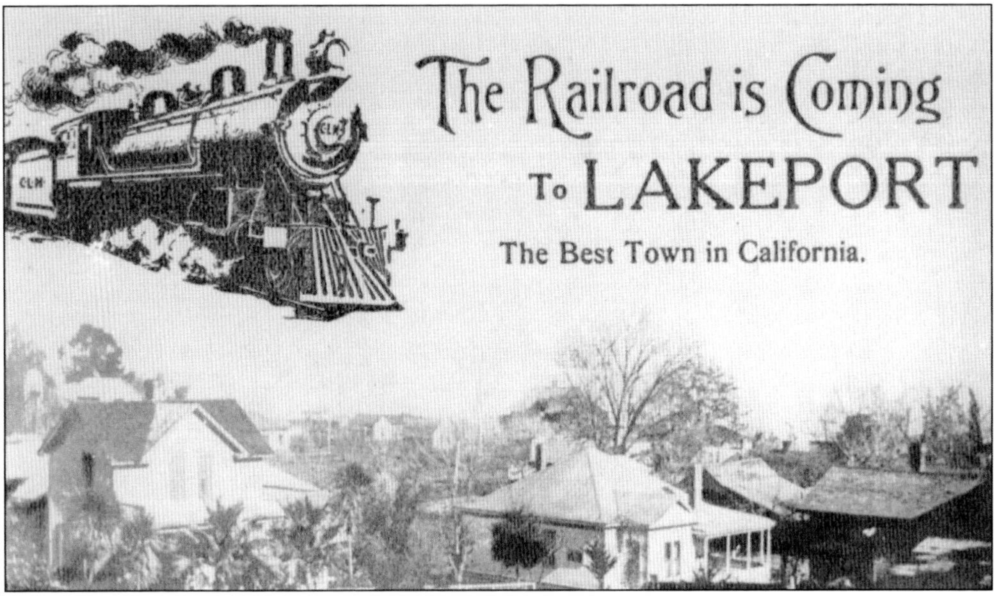

Starting in the late 1870s, companies began promising to provide the county with a railroad, but each attempt failed. Pictured above is a county postcard optimistically announcing the impending arrival of a train. The turn of the century saw a rapid increase in the number of these failed attempts, with no fewer than 10 enterprises in the first decade of the 20th century alone. In 1911, the Clear Lake Railroad Company was created. Although starting off promising, with a ground-breaking ceremony in November 1911 in Hopland, pictured below, this attempt also failed. Lake County is the only county in California not to be serviced by a railroad.

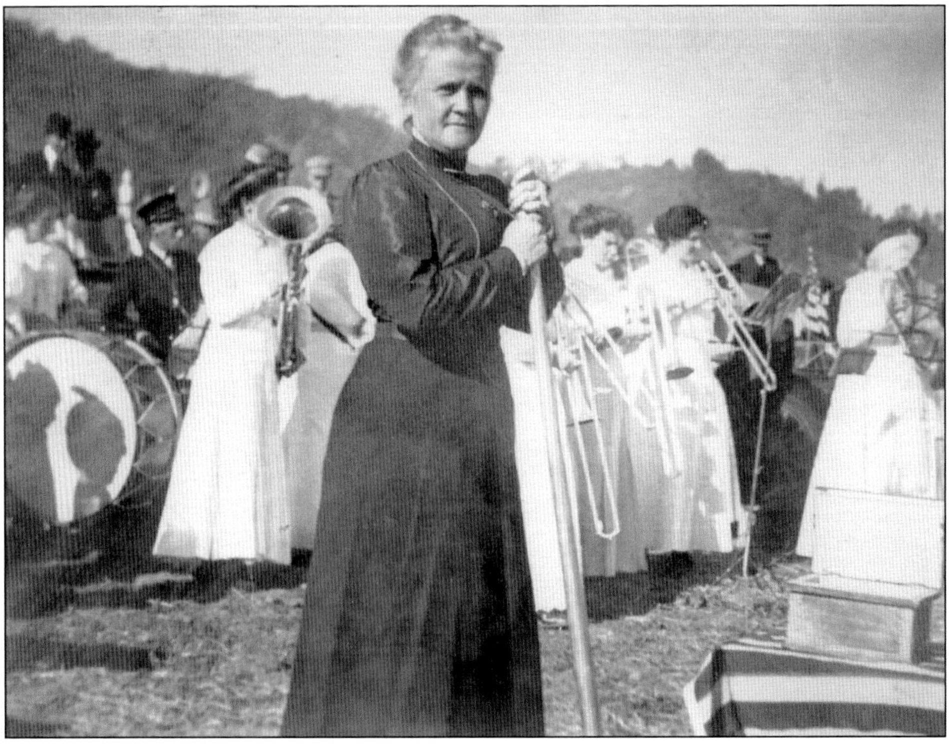

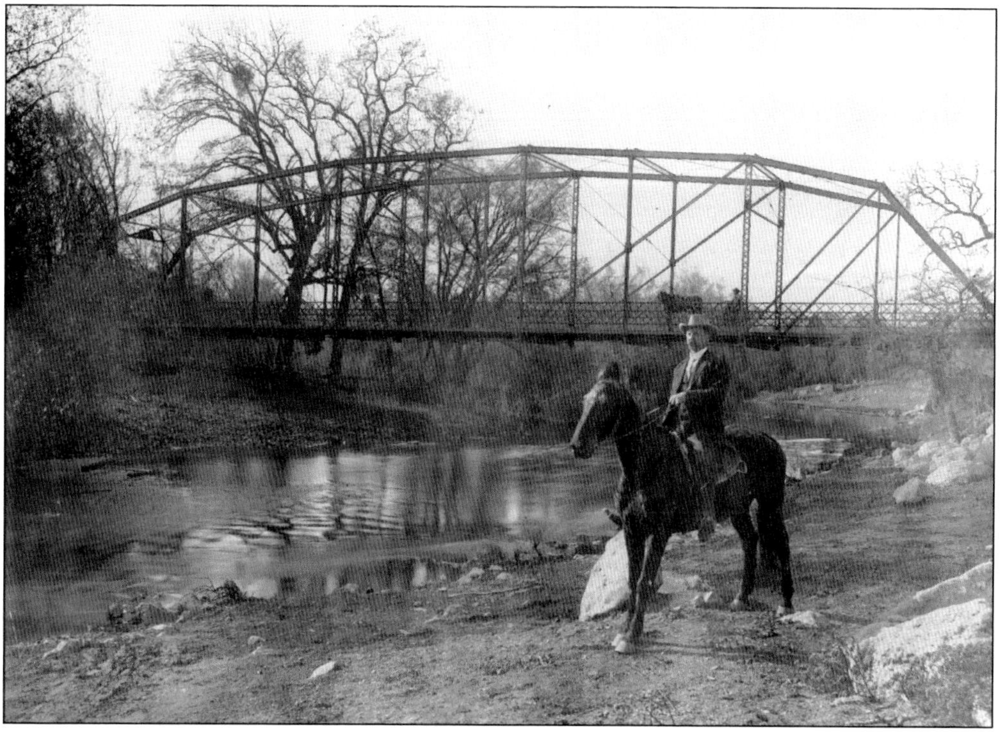

Between 1900 and 1928, the Lake County Board of Supervisors authorized 18 bridges to be constructed within the county. From large steel bridges, like the one constructed in 1914 across Cache Creek (pictured above), to smaller concrete ones, Lake County spent thousands of dollars in its campaign to modernize infrastructure. These bridges made travel throughout the county safer and more consistent, with the winter floods having less of an impact than they once had. The banks of Kelsey Creek in particular routinely suffered from erosion, and flooding was not uncommon. A steel-span bridge (pictured below) was built in Kelseyville in 1907 after the previous bridge had been washed out around the turn of the century.

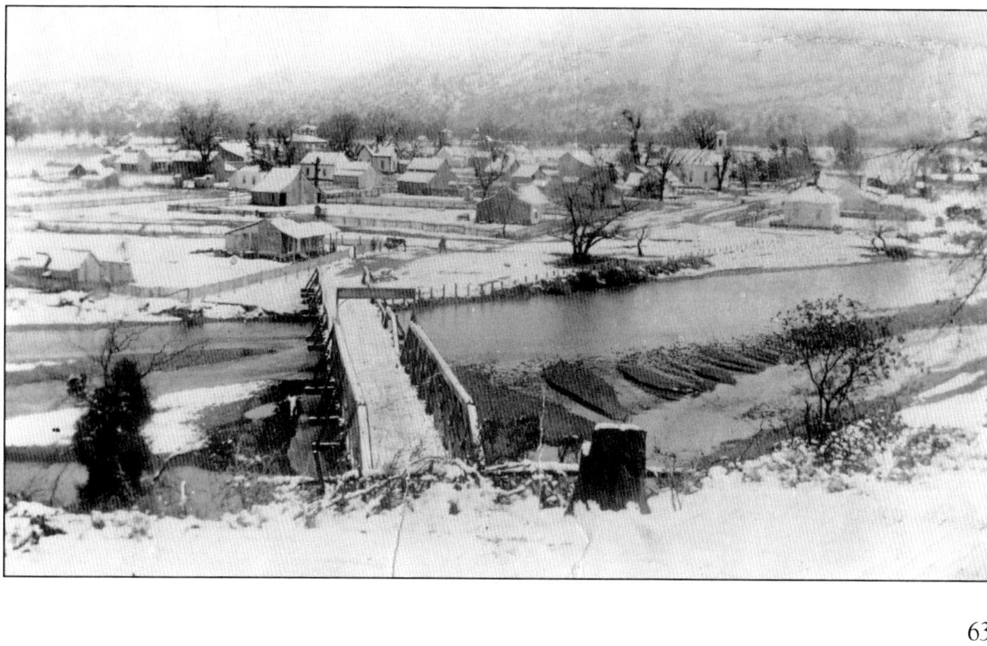

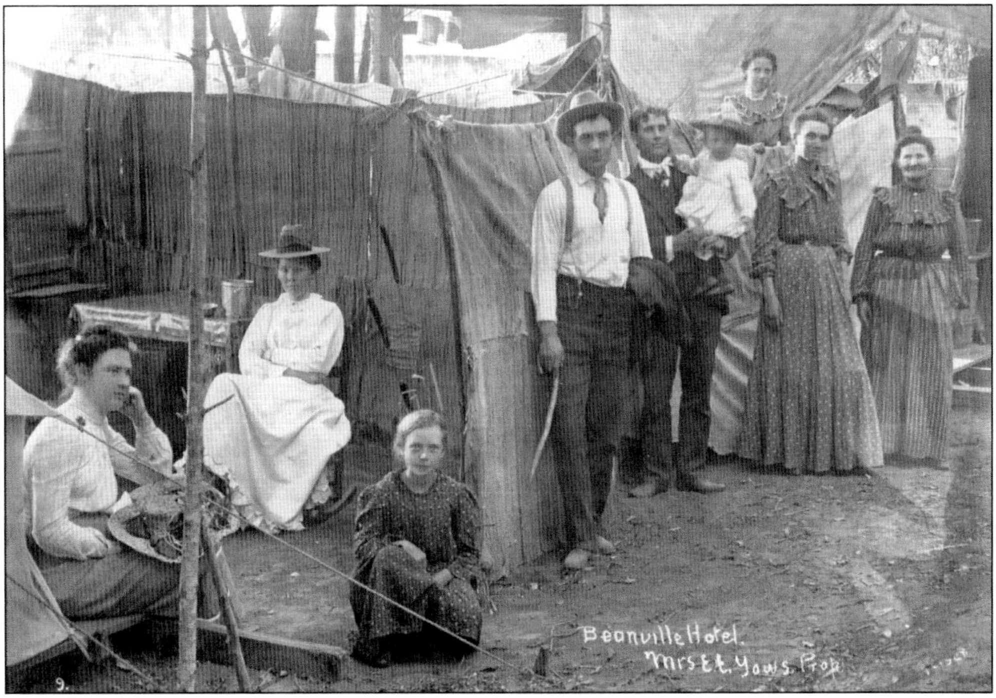

With the improvement of its infrastructure, the establishment of state highways, and a growing agricultural industry, Lake County experienced its second wave of immigrants since the first settlers of the 1850s. Pictured above is the itinerant farmworker camp the "Beanville Hotel," so named because many of the laborers came to work the growing number of acres of green beans in northern Lake County. With the construction of the Ukiah-Tahoe Highway (later renamed Highway 20) nearly complete, a new town on the eastern shore developed: Lucerne. Lots were laid and sewer lines were installed by 1932. Houses soon filled these once-empty lots, and a new community arose. Pictured below is Lucerne in 1949. Like in the 1850s and 1860s, these new communities necessitated the construction of new schools to service recently arrived families.

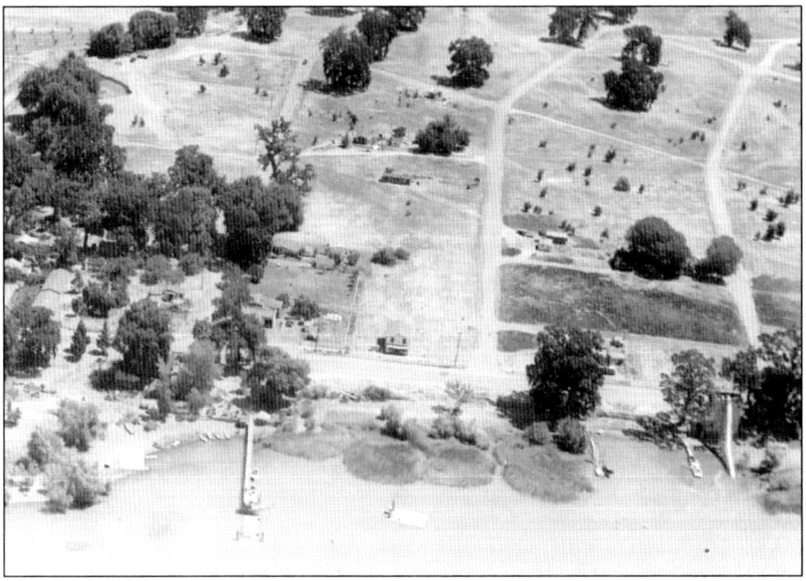

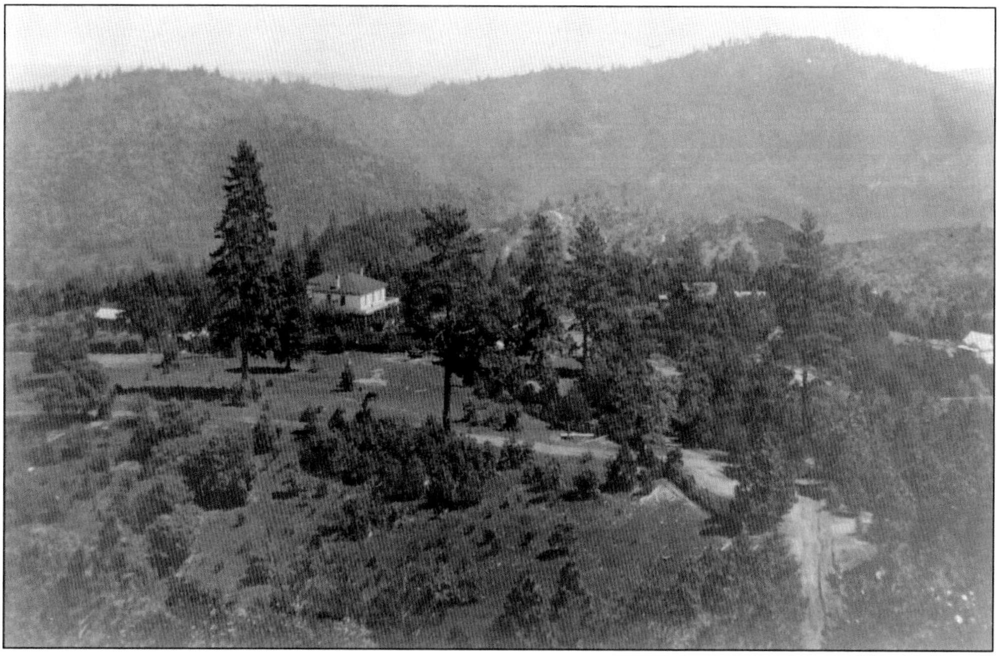

The new century sounded the death knell for widespread mining in the county. The Great Western Mine, which had produced millions of flasks of mercury over its decades-long operation, soon fizzled out. Pictured above is the house of the superintendent of the mine, Andrew Rocca, who resigned his position shortly before the mine's demise. Later operations over the next few decades sporadically worked the mine, but never again would such industry be seen in south Lake County. Pictured below is a furnace at the mine in 1937. Other mines followed suit, like the Sulphur Bank Mine in 1905, and the resulting exodus of laborers, miners, and Chinese workers accounts for the sudden drop in Lake County's population during this period.

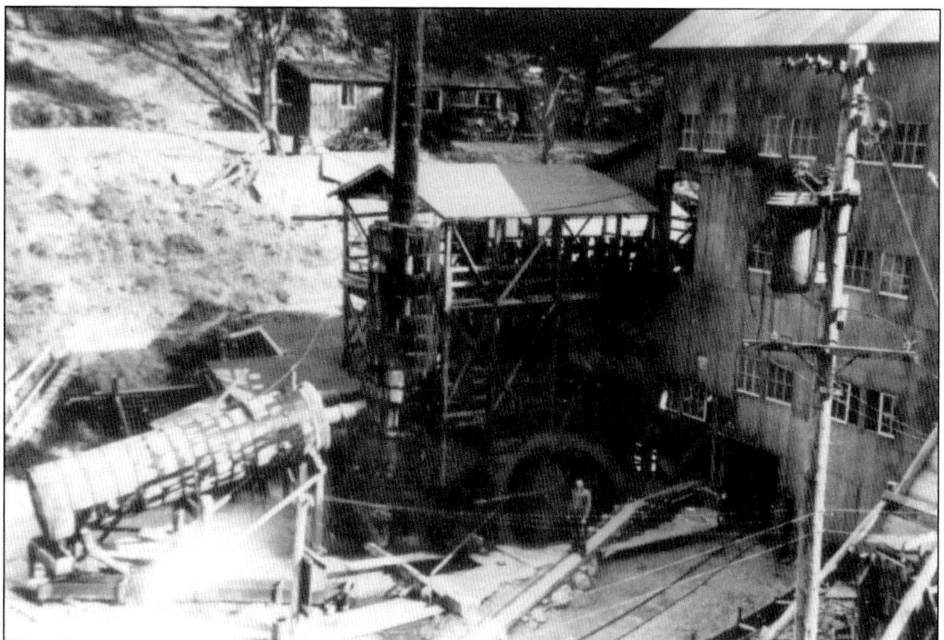

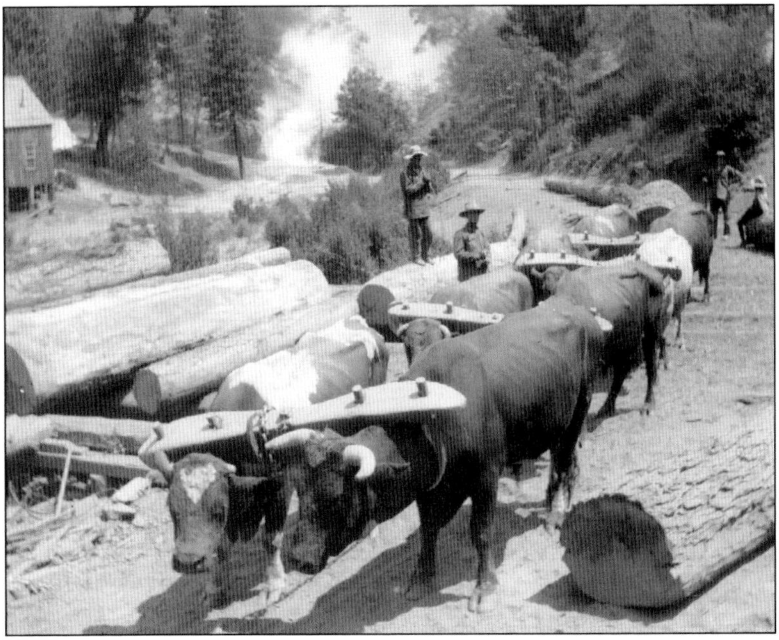

Logging remained an important industry in the pine-crested mountains of the county well into the 20th century. The Buckridge Mill operated on the slopes of Bartlett Mountain in eastern Lake County. As shown here, oxen haul felled trees to be processed at the mill.

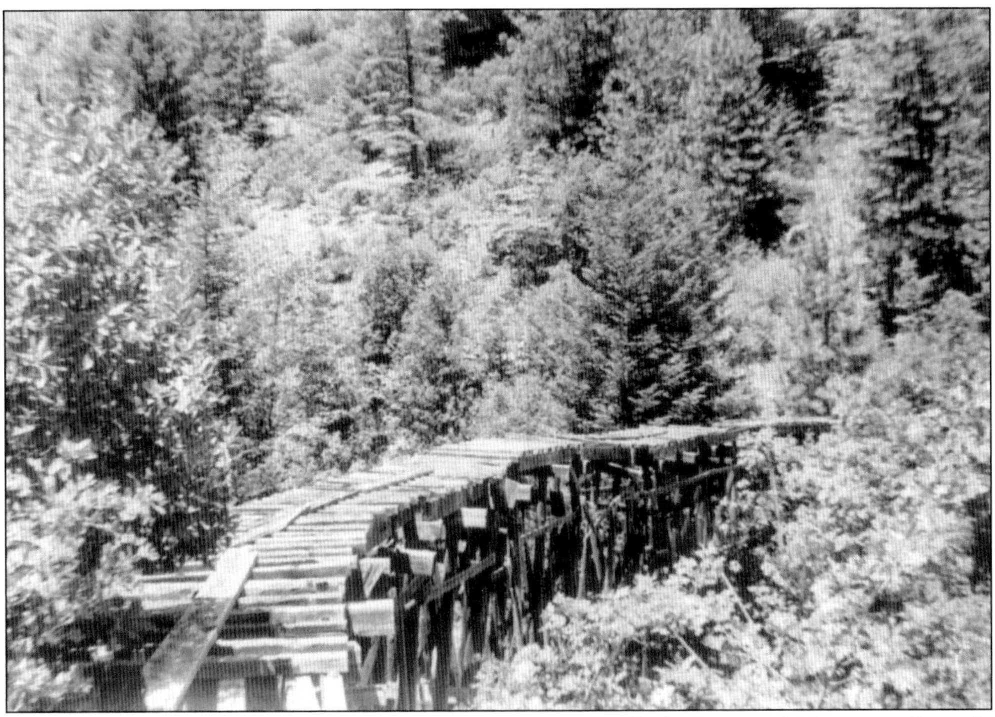

Starting in the 1920s, the Prather logging operation installed what would become the only operable train tracks in Lake County. Rather than hauling passengers and freight in and out of the county, though, these tracks allowed the Prather family to access more remote areas of the mountain and haul timber out on this homemade railway.

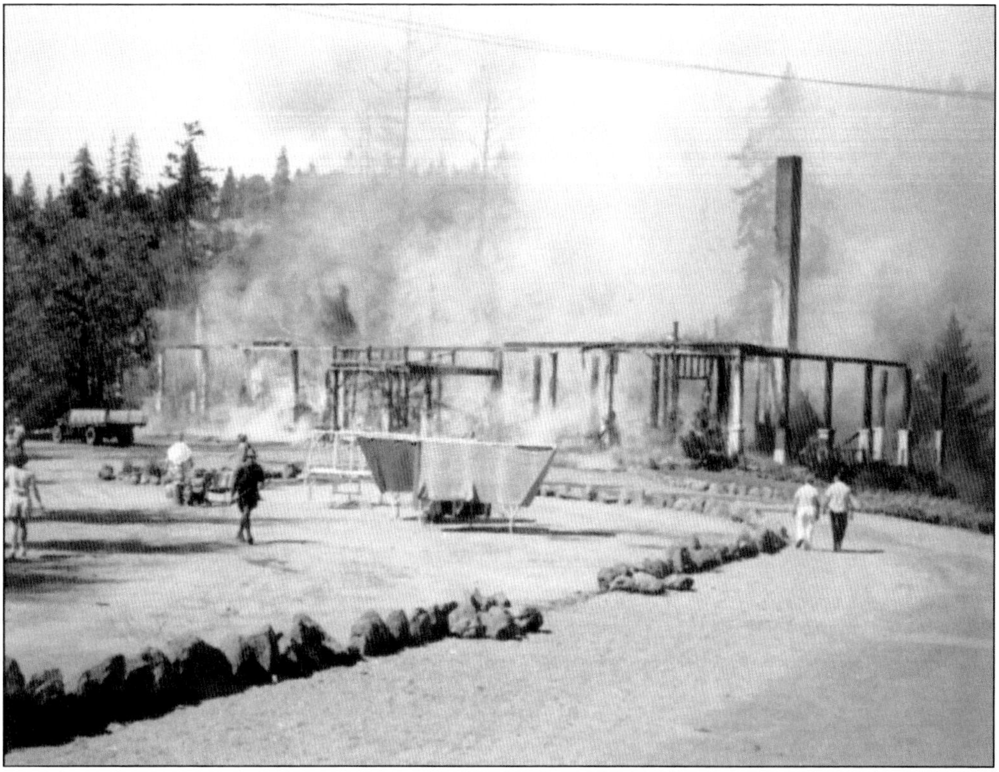

The first decade of the 20th century saw the resorts in Lake County operating as they had for the previous 50 years. But soon, travel to the remote resorts became less and less appealing to would-be guests. The advent of the automobile changed everything. Rather than catering to wealthy families who stayed for a whole season, the more adept resorts like Hoberg's and Harbin transitioned to serve the new breed of guests: weekend vacationers out on a family drive from the Bay Area. Many resorts, however, were not able to make the transition, and they gradually succumbed to a lack of business or perennial raging wildfires by the 1930s. Pictured here, Adams Spring is destroyed by a fire in the late 1940s.

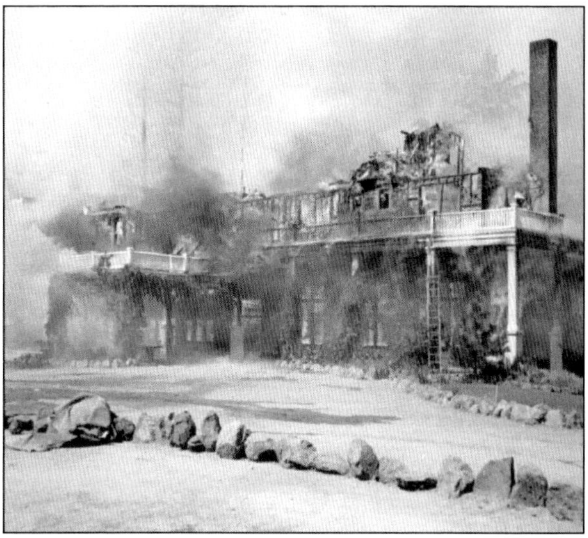

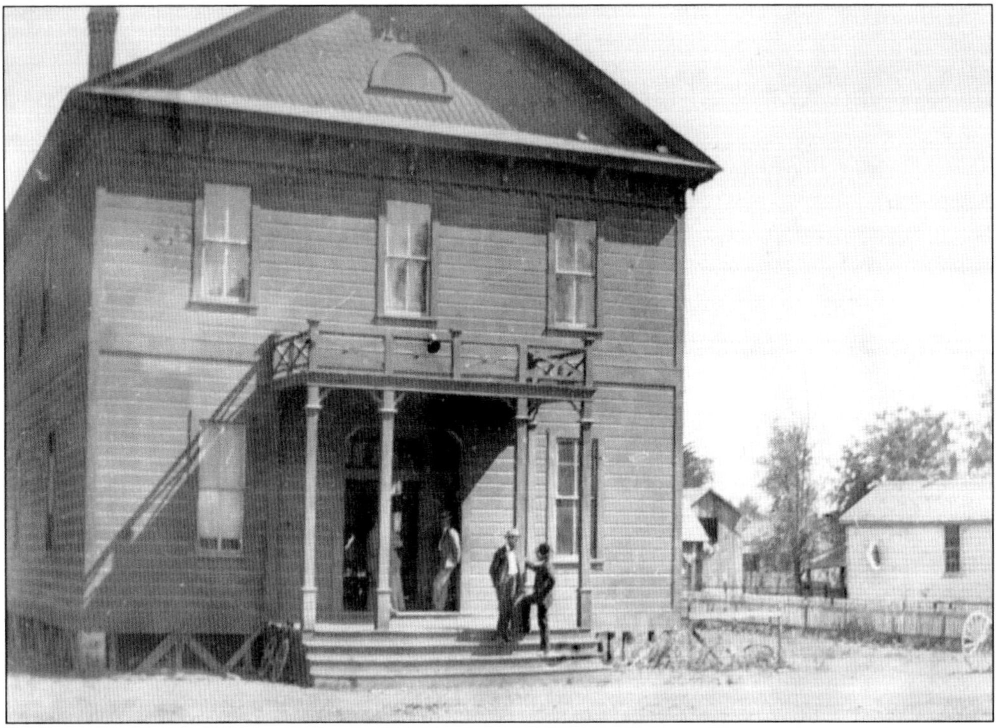

The Progressive Era of the early 20th century saw an explosion in the number of philanthropic social clubs within Lake County. Since the 1860s, Freemasons, Odd Fellows, and other fraternal benefit societies called Lake County home. Pictured above is the Upper Lake Independent Order of Odd Fellows hall, and below is the 1906 cornerstone-laying for Hartley Masonic Lodge No. 199's new lodge in Lakeport. The dawn of the new century saw a greater variety of clubs focused on community development like the Woman's Christian Temperance Union and the Federation of Women's Clubs. Both of these organizations raised money for schools to secure larger libraries and better facilities.

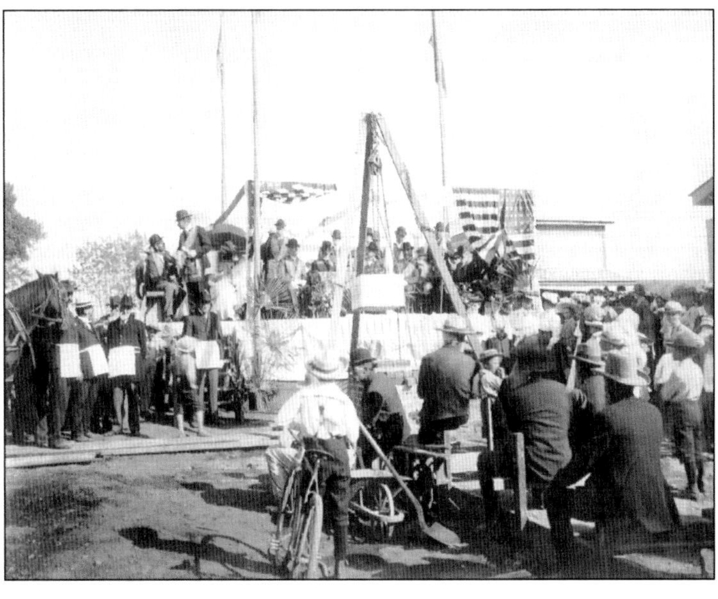

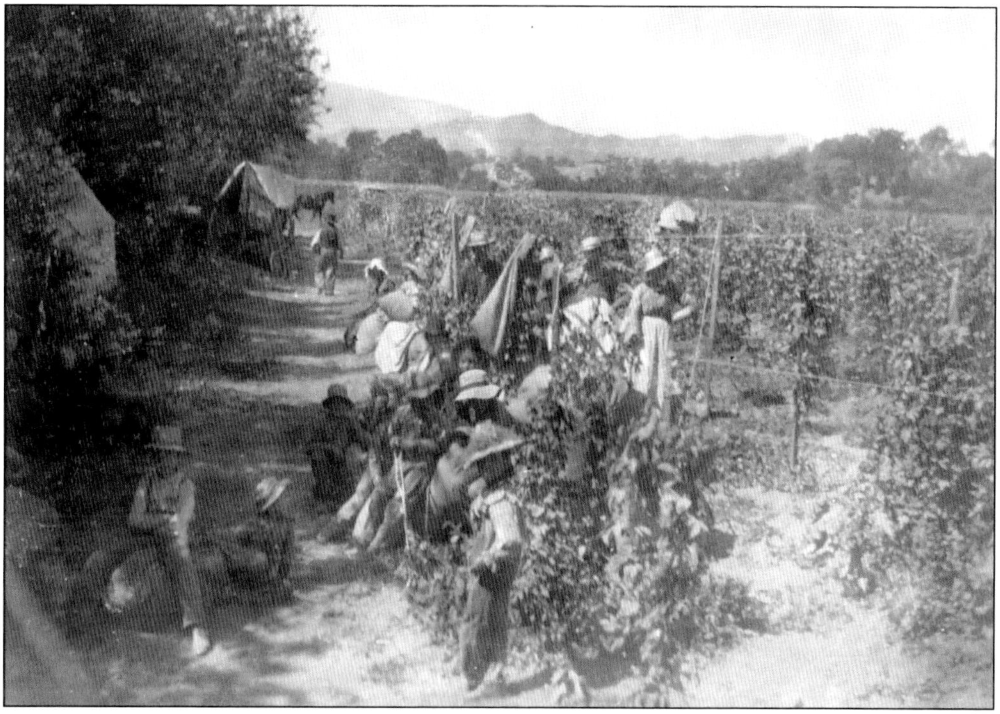

The rise of community-minded civic clubs and fraternal benefit societies corresponded to a sudden awareness of the plight of California's native population. In Lake County, the Federation of Women's Clubs successfully advocated for better—albeit still segregated—treatment of Pomo students during the 1920s. Native Americans themselves were also pushing for a better life with several tribes, like Upper Lake and Elem, purchasing large tracts of land to settle on. Pictured below is the Upper Lake sweat house around 1900. The 1910s also saw the creation of federal reservations, or rancherias. Despite these improvements, the day-to-day lives of the Native peoples remained unchanged. As before, many individuals found work in the agricultural industry. Pictured above are workers on Riggs's hop fields near Upper Lake.

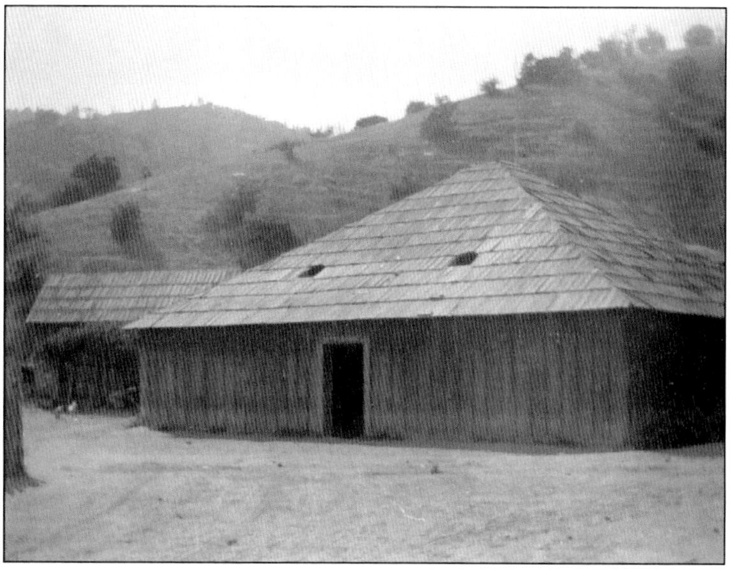

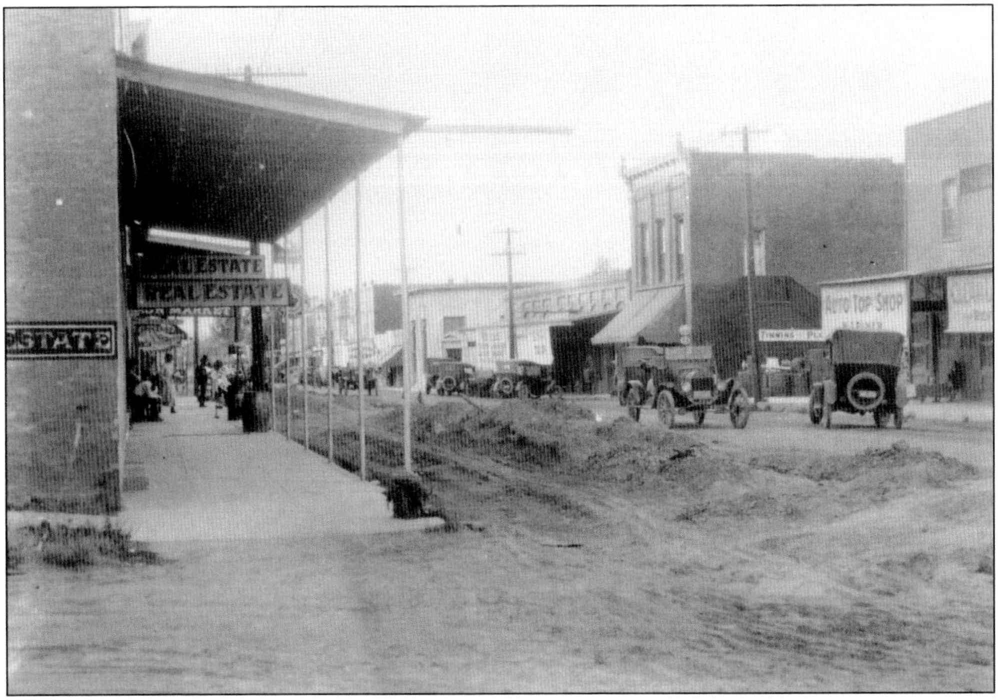

By the early 20th century, the town of Lakeport had risen to become the most populous town in the county. The towns of Upper Lake, Lakeport (pictured above), Kelseyville, Lower Lake (pictured below), and Middletown became the hubs of society. Despite the prominence of these "urban" centers, the county never lost its inherent rural culture. With agriculture and its associated industries like canning, Lake County's entire economic life force centered on the countryside. Even with the unification of schools in the 1910s and 1920s around these urban centers, rural one-room schoolhouses still dominated education in early 20th-century Lake County.

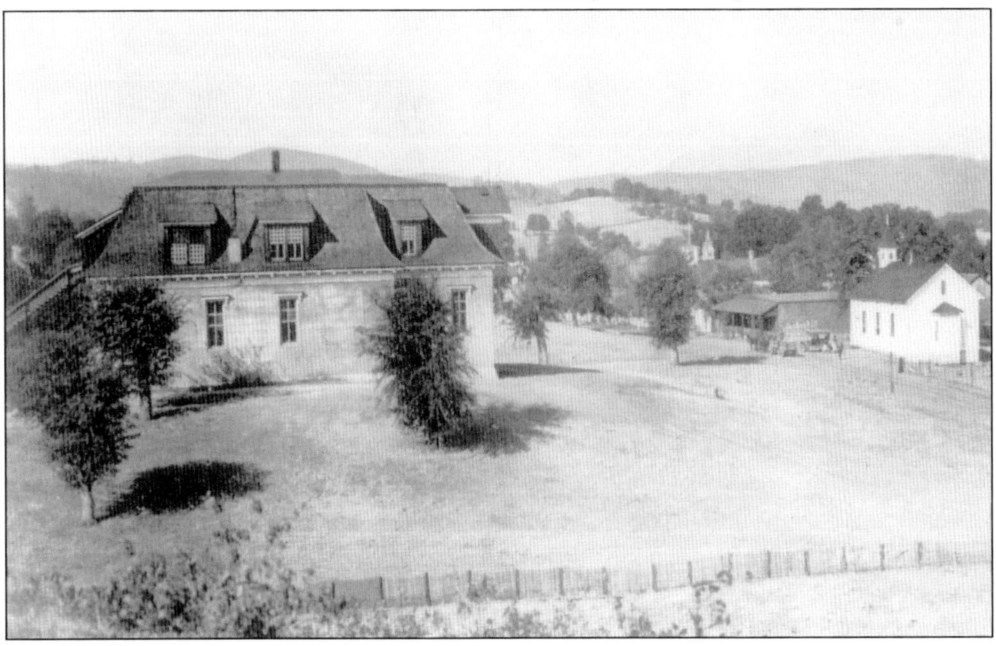

Five

Modern Schools 1901–1941

Up until the early 20th century, all public schools in Lake County were grammar schools; the highest level of education offered to children was the eighth grade. If a student wanted secondary education, private schools like Lakeport Academy were the only option. The law at the time did allow for public high schools to be built, but only by individual school districts. Of course, this only worked in the larger urban centers like San Francisco and Sacramento, where single school districts had enough eighth-grade graduates to justify a high school. But for a county like Lake County, finding at least 10 students for each grammar school was a challenge in itself. There were barely enough eighth-grade graduates in the entire county, let alone in a single district.

High schools were out of the question.

That is, until the passage of a state law in 1891 that allowed contiguous public school districts to unite and form a unified district and establish a unified high school, with the understanding being that at least two districts could supply enough students for a high school. Each unified high school had its own administrative apparatus, including trustees and separate forms of funding, which were beefed up after another law in 1903 provided state monies.

The simultaneous decrease in population and the improvement of roads (and the advent of automobiles) meant that fewer children lived in Lake County, but those who did were able to travel farther to get to school. These changes no doubt facilitated what became the period of school unification and consolidation in the 1910s and 1920s. Like most sudden changes to school policy, however, unification was easier in principal than practice.

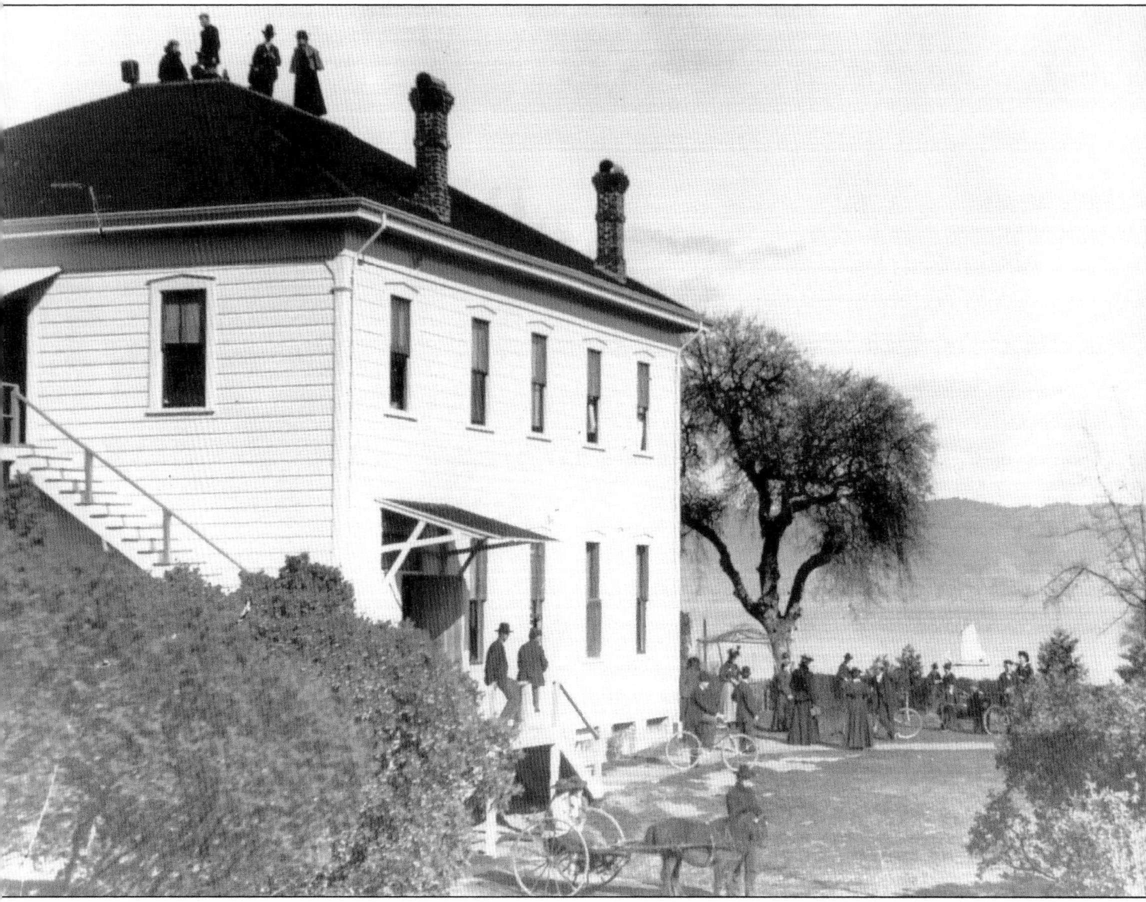

In 1901, the question of unification was posed in Lake County, with 19 different school districts ranging from Kelseyville to Upper Lake proposing to unify for the sake of a high school. It was a close call, with only five votes carrying the day in favor of unification. Lakeport nearly unanimously voted for, and Upper Lake nearly unanimously against unification. A further vote, divided along the same lines, decided the location of the new high school in favor of Lakeport over Upper Lake. In the fall of 1901, with the demise of the Lakeport Academy, Professor Overholser leased his now vacant school building (pictured) to the trustees of the Clear Lake Union High School District for $150 a year. After the first day of classes, the trustees hired Professor Overholser as the science teacher. (Courtesy of Lake County Historical Society.)

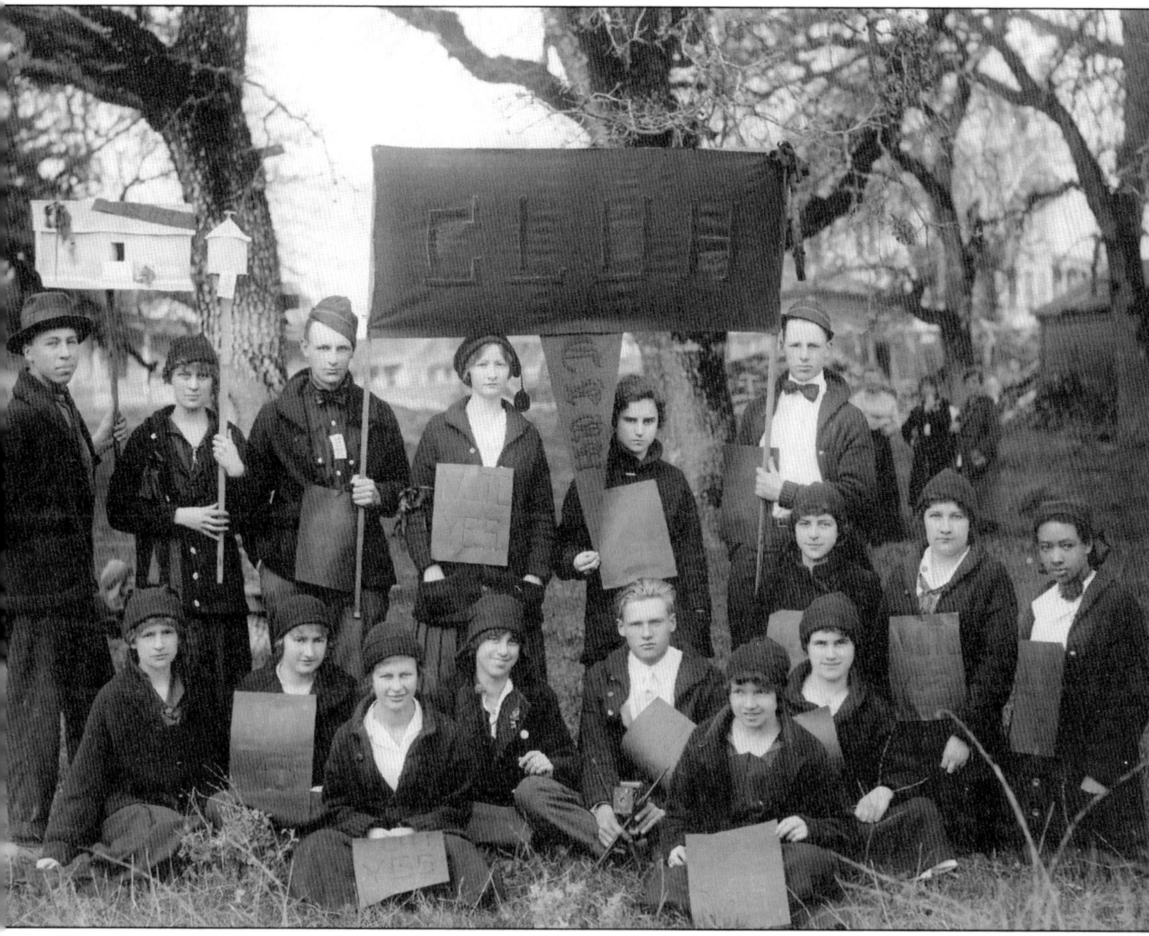

For over a decade, students of Clear Lake Union High (CLUH) attended classes in the old Lakeport Academy building. The rising class sizes necessitated a new building, and so, following the now age-old practice of voting for the sale of bonds, the unified school district put the issue to a vote, which failed. The same animosity over the location of the first high school evidently persisted, with Upper Lake residents still frustrated over the distance their children had to travel to the school in the first place. They were not willing to put out more money, and in 1915 Upper Lake and six of the northern school districts that composed the original 19 of the CLUH School District left to create their own, this one in Upper Lake. With the division of the unified school district, and with the students of CLUH drumming up support for a new building (one of their picket lines is seen in this image), the bond issue was passed in 1916.

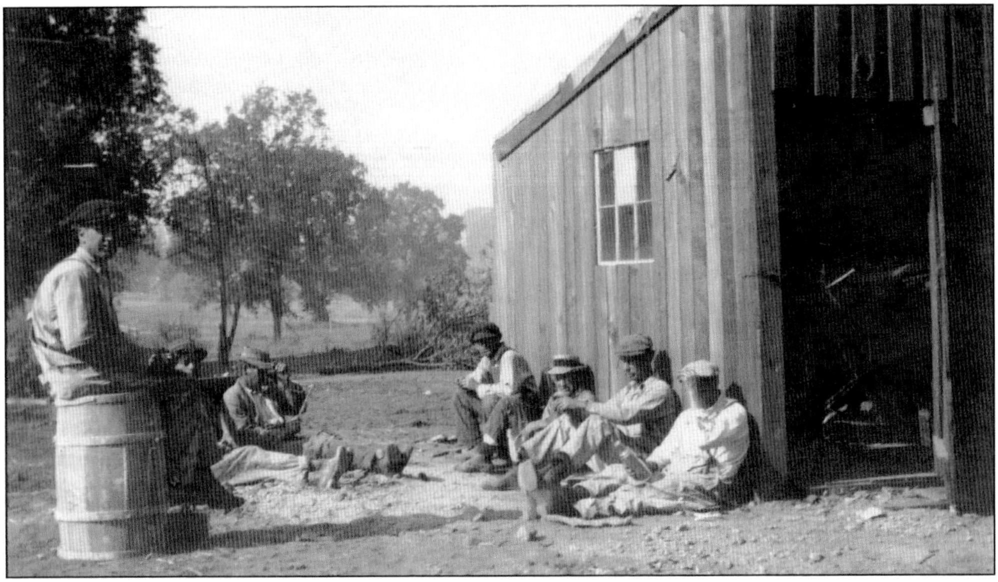

Authorized to sell $25,000 worth of bonds, the Clear Lake Union High School District, now seven districts smaller, immediately began construction on a new schoolhouse. The district bought a parcel of land for the site of the new school at the northwest end of Main Street in Lakeport. Despite the picture of the lounging construction workers shown above, the schoolhouse was completed remarkably quickly and by the end of the same year the bond issue was passed, the school building itself was complete. The old Lakeport Academy, now empty of schoolchildren, was bought and operated as a hospital until it burned down in 1928.

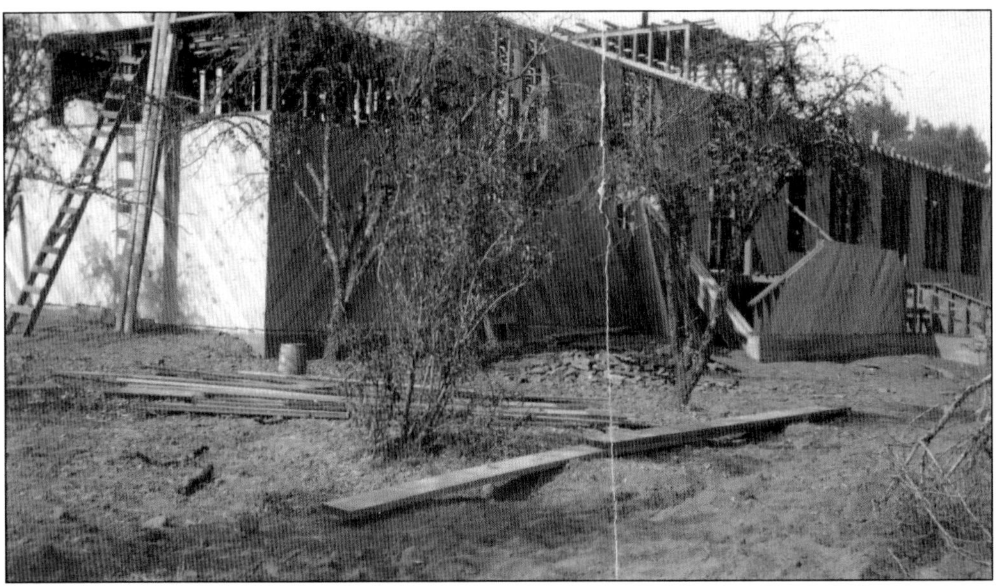

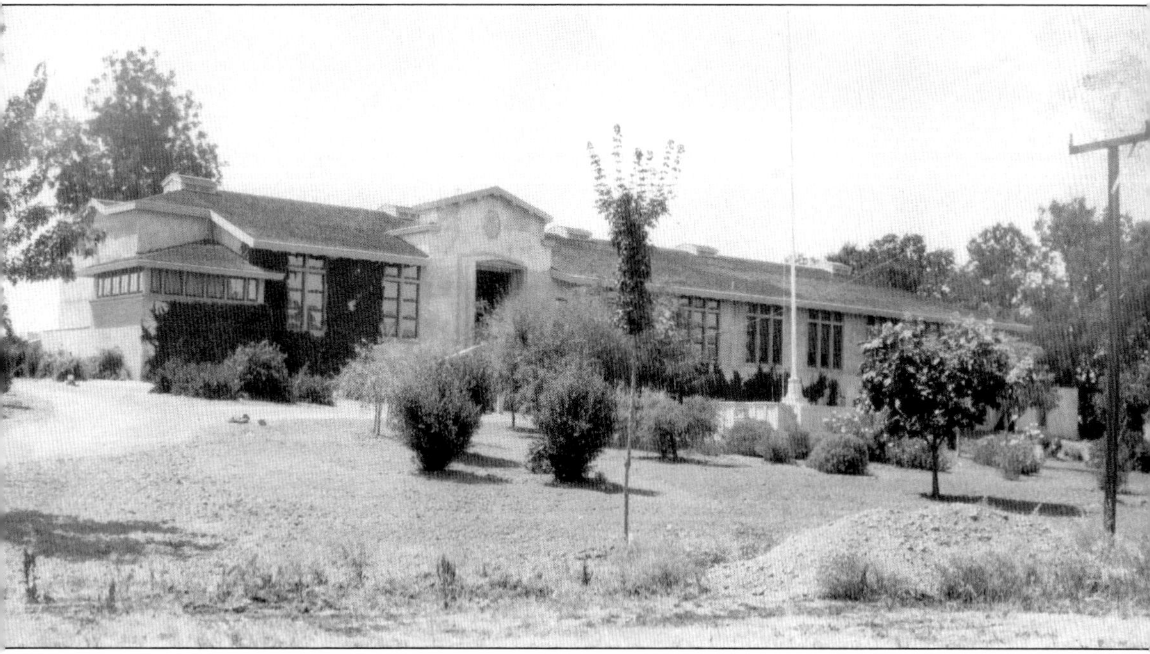

Just as the 1880 Lakeport Grammar School established the style of white clapboard, two-story schoolhouses that dominated the landscape for the rest of that decade, so too did the new CLUH establish a new style of school architecture in Lake County. The new schools being built throughout America at the time, to which CLUH aspired, built outwards, not upwards. These new, single-story schools looked nothing like the multistory structures of decades past. A growing trend among proponents for consolidated education was the demonization of "rural" schools. The image of a one-room school, in their minds, was one of backwards education where students rarely, if ever, got properly educated. The multi-classroom schools of the cities needed to be brought to the country. CLUH did just that. The new age of consolidated schools, with their multiple classrooms and bell-less rooflines, had come to Lake County.

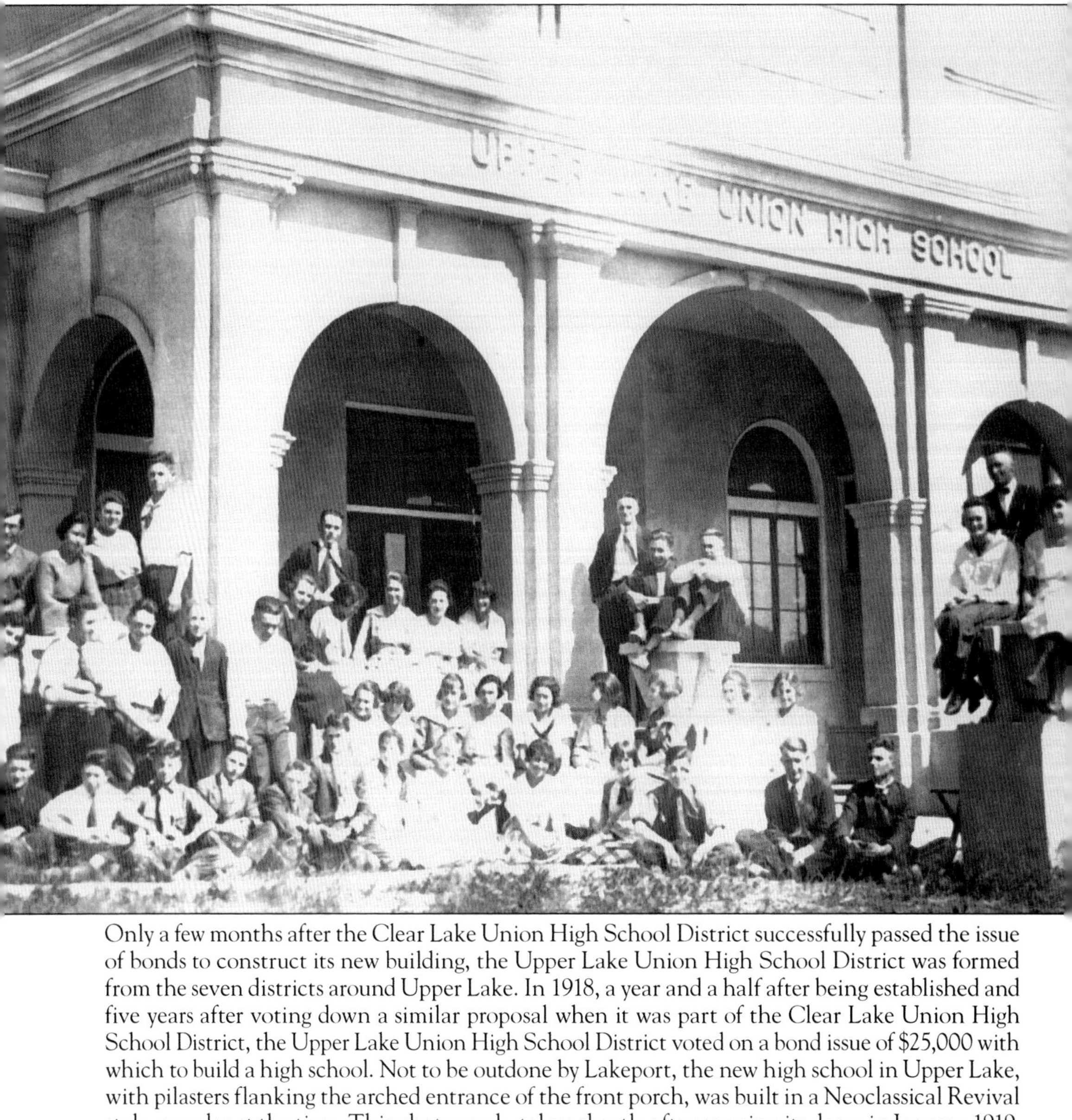

Only a few months after the Clear Lake Union High School District successfully passed the issue of bonds to construct its new building, the Upper Lake Union High School District was formed from the seven districts around Upper Lake. In 1918, a year and a half after being established and five years after voting down a similar proposal when it was part of the Clear Lake Union High School District, the Upper Lake Union High School District voted on a bond issue of $25,000 with which to build a high school. Not to be outdone by Lakeport, the new high school in Upper Lake, with pilasters flanking the arched entrance of the front porch, was built in a Neoclassical Revival style, popular at the time. This photograph, taken shortly after opening its doors in January 1919, shows these fine details as the students and faculty of the high school gather for a picture.

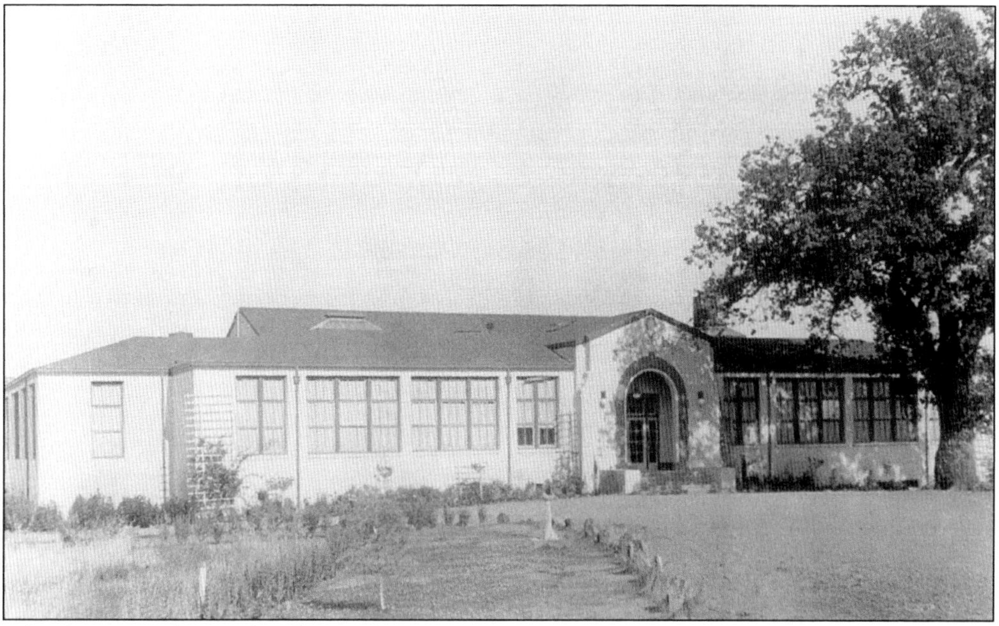

Like the wave of new schoolhouses built in Lake County in the 1880s, the 1910s and 1920s saw the other centers of education in the county following the lead of Lakeport and Upper Lake by creating their own union high schools. The citizens around Lower Lake voted in 1921–1922 to establish the Lower Lake Union High School District. But a lack of funds, and a general lack of students, meant that for the first decade, classes were held in the old 1877 Lower Lake Schoolhouse, which was still operating as a grammar school. Not until 1934 did the citizens gather enough money for the construction of the high school, shown above. Middletown was quicker on the draw and, even before Upper Lake, built a new high school in 1917, pictured below.

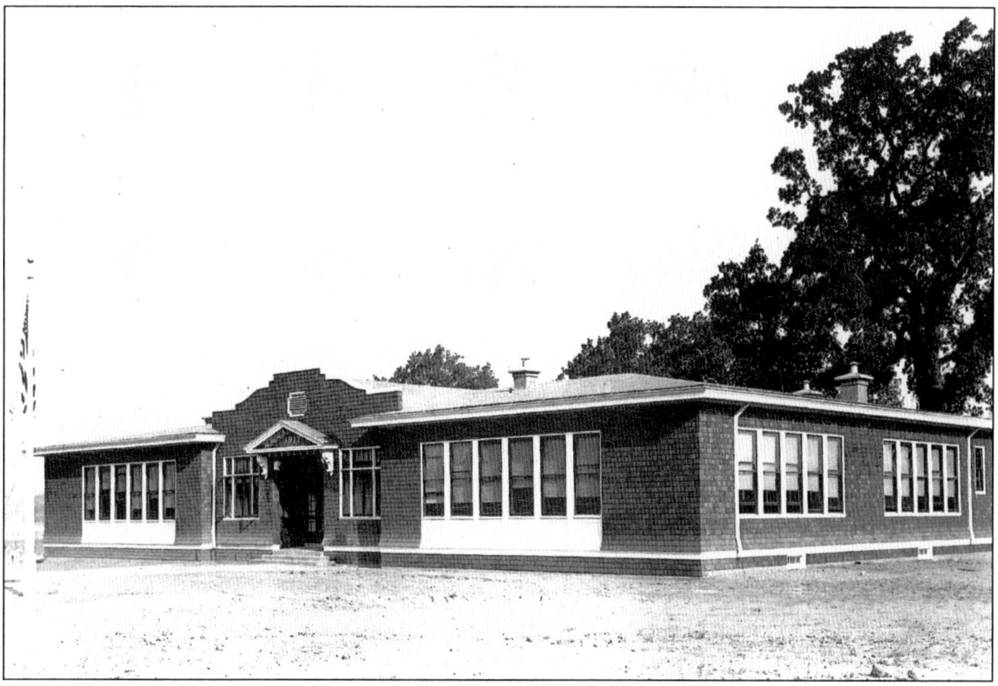

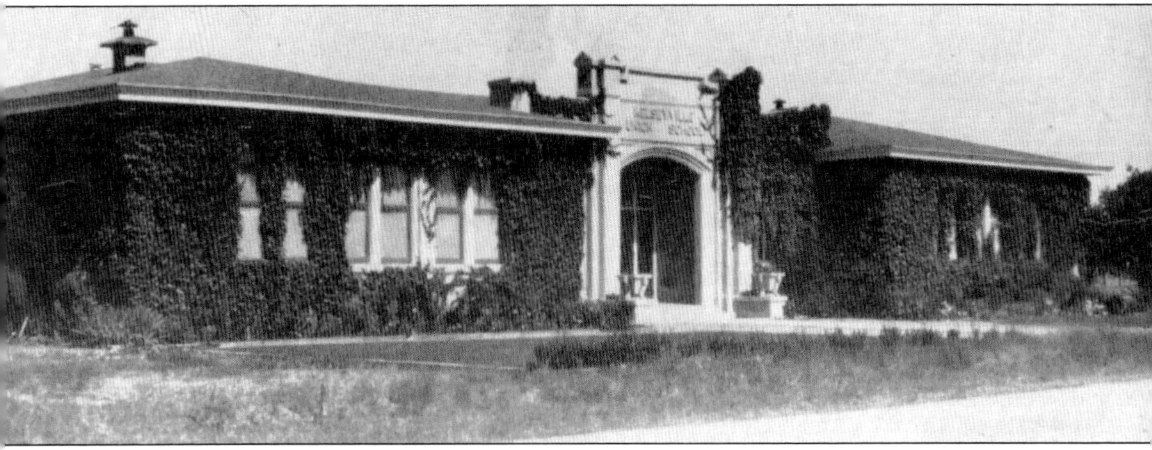

The same impetus behind the unification of schools to form high school districts also drove many of those same schools to consolidate, this time to form union grammar schools. This process was called annexation, as opposed to unification. Unlike unified high schools, which simply created an additional school district (high school district) on top of the individual grammar school districts participating, annexation actually resulted in fewer total districts, as the various rural schools coalesced into larger units. From the very beginning, Lake County had experienced forced consolidation as the population patterns in the rural outreaches ebbed and flowed, and districts lapsed and were consolidated with neighbors. However, the late 1910s saw a more conscious effort to consolidate schools, not out of a lack of attendance at one school or another, but in order to simplify the management of schools and to provide a better education for students. Kelseyville led the charge when, in 1919–1920, six districts consolidated to form the Kelseyville Union School District. Classes started at the new Kelseyville Union Grammar School (pictured) in 1920.

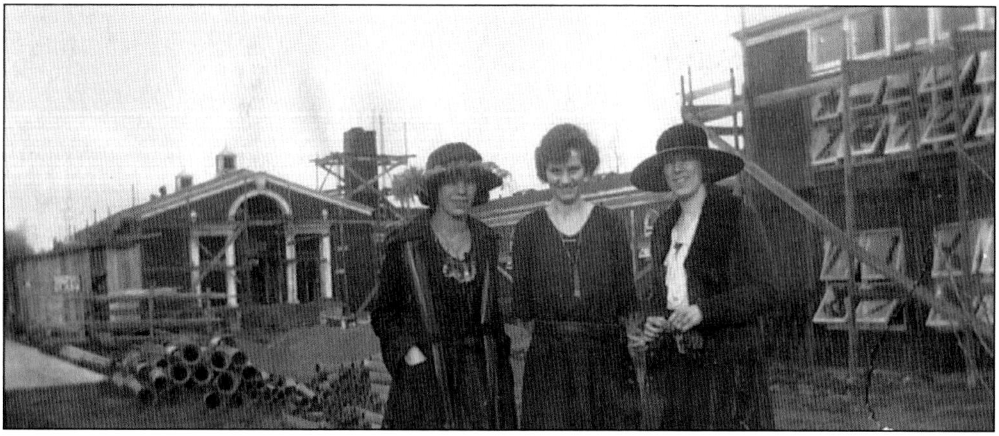

Playing second fiddle for the first time, Lakeport quickly followed the lead of Kelseyville, with several of the districts outside of the town consolidating to form the Lakeport Union School District in 1921. Shortly thereafter, construction of the new grammar school started. In the picture above, three young ladies pose in front of the school, still under construction. The final product was the largest grammar school built in Lake County yet. Even with the sprawling footprint of this school, the basic design of the front entrance, with a columned porch, stayed within the popular Neoclassical Revival style that the earlier Clear Lake Union High School started for school architecture in Lake County.

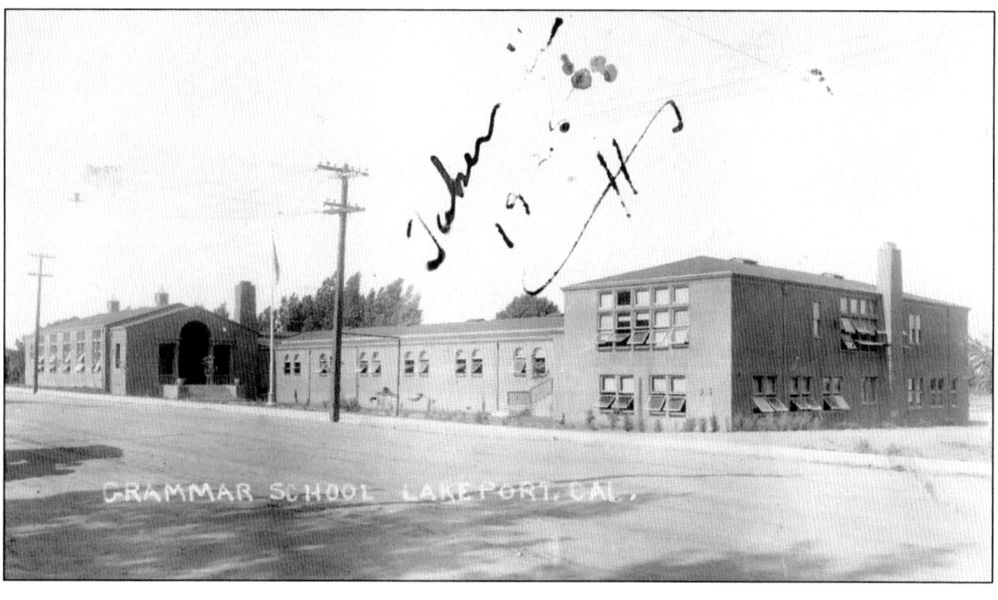

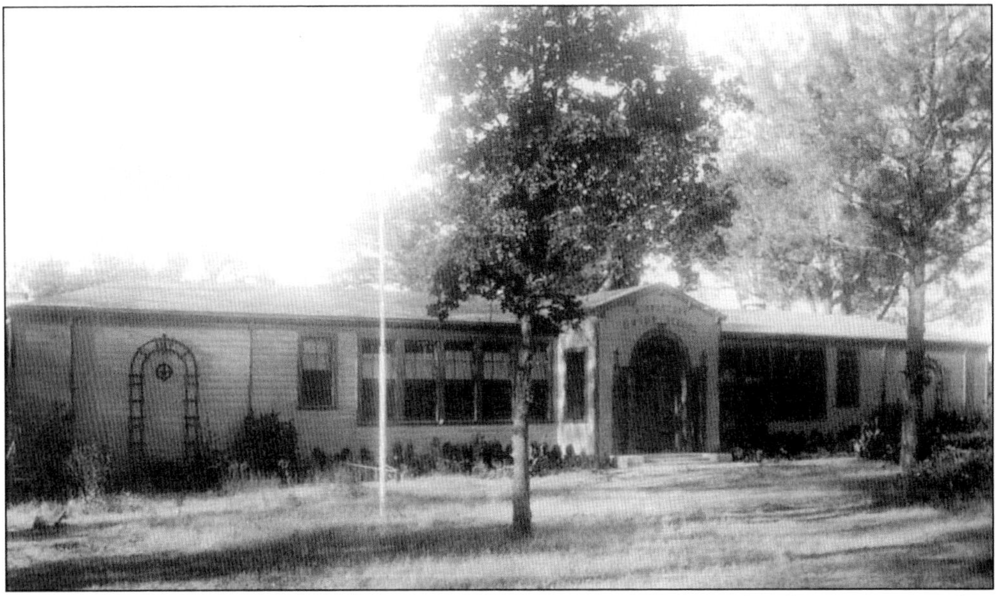

In 1925, the Callayomi, Loconomi, Middletown, and St. Helena School Districts voted to consolidate into the Middletown Union School District, with several other districts lapsing into it as well. Shortly thereafter, the new Union Grammar School opened its doors on the grounds of the old 1890s schoolhouse. Following the lead of the Lakeport Union Grammar school, this smaller version evoked the Neoclassical Revival style popular at the time, even going so far as to copy the design of the front porch of the Lakeport school building. Although consolidation of Upper Lake schools started as early as 1920, it was not until 1931 that the Upper Lake Union School District built the Union Grammar School.

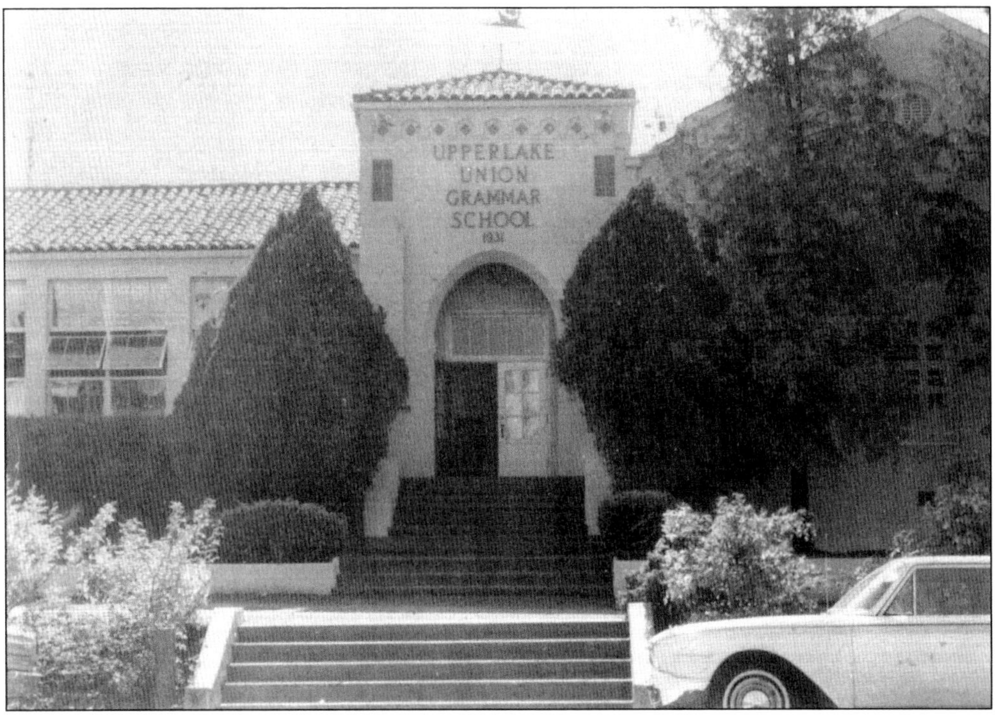

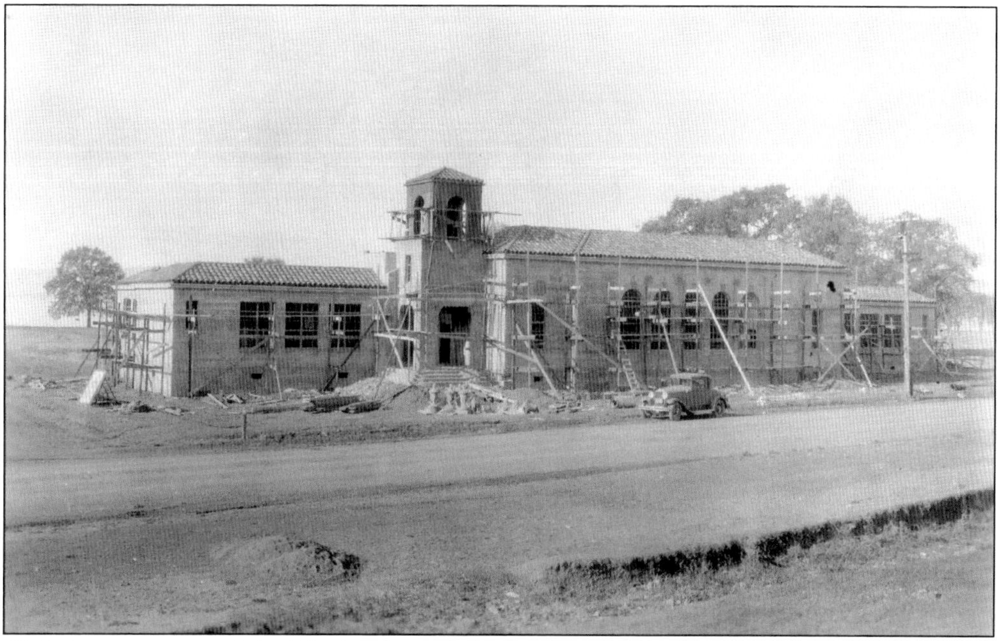

With the expansion of the Ukiah-Tahoe Highway into Lake County during the mid-1920s and early 1930s, the eastern shores of Clear Lake began to develop in earnest. Although always the site of some form of settlement, the small community of Lucerne coalesced into a more coherent town. With the highway came more people and, with them, a greater need for a school. The first classes of the Lucerne School District were held in a non-school building in 1929 until the new, modern school could be built in 1930 (pictured above). Also benefiting from the growing population, the East Lake School District, which had lapsed, reestablished, and lapsed several times over the years, was once more reestablished in 1931. A decade later, a newer, larger grammar school was opened (pictured below) alongside Highway 20.

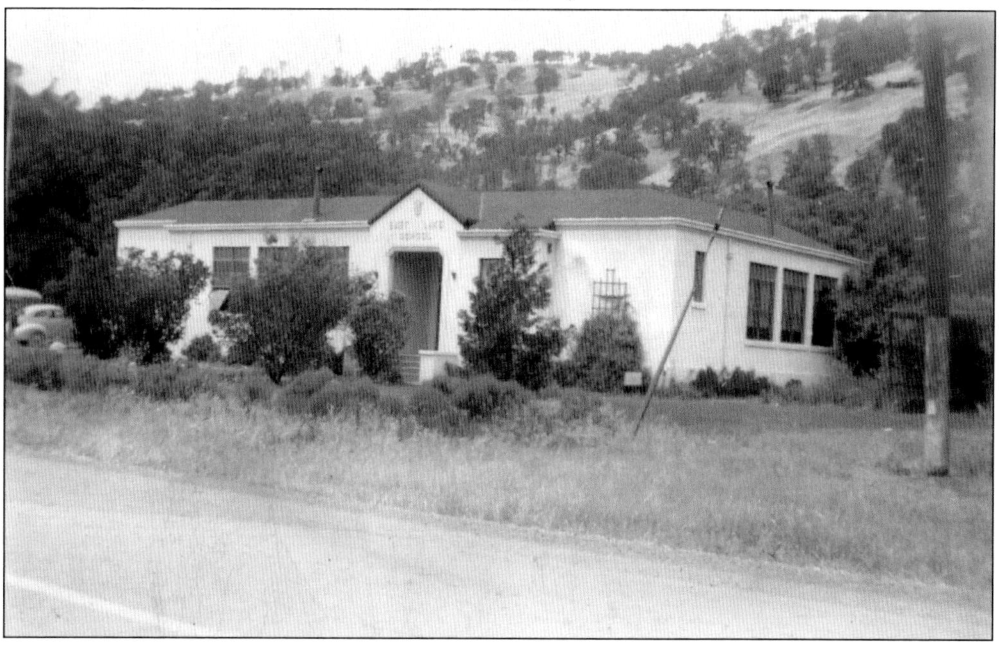

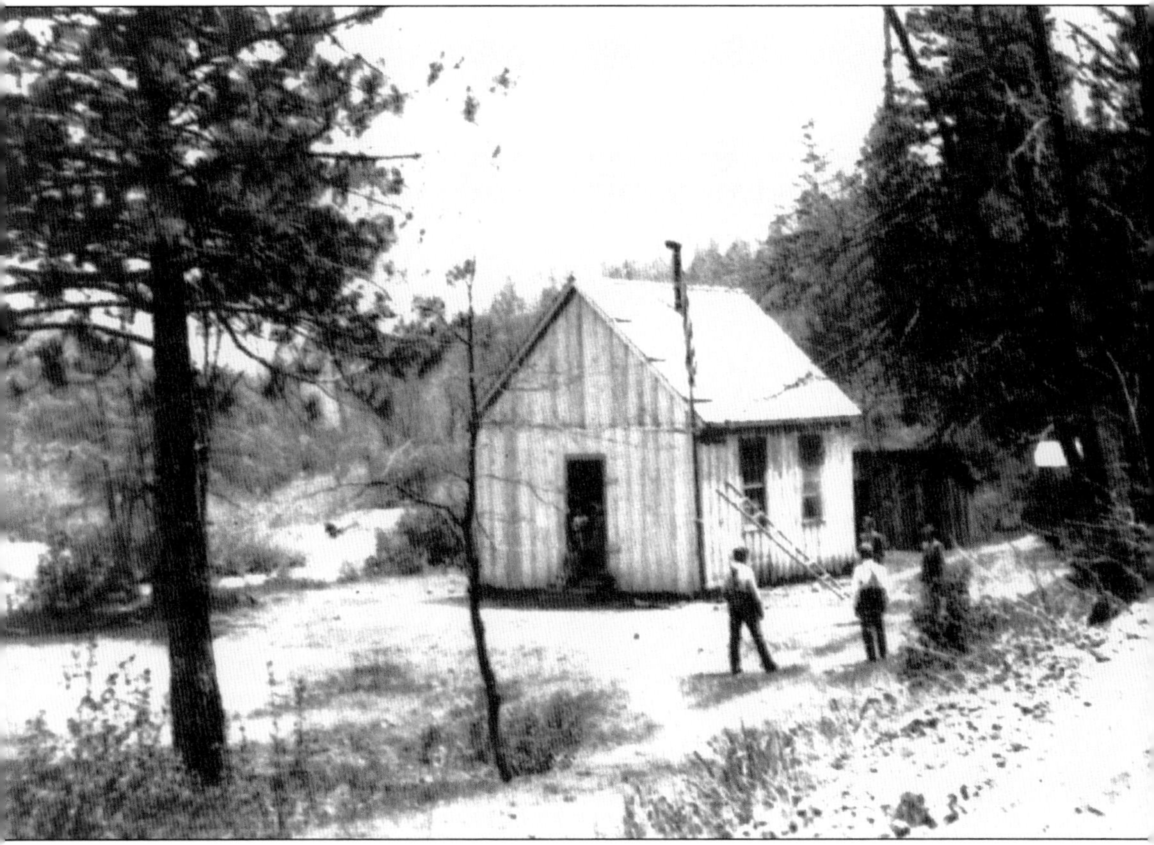

The rural character of Lake County determined, in some part, the way the county taught its children. For the isolated valleys and mountains of Lake County, the turn of the century did not mark a drastic change in school policy. The establishment of high schools and the increasing frequency of consolidation did not quite make it to these hidden valleys. The experience of most Lake County children for the first two decades of the 20th century did not differ much from previous decades. The one-room school was still very much alive, especially in the far-flung districts in the Mayacamas to the west and farther north in what is now Mendocino National Forest. When the Twin Valley School District in northern Lake County needed to build a new schoolhouse in 1906, the small clapboard building the county constructed would have seemed at home in the 1880s. Following the life cycle of 19th-century school districts, the Twin Valley School District lapsed in 1918 due to a lack of students.

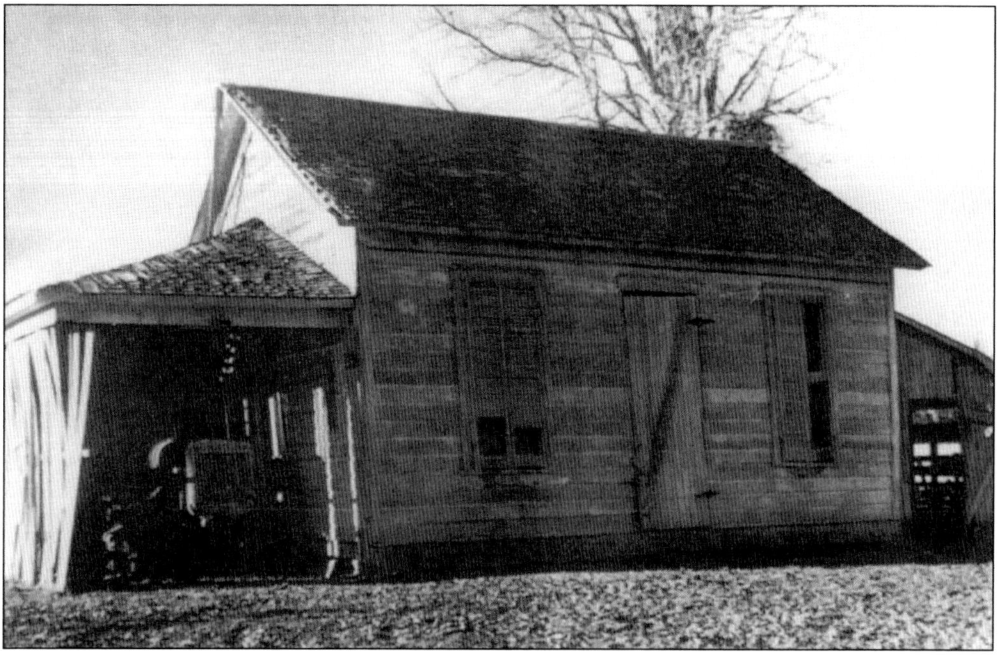

Shifting populations continued to plague the Lake County school system, and the early 20th century saw the creation of several new districts in addition to Twin Valley. The sudden growth of logging in the area of Big Canyon necessitated the creation of the Big Canyon School District in 1913. The schoolhouse seen in the below photograph was only used for a few years until the district lapsed after many families moved to gain employment towards the war effort in 1918. The Alcove Schoolhouse, pictured above, had a similarly short life as a school. After being built in 1903, it was sold in 1919 when the Alcove School District consolidated with Kelseyville.

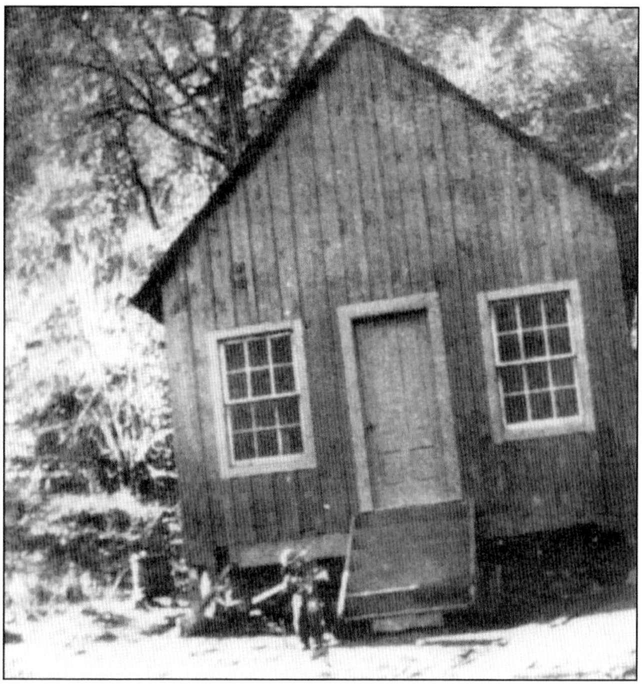

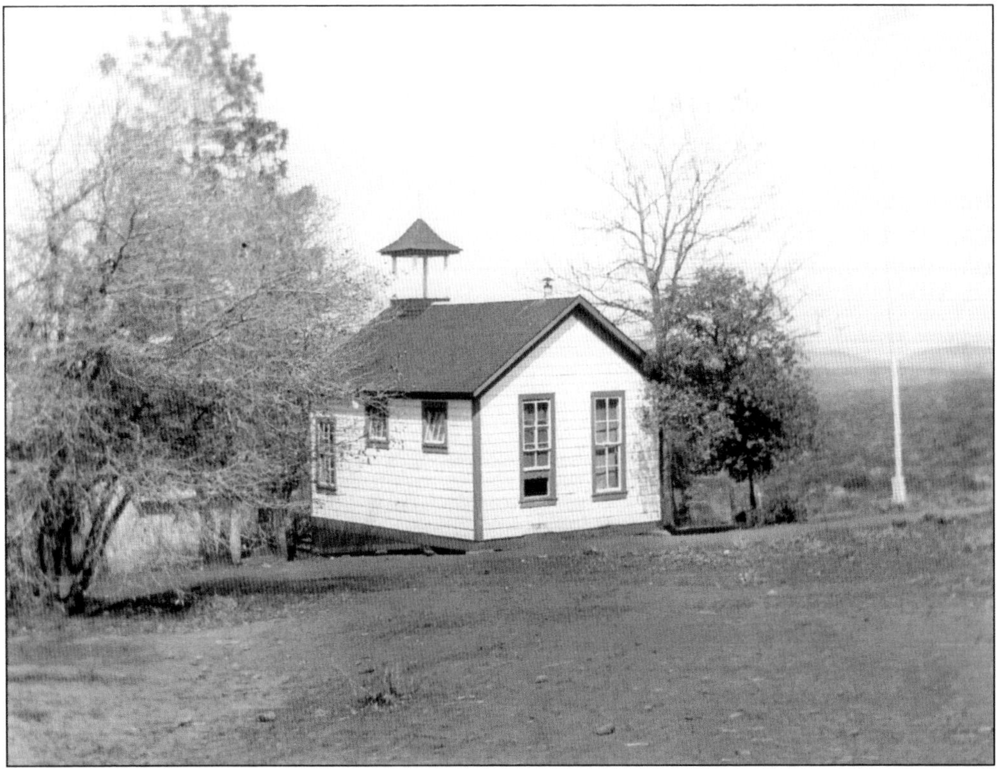

Not all rural districts in Lake County got swept up in the consolidation of the 1910s and 1920s. The Mountain School District, for instance, continued autonomously for several decades into the 20th century. Its isolated location in the Mayacamas Mountains in western Lake County made consolidation with other districts impractical. In 1901, the by then decades-old district issued $600 in bonds to build a new schoolhouse (shown above). After outgrowing this schoolhouse in a few years, classes were moved to the Mountain Improvement Clubhouse community center nearby (pictured below). The Mountain School District continued to operate until 1948, when it finally consolidated with Kelseyville.

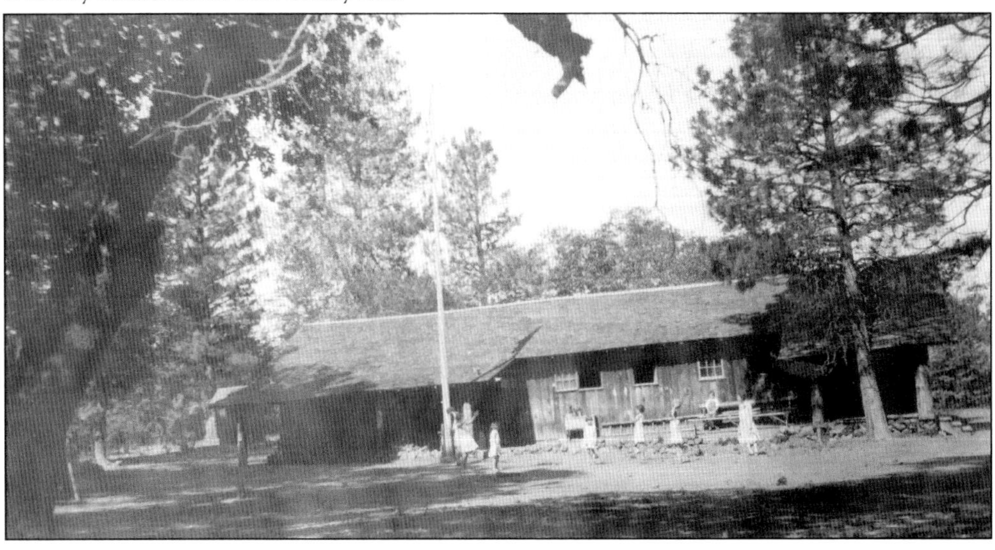

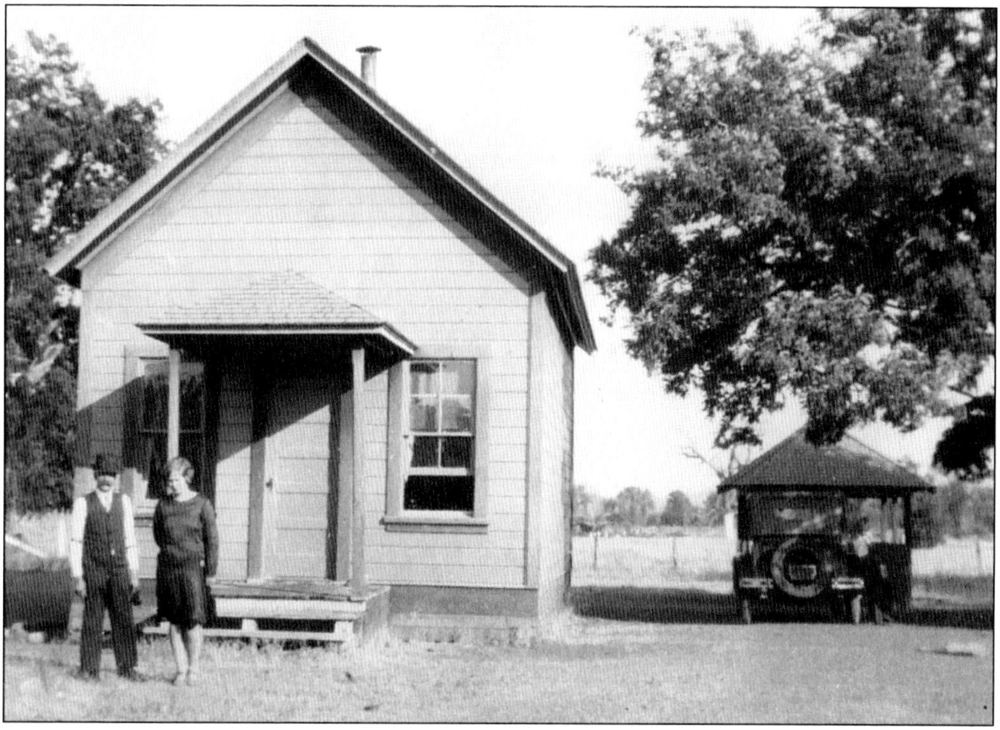

Several other school districts, also located within the Coastal Range in western Lake County, fiercely retained their autonomy and resisted consolidation. Even when the district itself consolidated with Middletown in 1925, classes were still held in the 1910 Loconomi Schoolhouse, pictured above, until lack of pupils finally forced it to close in 1937. The Cobb Valley Schoolhouse, built sometime in the early 1900s, remained one of the longest-used schoolhouses in Lake County history. The district eventually consolidated with Middletown in 1950, but classes continued to be held in this one-room schoolhouse until 1973. It was the last of the one-room schoolhouses used in Lake County.

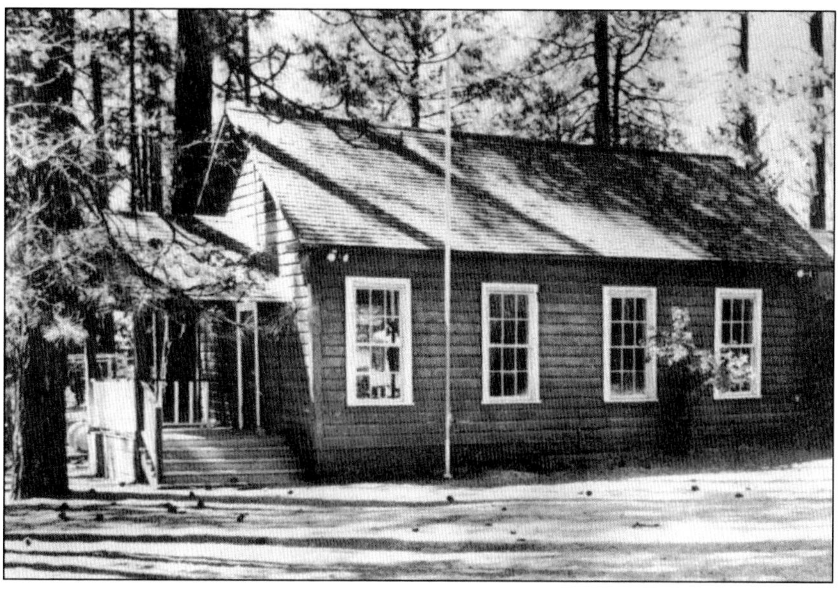

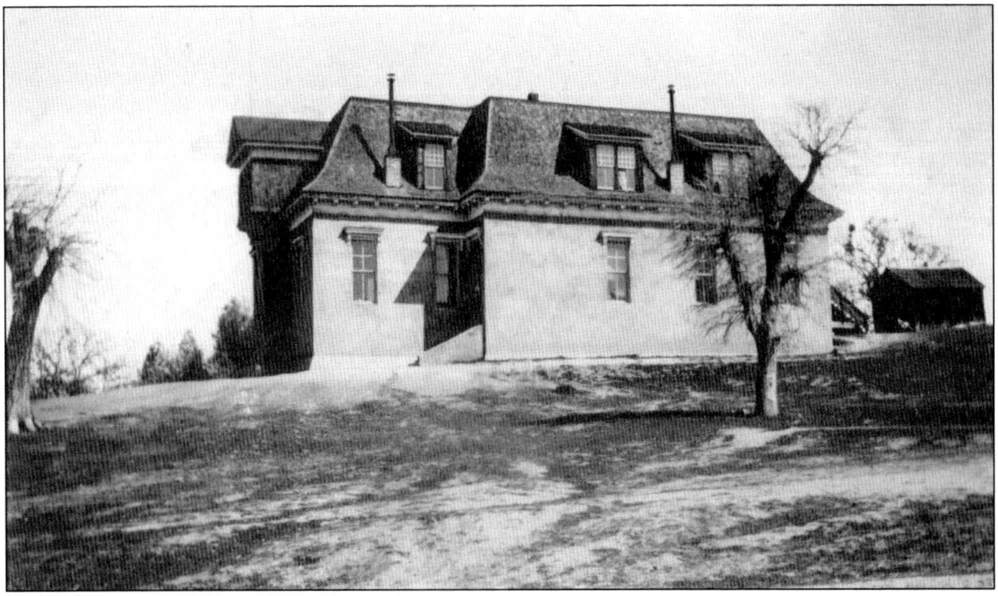

Many of the schoolhouses built in the twilight of the 19th century remained usable well into the 20th century. For 52 years, from 1877 until 1934, the Lower Lake Schoolhouse (above) saw hundreds of schoolchildren pass through its doors. Other than the replacement of the towering belfry and roof in 1906 following the Great San Francisco Earthquake, this building underwent no significant alterations. Unlike many other schoolhouses, which had to be altered or altogether replaced when nearby school districts were absorbed, the Lower Lake Schoolhouse was large enough to accommodate these influxes. Like the Lower Lake Schoolhouse, the Big Valley Schoolhouse, built around the same time, served the district for decades until finally consolidating with Kelseyville in 1920.

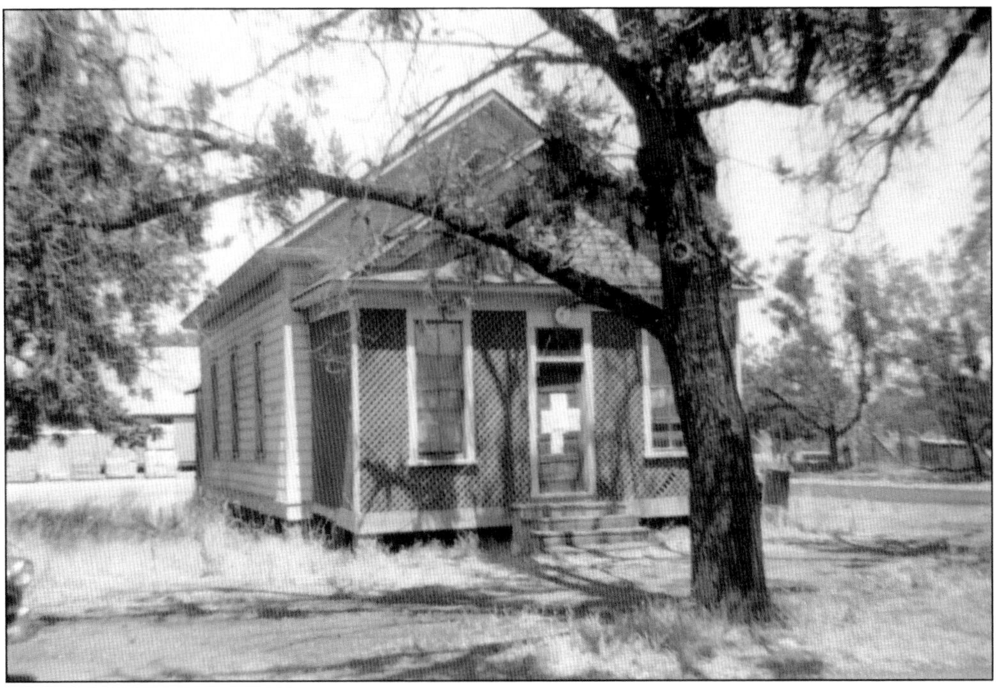

Six

Teaching and Learning in Lake County 1901–1941

The changes of the 1880s and 1890s were minor compared to those that the new century brought. Thinking back to his own childhood in 19th-century Lake County, William M. Nobles recognized this: "Our grandkids have palaces to go to school in, and buses to take them there. We were lucky . . . if we had any kind of old shanty school house to walk miles to." In a single man's lifetime, schooling as he knew it had fundamentally changed.

The nationwide Progressive movement of the 1890s had altered the concept of schools, even in far-flung places like Lake County. Sociopolitical groups like the temperance movement raced like wildfire across the country, and by the 1890s, Lake County had its own chapter of the Women's Christian Temperance Union. In education, Progressive changes included pedagogical innovations, expansion of the curriculum, addition of extracurriculars, and improvement in the education of teachers. The last decade of the 1800s and first decade of the 1900s saw the birth of a modern education system, and Lake County rode the wave along with the rest of California. Of course, being a rural county also meant Lake County did not see all of these national changes effected, and there still existed one-room rural schoolhouses well into the 1930s locally (and indeed, all the way into the 1970s).

The large, consolidated schools of the late 1910s and early 1920s, which soon became the norm, represented a major shift in Lake County education. Remembering the move to the new consolidated school in Lakeport in 1923, retired teacher Helen Davis especially recalled that, for the first time in her career, she was able to teach a single grade in a single classroom. Indeed, the very profession of teaching saw dramatic changes, with the authority to certify teachers gradually shifting from the local back to the state level.

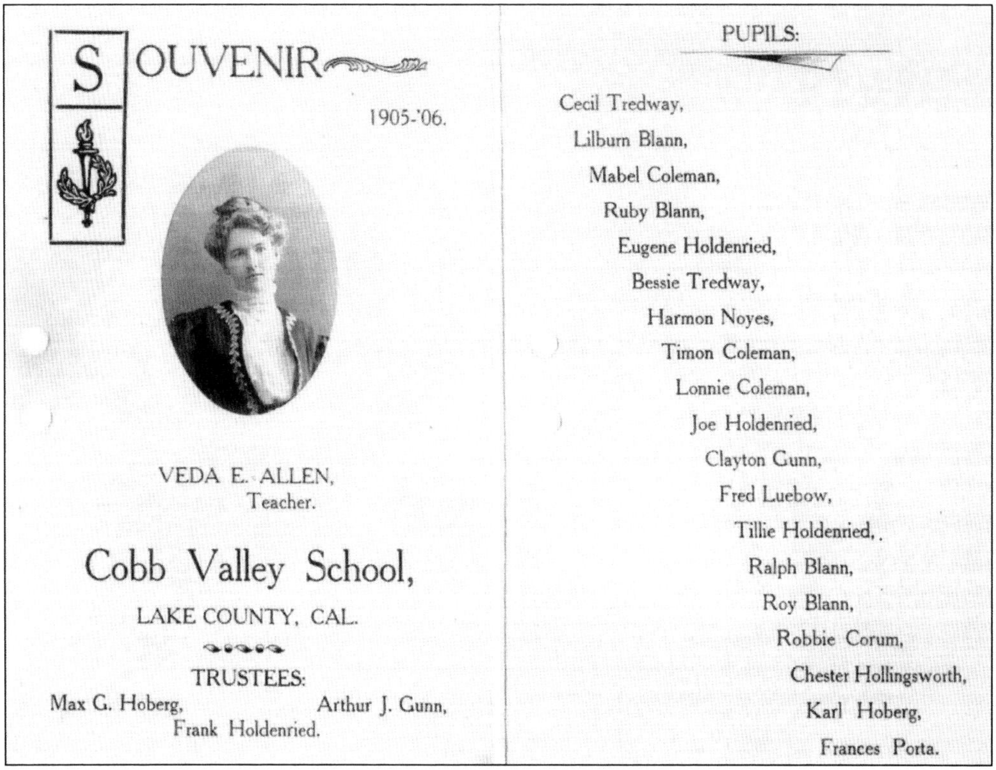

As shown above, school districts continued to issue the same quaint souvenirs as they had a decade earlier. In fact, teaching in 1905 seemed remarkably similar to teaching in 1895, unless one was a new teacher. The most desired and permanent credential for a teacher to obtain was the "life diploma," which could only be issued by the state. Counties like Lake County were still able to issue six-year grammar grade diplomas (which allowed teachers to teach at a grammar school) on the basis of county-level examinations, but these were only valid within the county of issuance. By the turn of the century, the state had most of the power in credentialing teachers, with counties allowed to issue certificates only after the state had issued credentials.

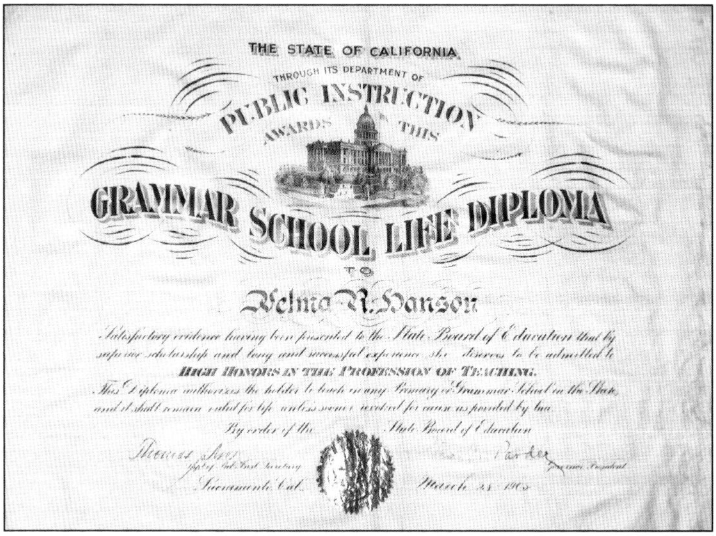

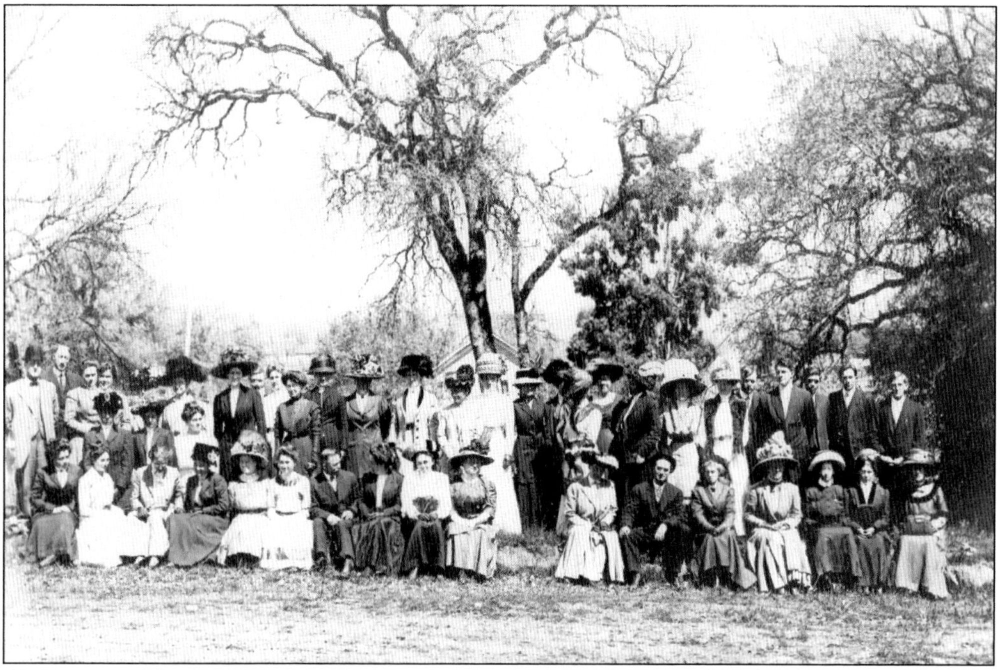

With a greater focus on hiring professionals to be teachers, the annual teachers' institutes that had started in the 19th century became even more important as a means of continued professional development. Several of the actual programs used at the institutes in Lake County during the 1910s currently reside in the Historic Courthouse Museum. These documents provide an insight into the topics thought most important to convey to teachers at that time. Pictured above are the teachers who attended the 1911 institute and below is the program for it. Of particular interest that year was the notion of manual training in schools, with guest lecturer from Berkeley Arthur H. Chamberlain discussing this topic over the course of several workshops. Another presentation was made especially for school trustees on "Beautifying Schoolrooms and School Grounds; Sanitary Measures; Employment of Teachers etc."

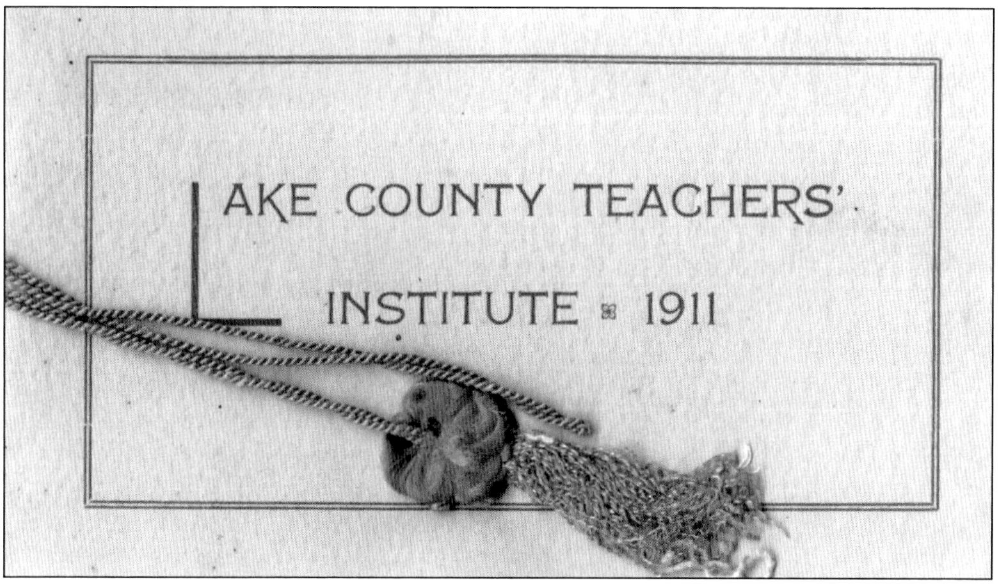

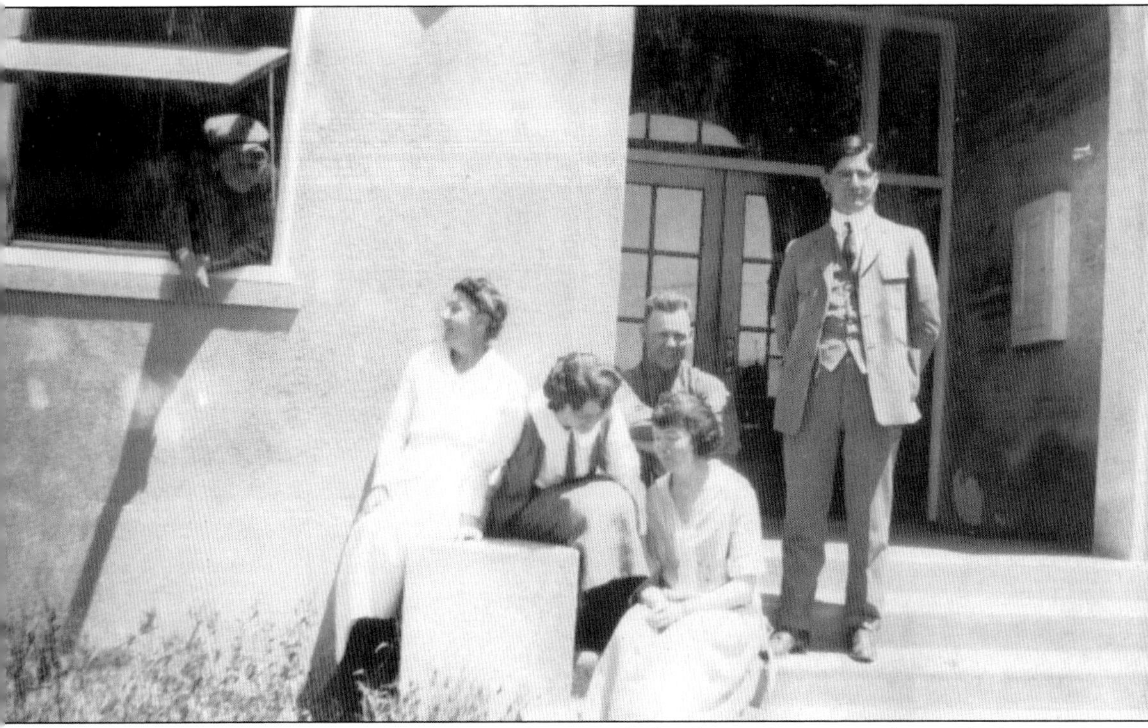

It is important to note that until the unification of schools in Lake County during the late 1910s and early 1920s, the vast majority of schoolhouses remained the one-room wooden structures of the previous century. Like their earlier counterparts, these 20th-century one-room schools were taught by a single instructor and were attended by students as young as 5 and as old as 17. Even with the construction of Clear Lake Union High School in 1901, most of the several dozen school districts in the county were too far away from Lakeport to send their students. It was not until the establishment of several other high schools in the 1920s that most Lake County students were able to take advantage of a free secondary education. In many ways, this picture, which shows the faculty of Kelseyville Union Grammar in 1924 posing on the steps of their new modern school, is an anomaly for the still-rural Lake County.

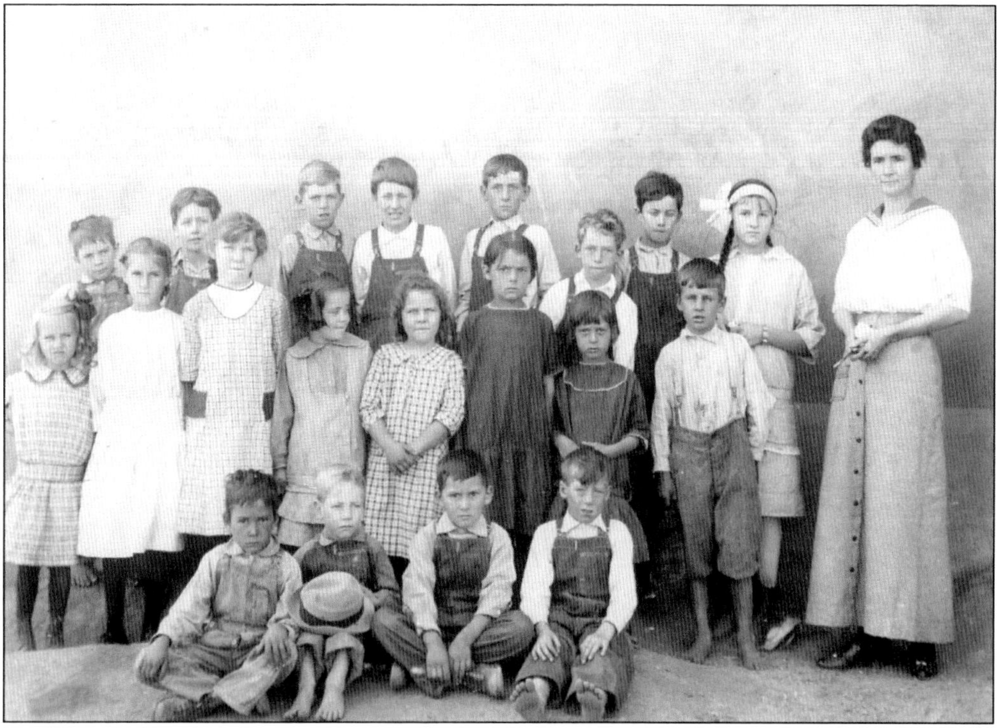

In this image, young students pose in front of the Lower Lake Grammar School in 1914. The mostly barefoot, somewhat ragtag bunch of kids is more emblematic of the rural school experience of early 20th-century Lake County. (Courtesy of the Lower Lake Historic Schoolhouse Museum.)

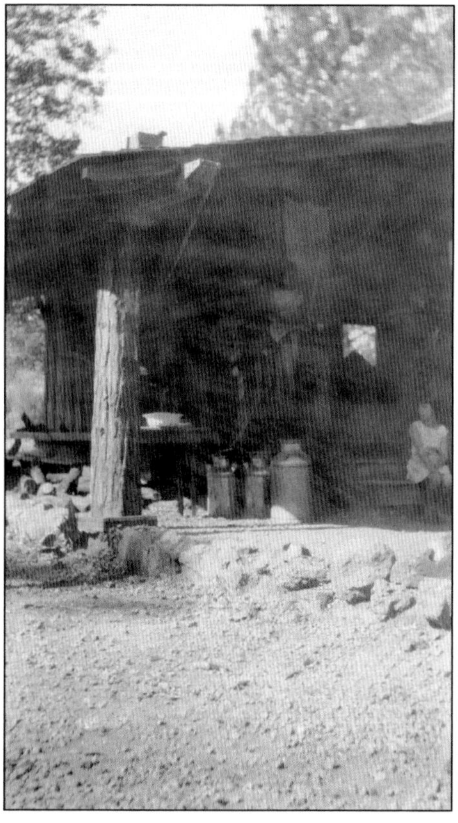

Even as late as the 1930s, the more rural school districts in Lake County operated one-room schoolhouses in a manner that had not changed much since the 1860s. In this image, two young girls sit on the porch of the Mountain Schoolhouse. The barrels shown in the photograph were filled with water and had to be brought to the school each day.

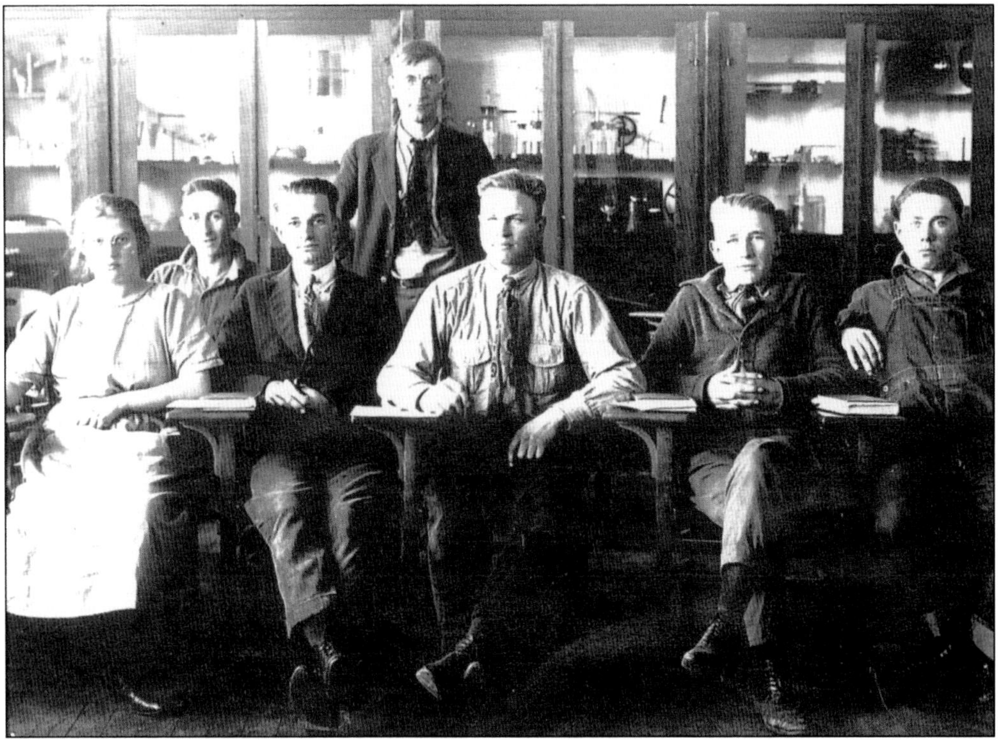

Meanwhile, high school students were being exposed to an entirely new set of classes, with special focus on sciences. With these classes came an obvious need for a greater variety of educational tools. Gone were the days of McGuffey's Color Chart. Pictured is an Upper Lake Union High physics class around the 1920s; notice the cabinets in the back full of scientific equipment.

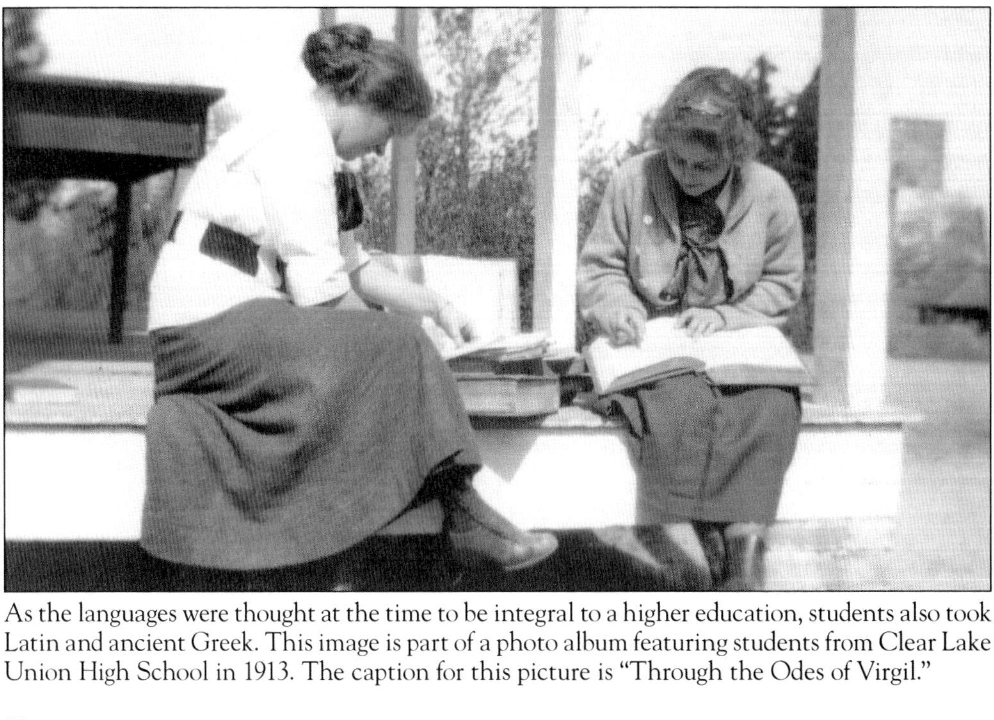

As the languages were thought at the time to be integral to a higher education, students also took Latin and ancient Greek. This image is part of a photo album featuring students from Clear Lake Union High School in 1913. The caption for this picture is "Through the Odes of Virgil."

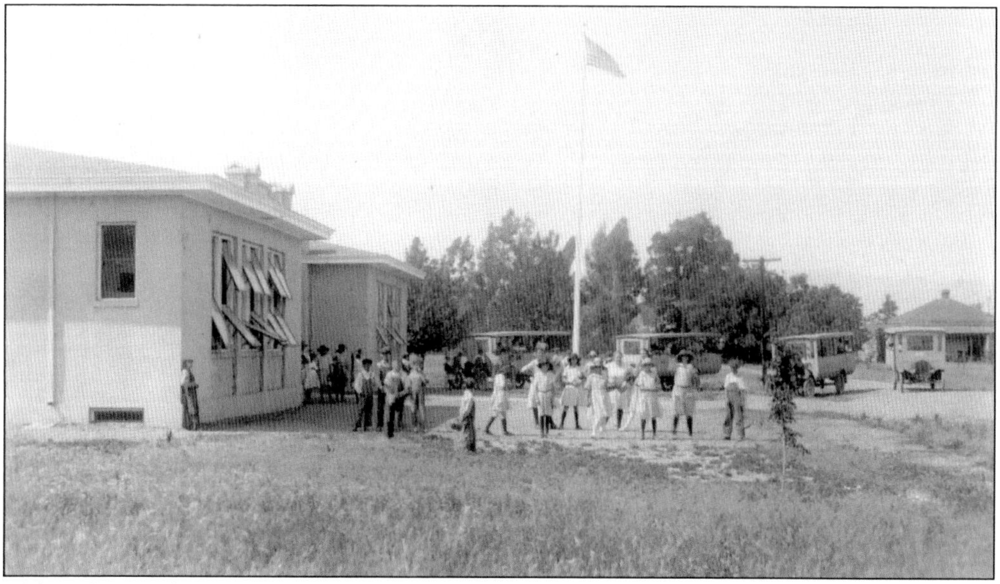

Although providing numerous benefits, including these new additions to the curriculum, unified schools also created some problems. In the past, students had usually lived within walking or horse-riding distance to their schools. However, with school consolidation, trustees of these new districts had to find a means of transporting students to the now-distant school. When it opened its new Union Grammar School in 1924, the Lakeport district solved this problem by contracting with the Spiers Stage Company to transport students, until the school was able to purchase its own fleet of buses. Pictured above are the earliest photographs of school buses in Lake County, dropping students off at the Kelseyville Union Grammar School in 1919. Below, a bus driver for the Cobb Valley district poses with his passengers.

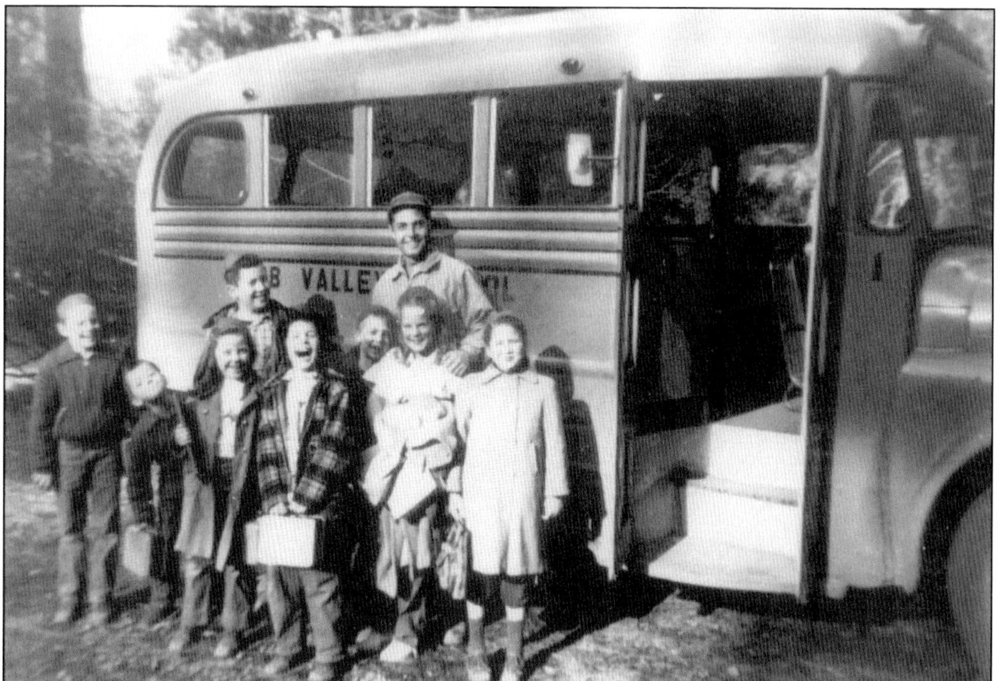

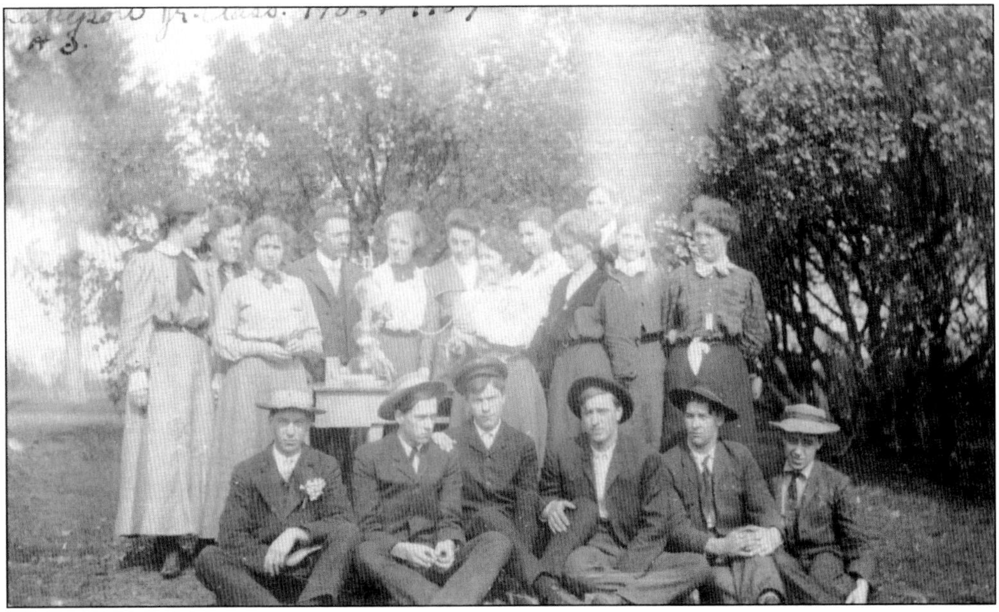

After closing his private school in 1901 and taking on the post as science and math teacher at the newly established Clear Lake Union High, Prof. John Overholser frequently took his students on expeditions throughout Lake County. Seeming to spurn the classroom, Overholser teaches his junior physics class of 1906–1907 in the photograph above. Notice what appears to be a distilling column on the table at the center of the group. Below, he teaches his 1913 class the physics of a pendulum and gravity with the aid of two pieces of fruit.

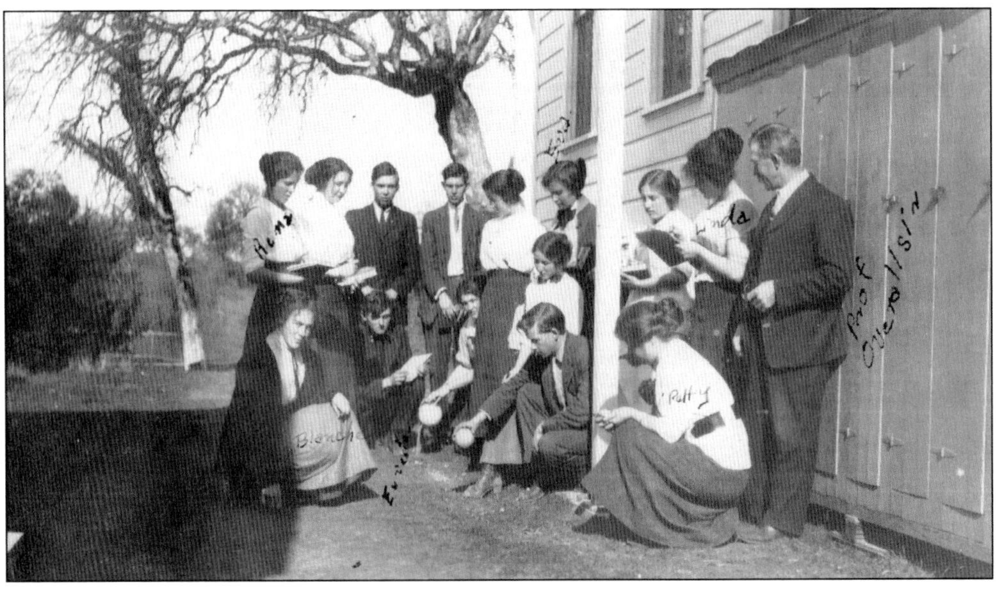

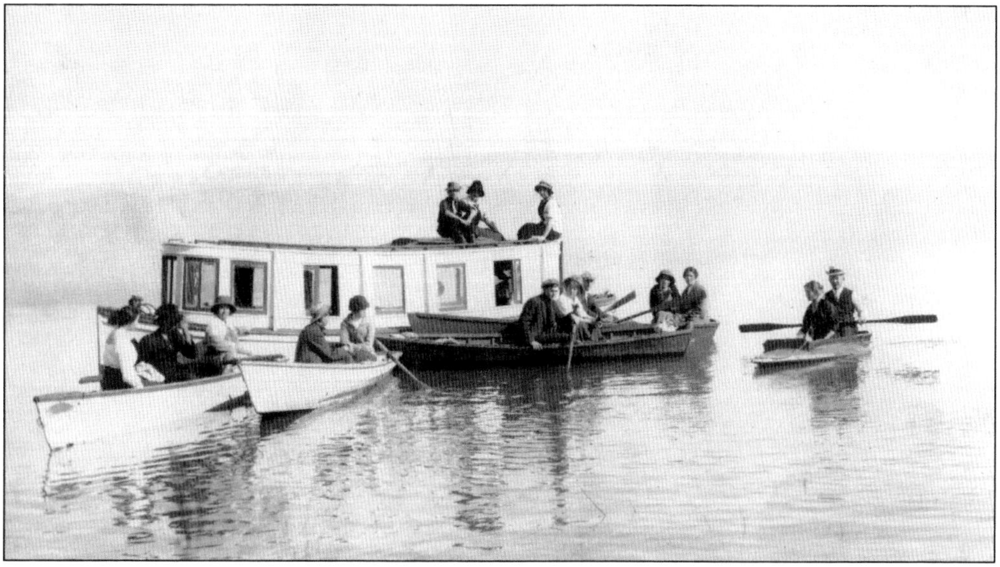

Living in Lake County for any length of time, with its abundance of natural beauty and sheer agricultural bounty, would make anyone an environmentalist soon enough. For Professor Overholser—and surely for other teachers in Lake County—the very land provided for him ample inspiration. Pictured here, he takes a class out on the lake to travel quite a distance from Lakeport to near modern-day Clearlake, a journey of over a dozen miles. The destination was the abandoned Sulphur Bank Mine. The lesson that day, according to the cramped white caption written next to this photograph in the scrapbook, was on the properties of sound and echoes.

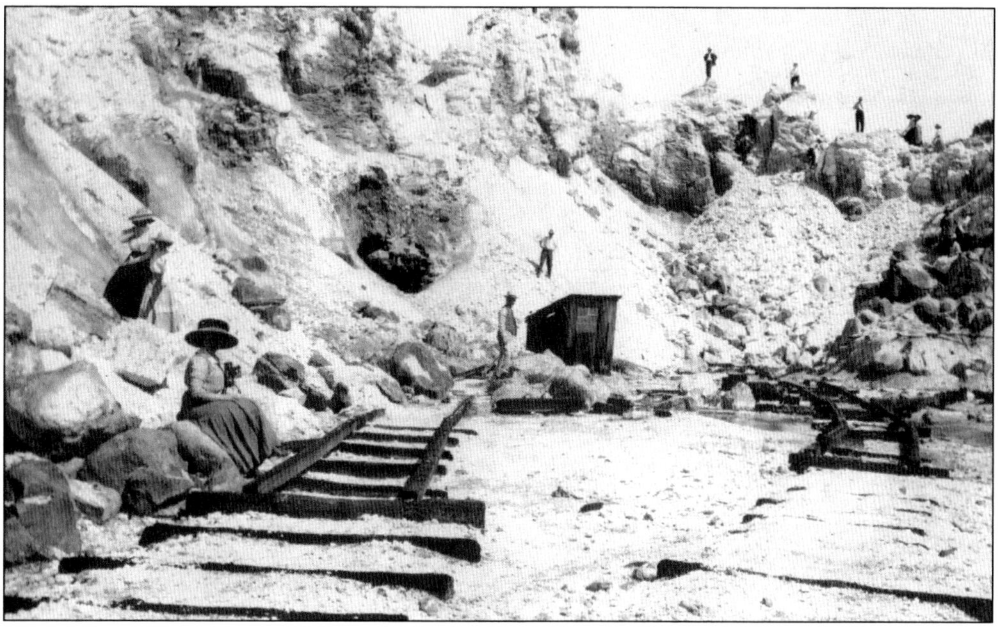

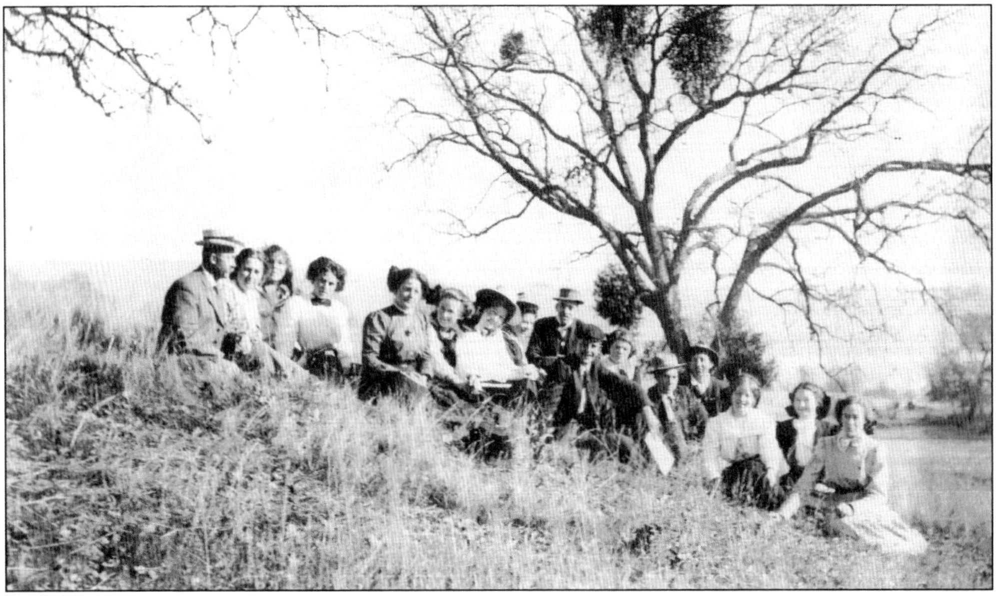

Not limiting himself to the shores of Clear Lake, Professor Overholser also dragged his students up and down the oak-dotted hills outside of Lakeport. On the particular outing pictured here, he teaches his students the rudiments of contouring.

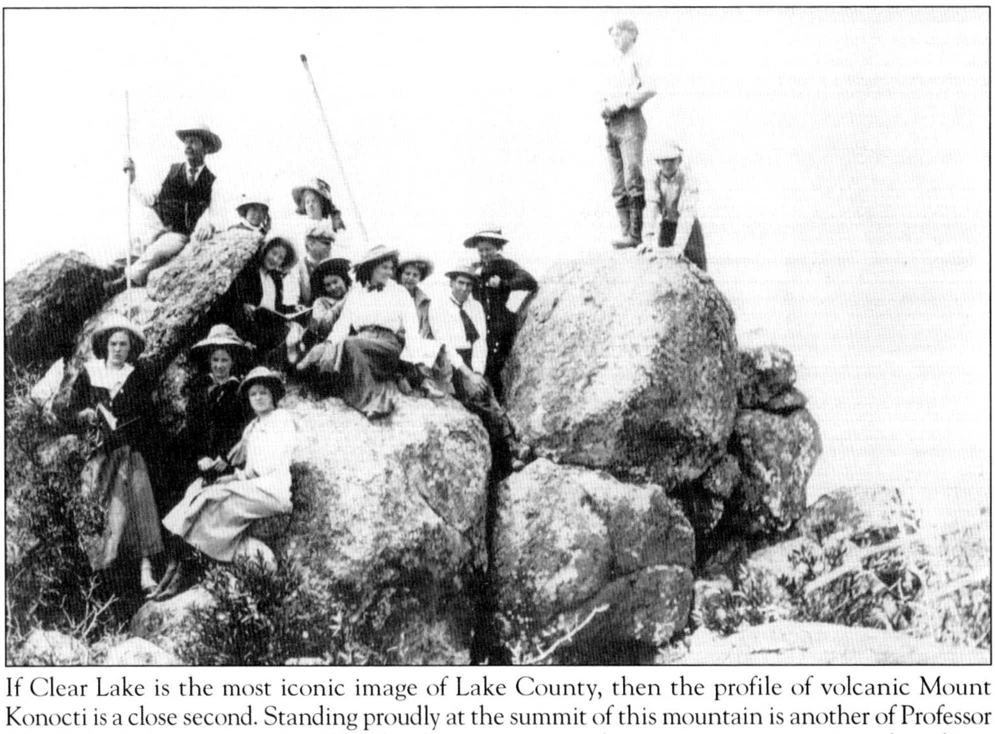

If Clear Lake is the most iconic image of Lake County, then the profile of volcanic Mount Konocti is a close second. Standing proudly at the summit of this mountain is another of Professor Overholser's classes, again in 1913. Thanks once more to the accompanying caption, the subject of that day's lesson is known: volcanoes.

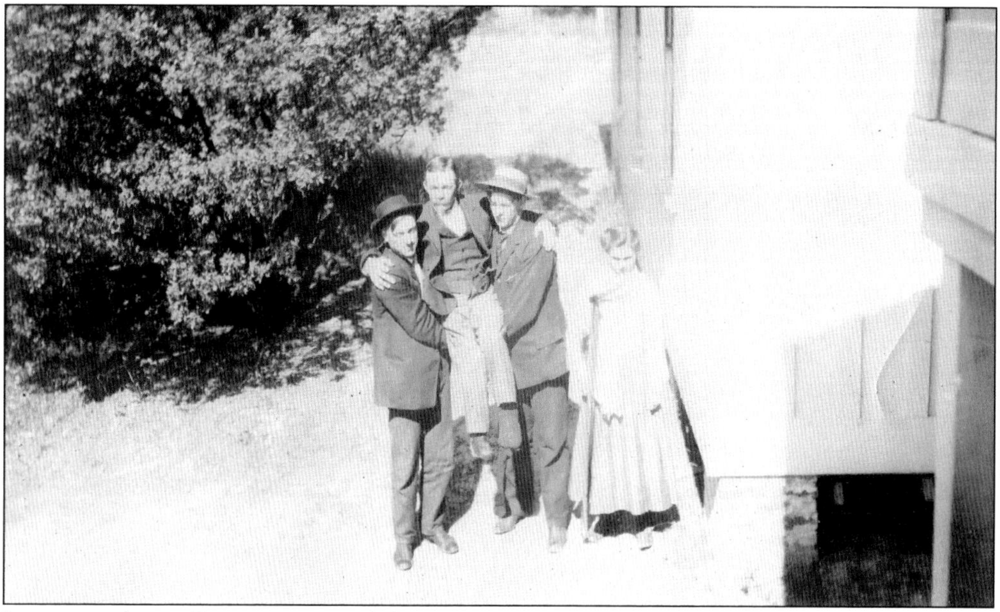

It appears that gallivanting around the countryside had its downsides, especially for an aging schoolteacher. Professor Overholser is shown here being carried back to town by two of his students after taking a fall and breaking his leg during one of his school trips.

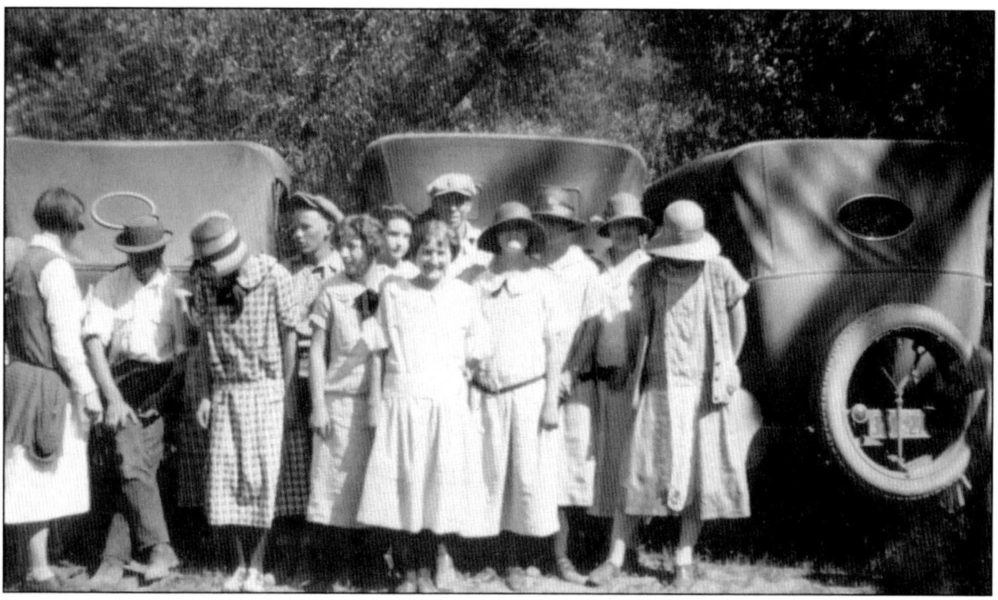

The students of Clear Lake Union High School were not the only ones in Lake County to enjoy the occasional field trip to take in the natural beauty of the land. The 1925 senior class of Kelseyville Union High School poses while on a trip to Seigler Springs, one of the world-famous mineral springs still operating in the surrounding mountains.

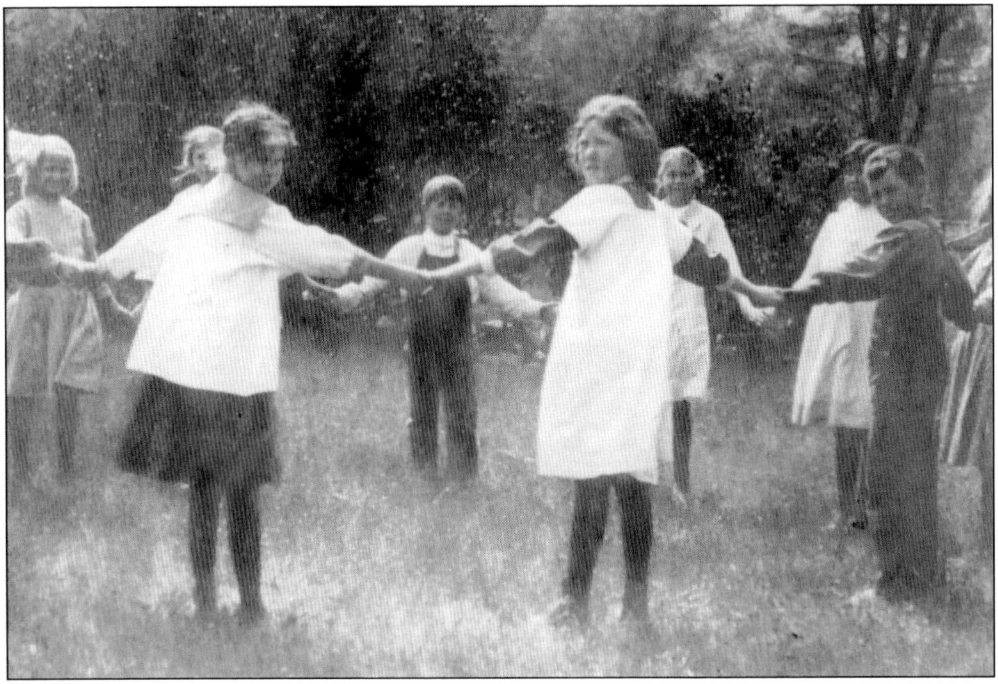

Pictured above is a group of students at the Middletown Grammar School enjoying a game of ring-around-the-rosy in 1913. By 1929, with many schools in America beginning to be consolidated, the isolated, rural one-room schoolhouses of years past were already being looked upon with a sense of nostalgia. Writing in the January 1937 edition of the *Sierra Educational News* journal, Mrs. Lewis, a teacher in Lake County, remarks that the Mountain Schoolhouse "has one of the most beautiful playgrounds in all of California," as pictured below. She plays down the fact that the schoolhouse was in fact built as a clubhouse to begin with and that teachers had to put up partitions to break up the space. Instead, Lewis laughs it off by saying "the children have lost nothing by the change."

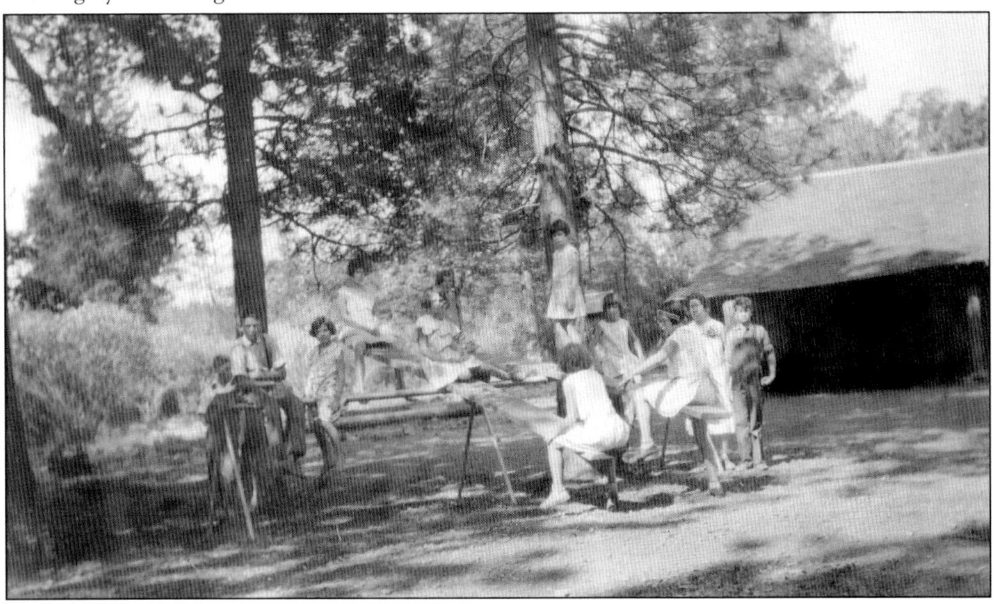

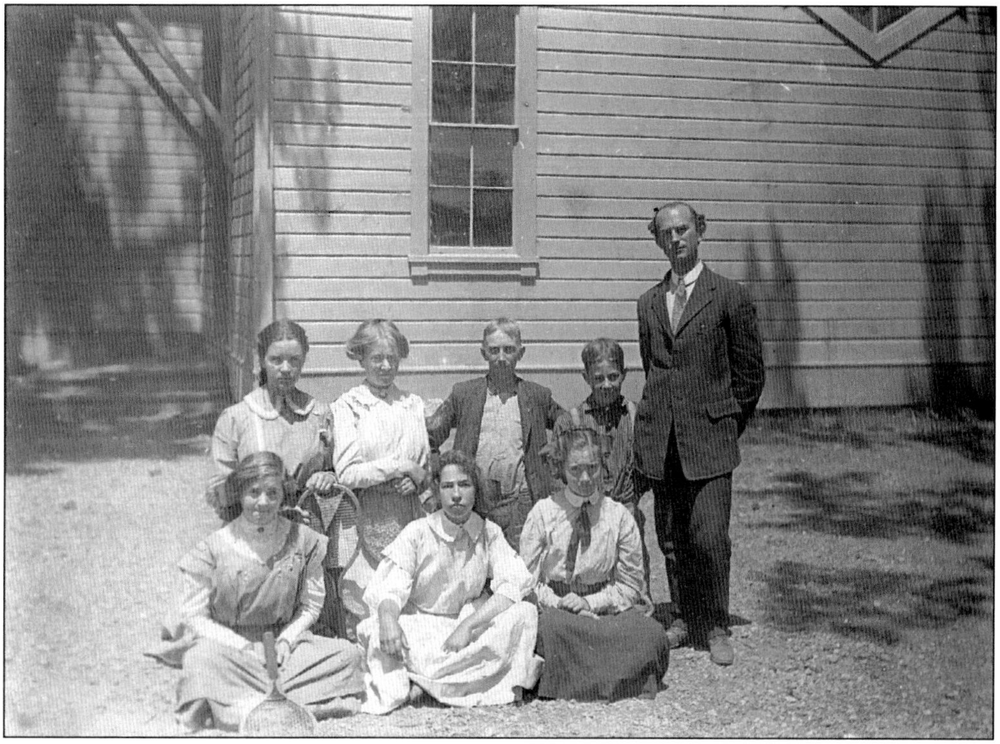

Even the most cherished part of the student's school day could not escape the changes that came with the new century. Recess, especially in schoolhouses out in the country, provided children with pent-up energy a time to run wild. Some schools, like Middletown (pictured above around the turn of the century), gave students organized sports to play; notice the badminton rackets the girls hold. With the new, larger, consolidated schools built in towns like Lakeport, the students were finally given fenced-off spaces to play games. Before, as retired teacher Mrs. Davis Mckee recalled years later, "what bothered the boys [about the old grammar school] was the way their playground balls would take off downhill for Main Street." Pictured below, grammar school students enjoy their brand-new playground in 1924.

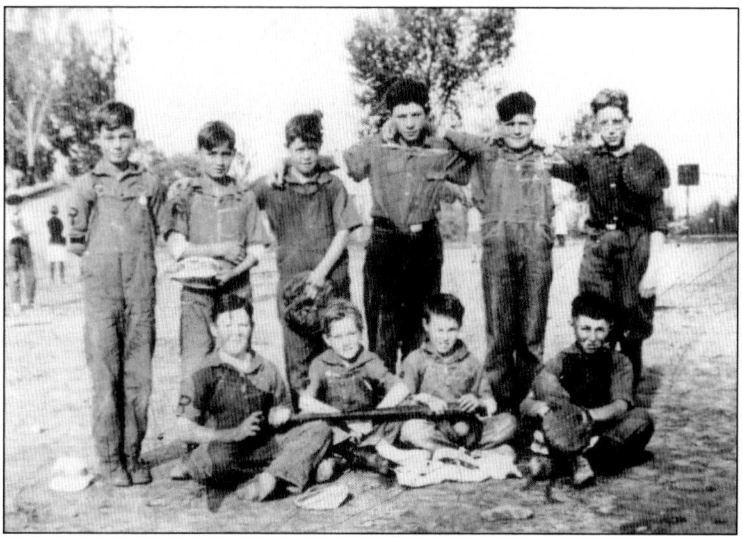

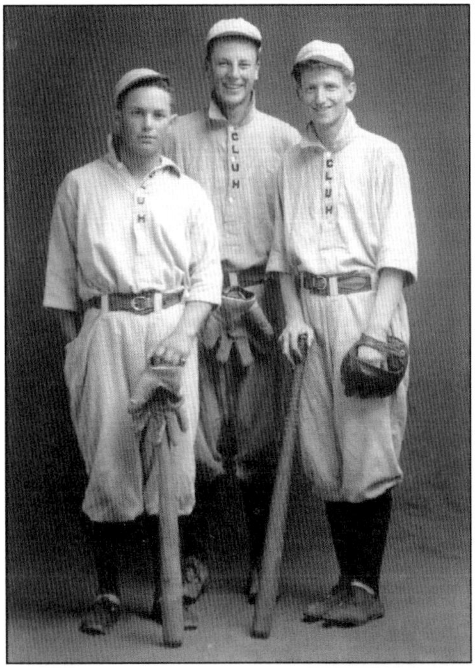

If grammar school students enjoyed their new playground space, high school students in Lake County took to the extracurricular sports offered at school with a vengeance. With the birth of unified school districts and high schools came a level of organized sports that had not yet been seen in Lake County. At left, three Clear Lake Union High School baseball players pose for a photograph that was soon made into a postcard. Below, the Upper Lake Union High championship team of 1920–1921 poses in front of its new school building, just a few years old at that time.

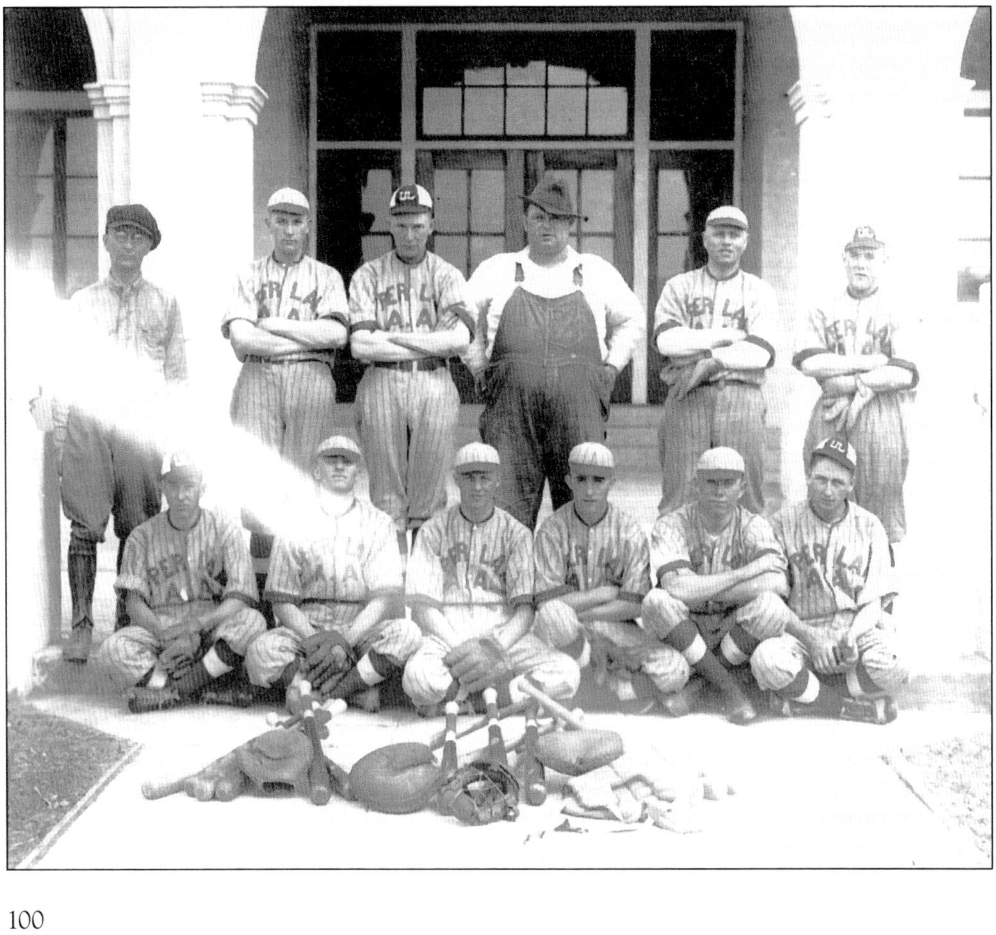

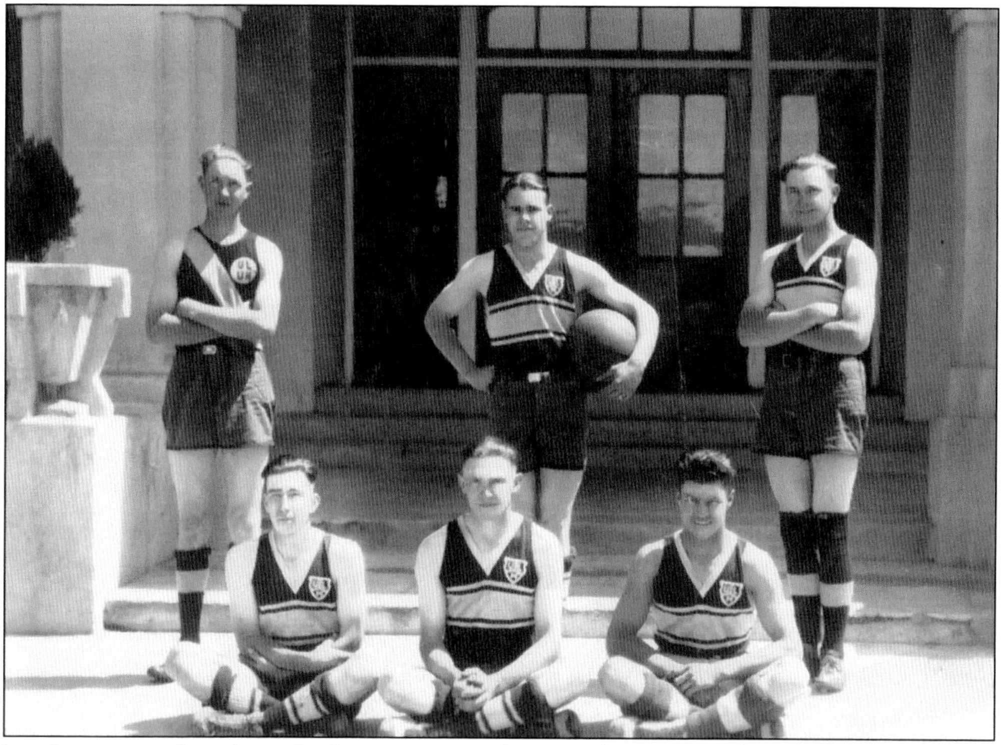

In what seems to have been the favorite spot to take team photographs, the Upper Lake basketball team of the early 1920s poses in front of the high school building. The birth of school sports teams provided an outlet for what had always been a rivalry between the major towns in the county.

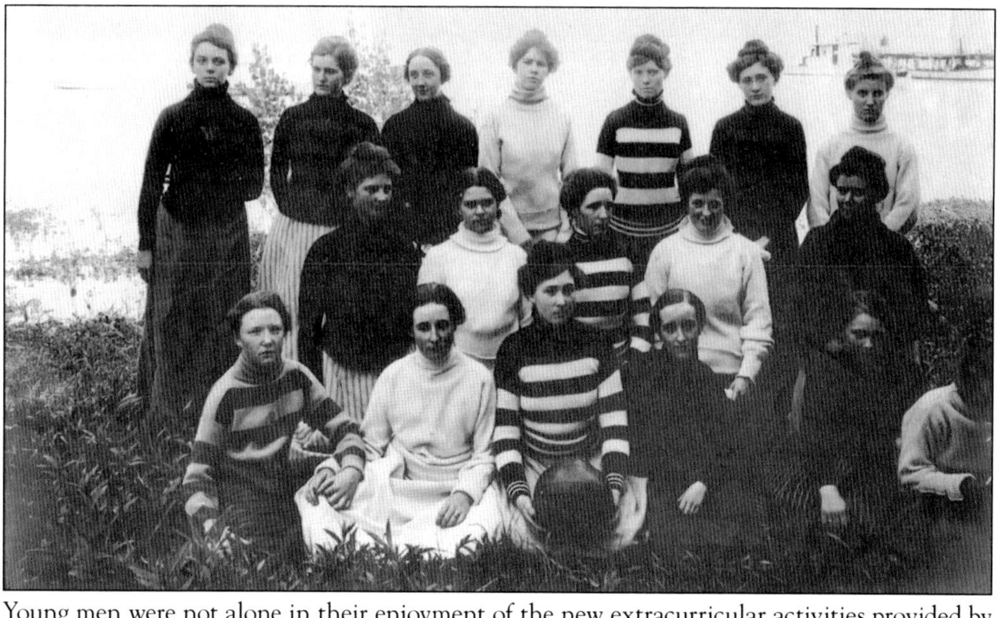

Young men were not alone in their enjoyment of the new extracurricular activities provided by the Progressive Era educational reforms. This is a women's basketball team in Lakeport. It is not certain whether this was a civic team or one associated with Clear Lake Union High School, but by the mid-1910s each high school in the county had women's sports teams.

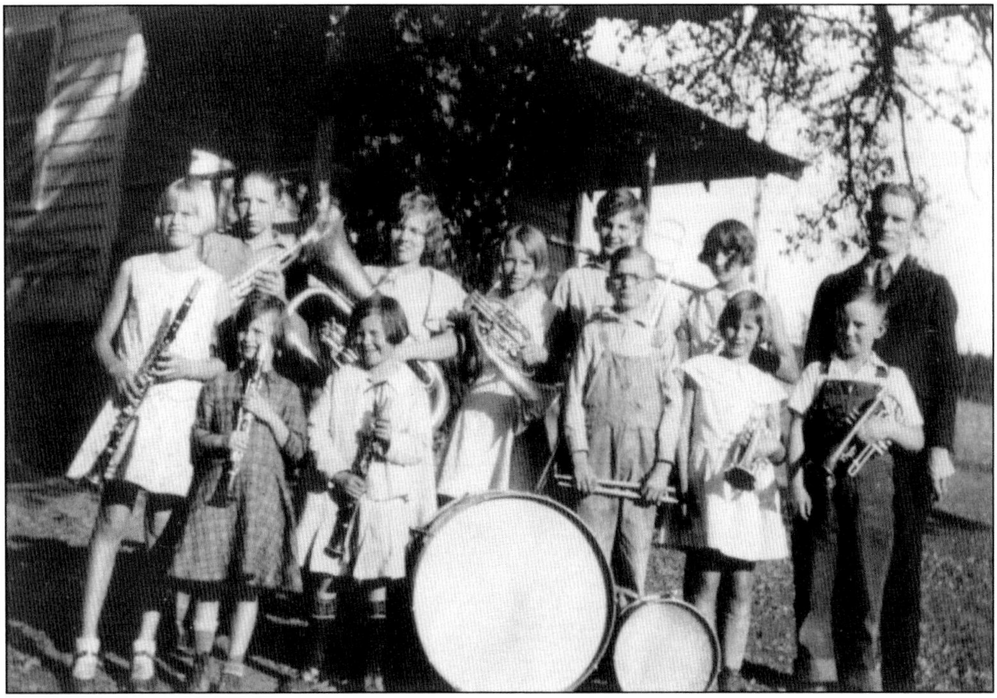

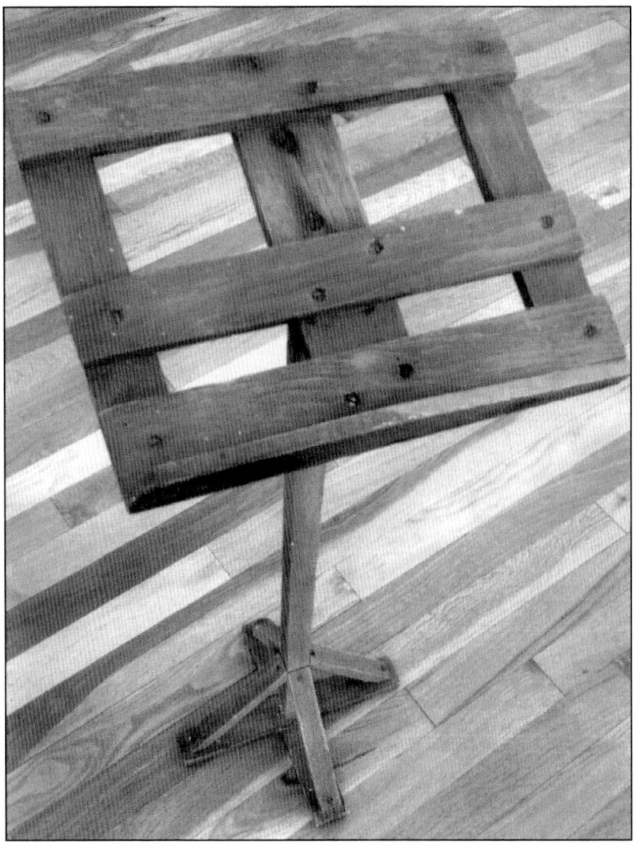

Organized sports teams were not the only extracurricular activities in vogue in the early 20th century. In an age before radio, someone with musical talent provided people with some of the only entertainment to be had in rural areas. Pianos would be hauled into the backs of pickups and driven to the remotest parts of the county just for a celebration. Before the 20th century, music education in Lake County schools was a haphazard affair, with private lessons providing the only means of instruction. Starting in the 1910s, however, school music groups and whole bands began to appear. Above is the Morgan Valley School band of 1930–1932. At left, one of the music stands used in school is on display in the Lower Lake Historic Schoolhouse Museum. (Above, courtesy of the Historic Courthouse Museum; left, from the author.)

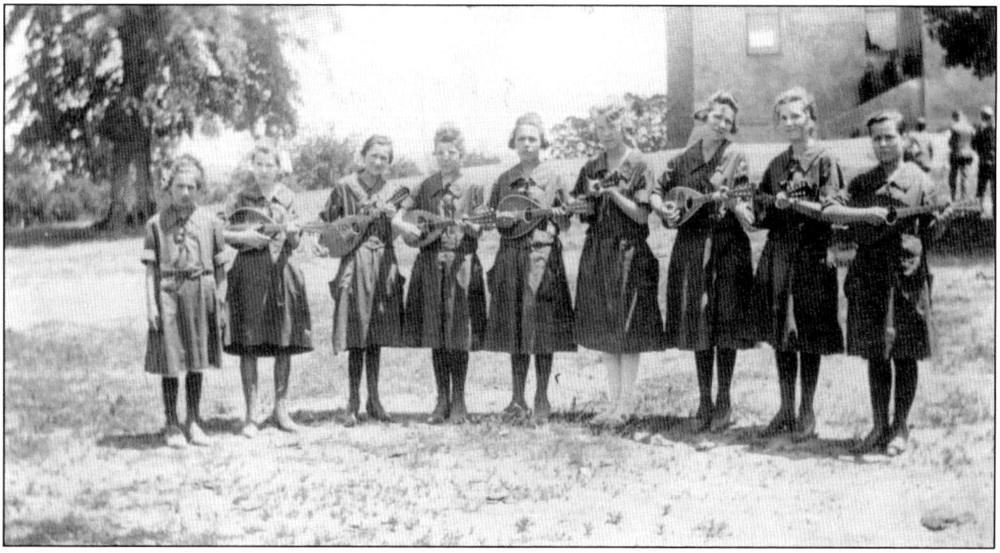

Depending on the proclivities of the music teacher and the financial capabilities of the school district and parents, some schools developed themed music groups. Pictured here is the girls' mandolin band of Lower Lake Grammar School in 1920. (Courtesy of the Lower Lake Historic Schoolhouse Museum.)

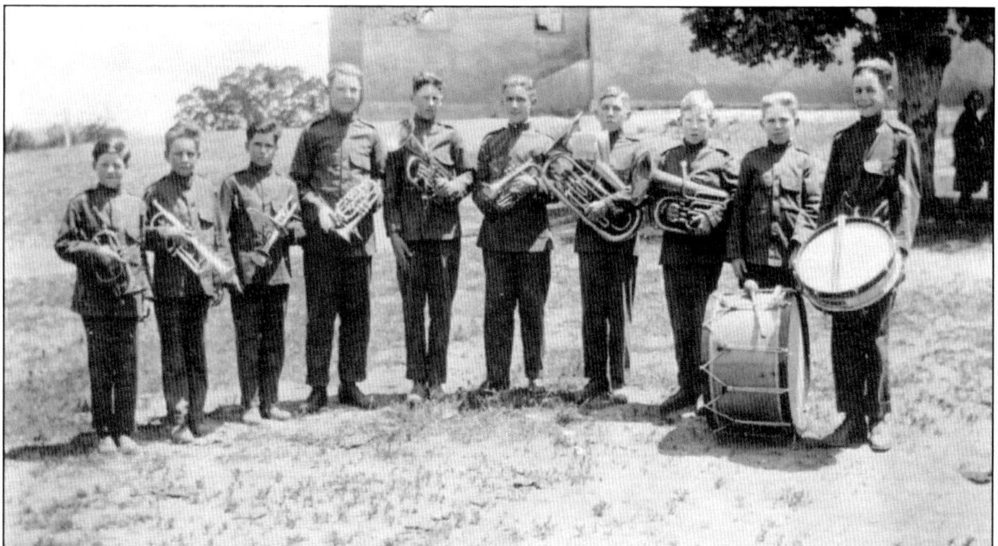

Lower Lake Grammar School also had a boys' trumpet band, shown here. In 1920, the boys' trumpet band and the girls' mandolin band gave concerts to earn money to spend a week in Sacramento, which they were able to do—chaperoned, of course. (Courtesy of the Lower Lake Historic Schoolhouse Museum.)

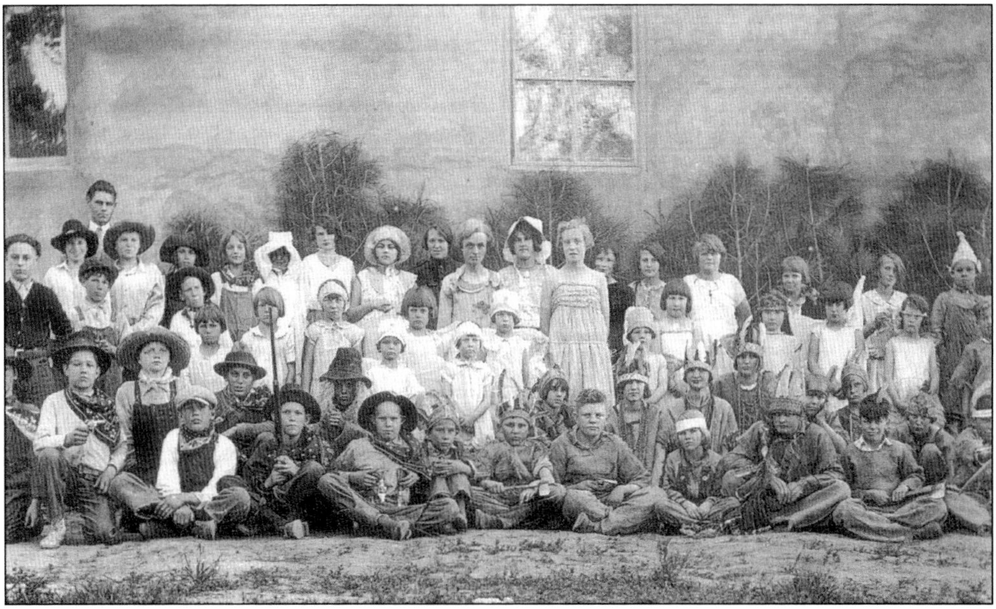

Some of the larger, newly unified schools, like Upper Lake and Lakeport, even had auditoriums built. These spaces allowed for student-led plays and pageants, and theater clubs sprouted up quite quickly. Although still housed in the 1877 schoolhouse, the Lower Lake Grammar/High School had a theater on the second floor of the building. The scene of traveling circus performances and town dances, this space was also utilized for student plays. Above, the 1925 cast of the school's performance of *Johnny Appleseed* poses in front of the school. Below, the older students from that same year pose onstage, dressed in their costumes for *In the Shadow of the Rockies: A Romance of the Golden West.* (Both, courtesy of the Lower Lake Historic Schoolhouse Museum.)

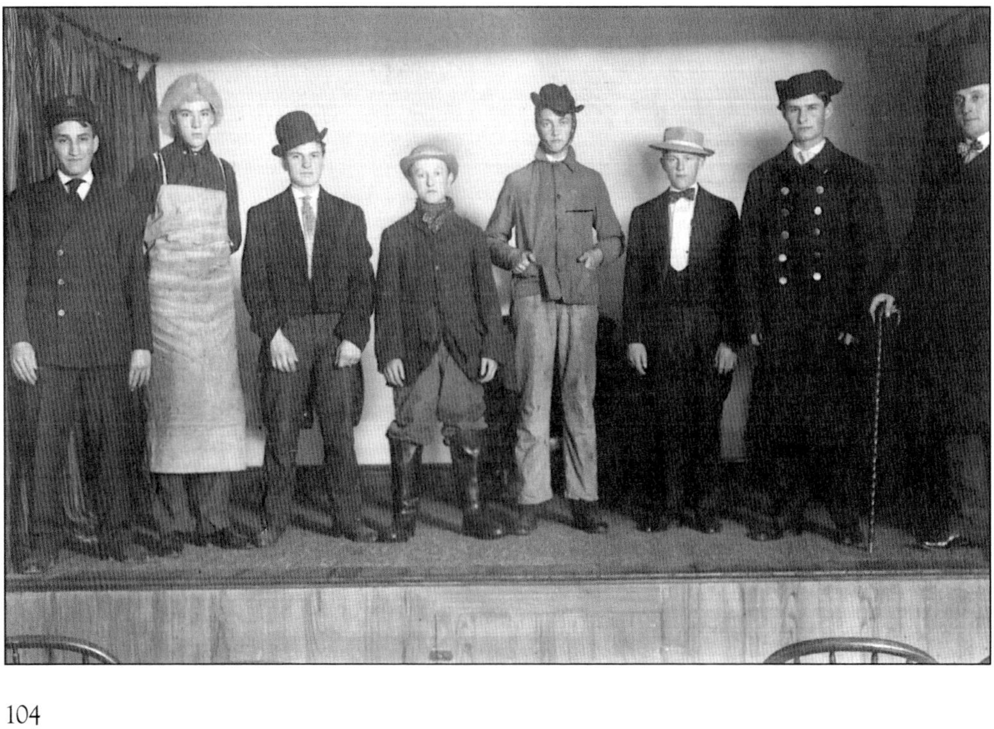

Peace Day in California Schools

MAY 18, 1915

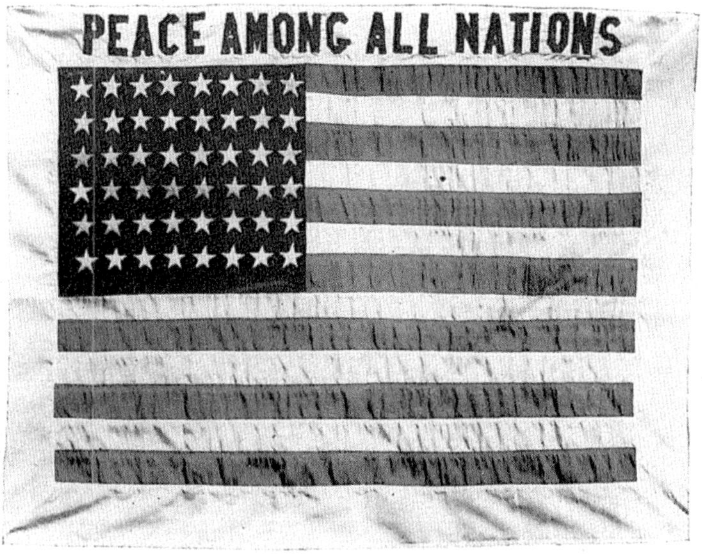

This is the flag of a peace loving Nation. As the stars represent neighbor states living together in peace, so the whole flag is an emblem that the Nations will so live also.

ISSUED BY
THE STATE DEPARTMENT OF EDUCATION

PRINTED AT CALIFORNIA STATE PRINTING OFFICE

In a process that has since been identified as "Americanization," American schools after the late 19th century—faced with an unprecedented wave of immigrants from Central and Eastern Europe—attempted to indoctrinate its students with the ideas and values that supported the cultural status quo of the period. That meant maintaining the mores of white, Anglo-Saxon Protestants. Despite its isolation, Lake County was not averse to this influx of new citizens, with European and Hispanic families making their way into the Clear Lake basin. Patriotic pageants, American flag-waving students, and other nationalistic trends appeared with increasing frequency in schools in the 1910s. World War I exacerbated these displays. Pictured here is a pamphlet handed out to Lake County teachers, encouraging them to buy and display a flag in their classrooms in a call for peace. (From the author, with permission from Melinda Moranda.)

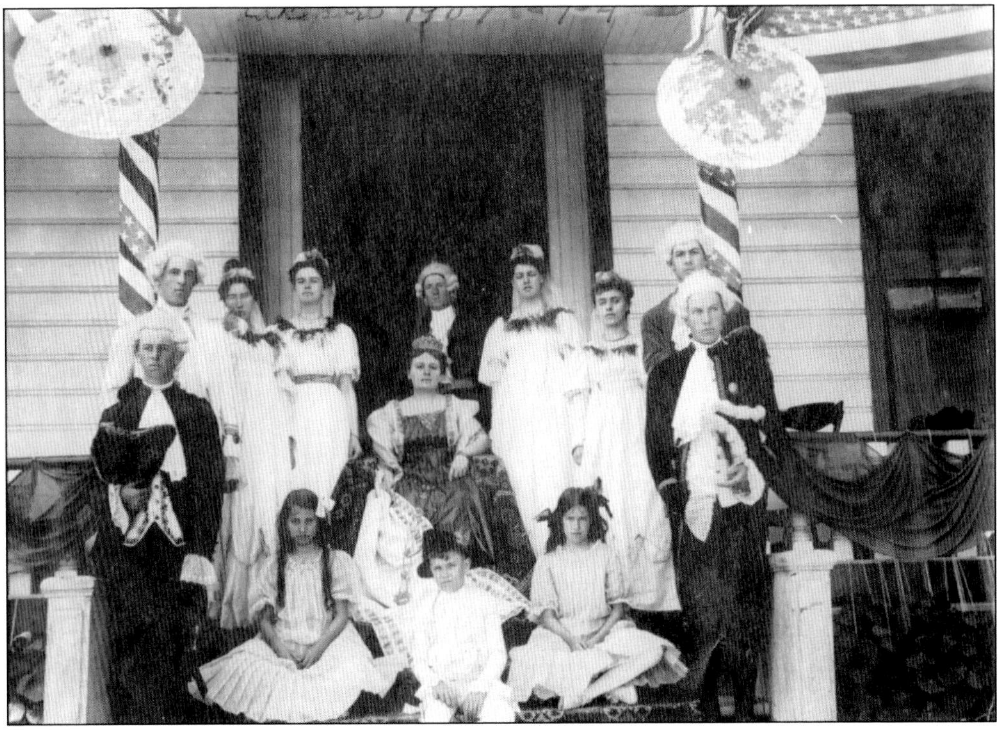

Starting in the late 19th century with elaborate Fourth of July parades in Lakeport and Upper Lake, Lake County residents developed a hankering for powdered wigs, tricorn hats, and ball gowns. Pictured here, Upper Lake students pose for a Fourth of July celebration in 1907.

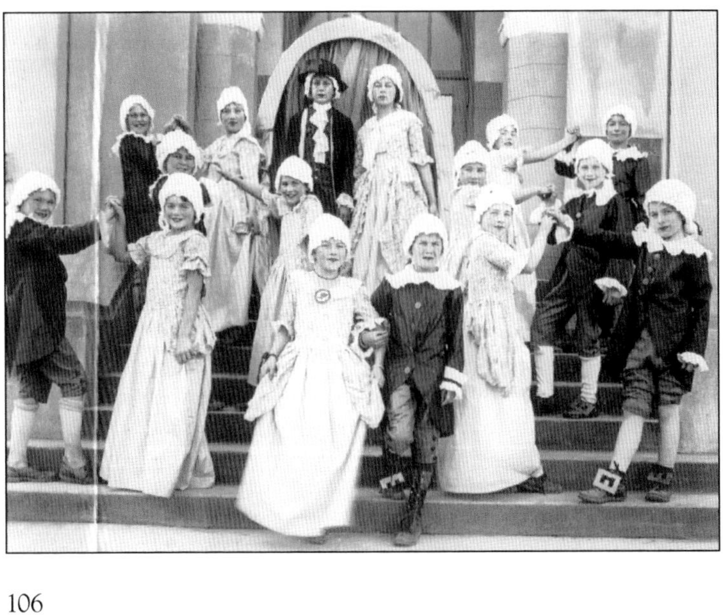

Fourth of July was not the only patriotic celebration observed in Lake County schools. Here, young boys and girls pose on the front steps of the Upper Lake Union Grammar School in their regalia as part of a celebration of Washington's Birthday.

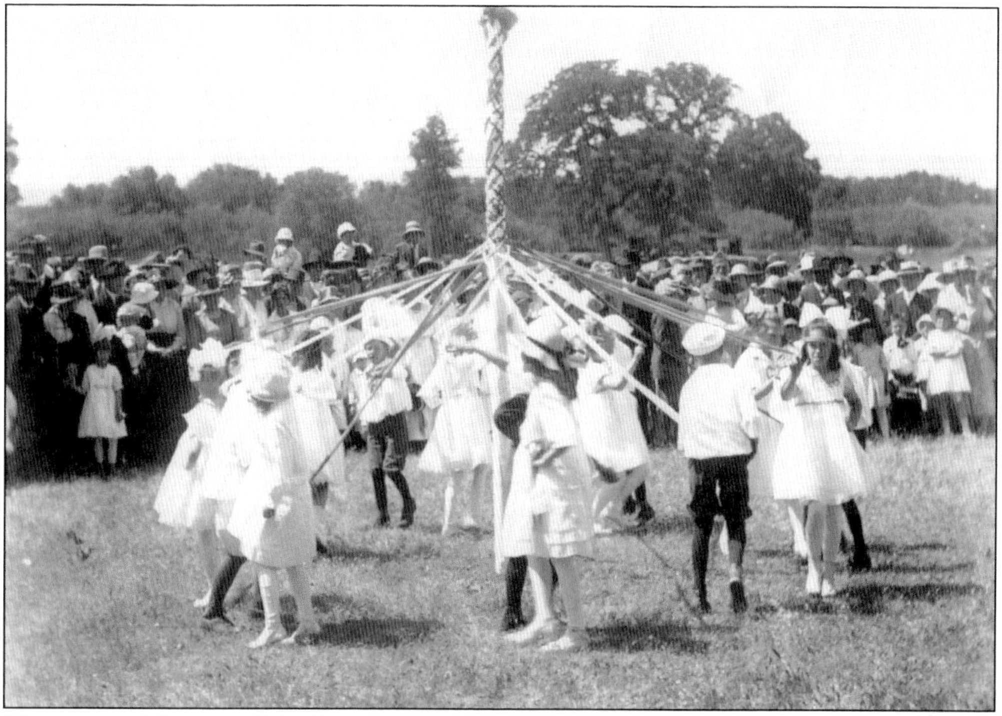

The spring celebration of May Day also became quite popular, especially after World War I. Above, Kelseyville Grammar School students dance around the maypole in 1919 for their families and friends to enjoy. Below, an empty maypole stands in the playground of the Mountain School in 1929. A piano was hauled cross-country to the schoolhouse so that music could enliven the pageantry. Like in other farming communities across America, May Day in Lake County offered its residents another opportunity to come together in celebration of their common, rural American culture. For students whose families had recently immigrated, these celebrations—whether seen as indoctrination or cultural integration—initiated them into their new communities.

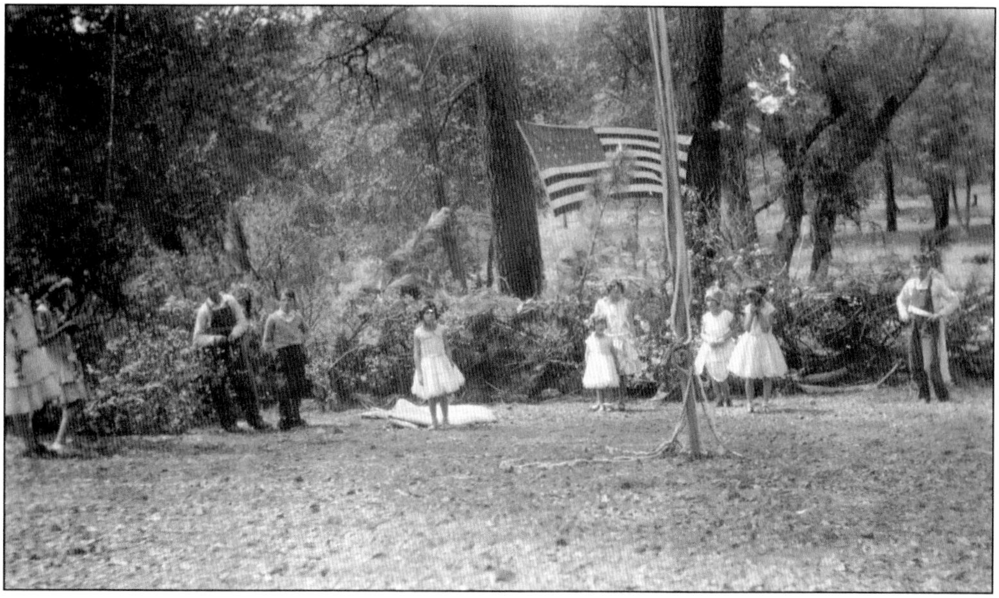

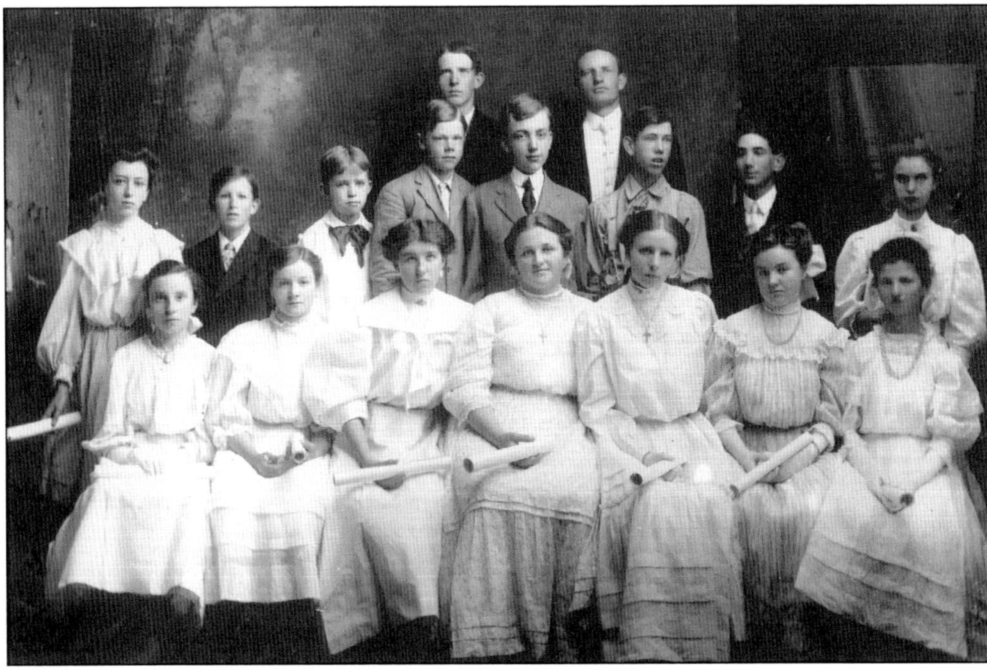

Pictured here is the eighth-grade graduating class of Lakeport Grammar School in 1907. Just six years earlier, this would have been the end of education for some of these students. By 1907, however, Clear Lake Union High School was in full swing and these students were on their way to a secondary education.

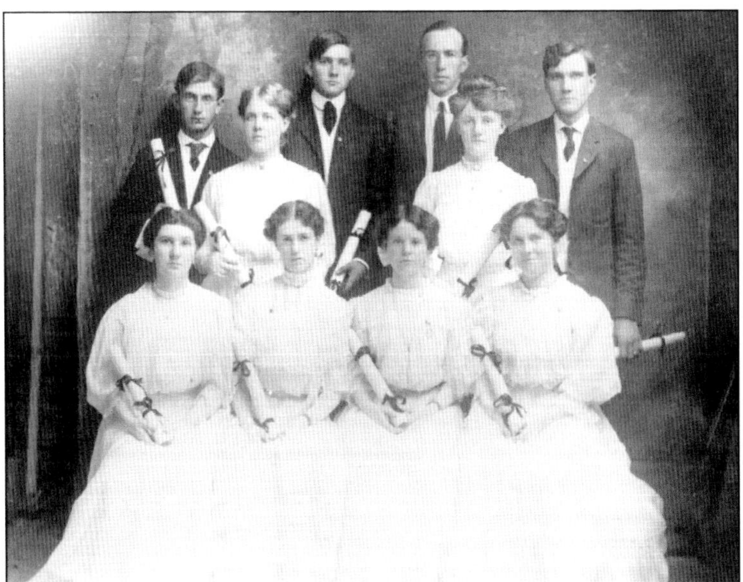

That same year, one of the first classes to have attended all four years and then graduated from the Clear Lake Union High School also posed for photographs, one of which is shown here. From later yearbooks, it is known that some of these students continued on to attend college, some became teachers themselves, and still others moved into the business world.

Seven

Lake County Schools
A History of Segregation

California has a mystique about it that forces blinders on people when questions of race and prejudice arise. There is a notion that these evils were a thing for the South, or at least the East Coast. The reality, when one but scratches the surface of the historical record, proves these notions naive at best and purposefully forgetful at worst.

Lake County was largely settled by immigrants from Missouri, who made the trek across the plains, over the Sierra Nevada, and through the central valley to the Clear Lake basin in the 1850s. Along with their faith, families, and furniture came their preexisting prejudices. Whereas segregation in the American South largely affected African Americans, in Lake County, there never existed a significant enough population of African Americans to force the issue. Throughout the 19th century, California law allowed segregated schools for nonwhites only when there were enough to create their own school district. The only such groups in Lake County were the indigenous Pomo, Miwok, Wintun, and Wappo tribes.

By the end of the 1850s, several groups of pioneers had laid claim to prime farming and logging land, completely ignoring the Native tribes, whose own claims went back thousands of years. This same racially charged indifference towards the Native tribes persisted decades after in the segregated education system practiced in Lake County.

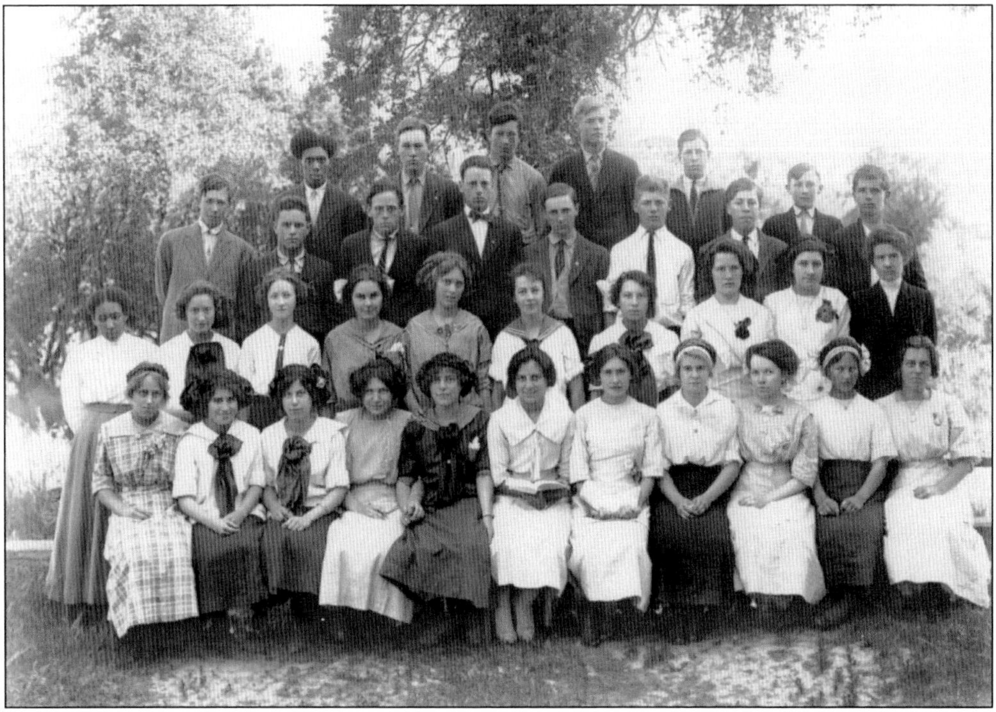

The reports sent to the state by the county superintendent of common schools throughout the 19th and early 20th century indicate a near complete absence of African American children in Lake County. Pictured above are the two Knox children, who attended Clear Lake Union High School in the mid-1910s. Even though African Americans were taught in the same schools as white children in Lake County, it does not mean that they did not suffer prejudice, as shown in the below picture, which was taken at the Rincon School. A young African American student stands at far left, separated from the rest of his classmates. On the back of the photograph, he is simply identified as "darkie."

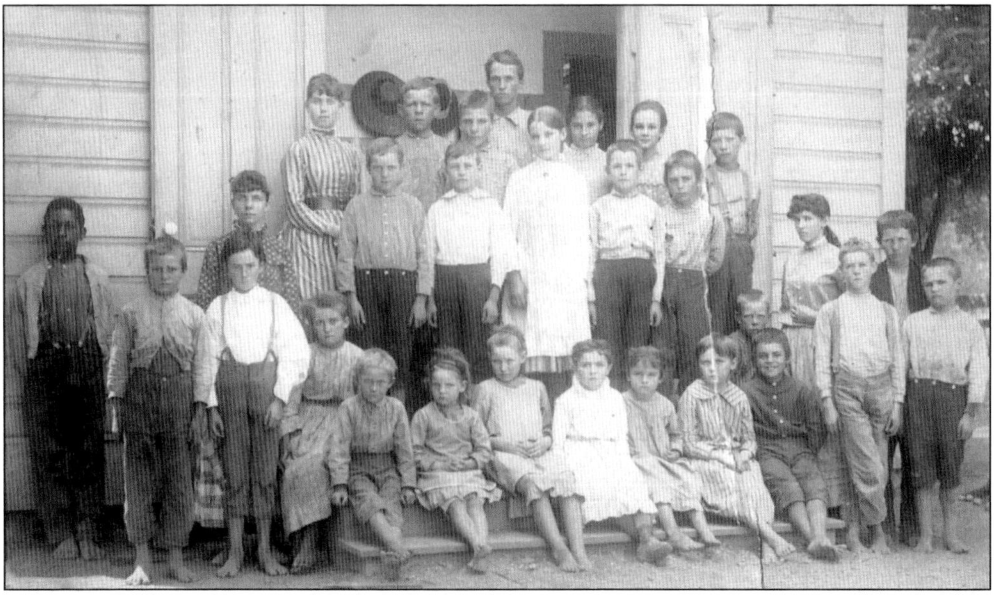

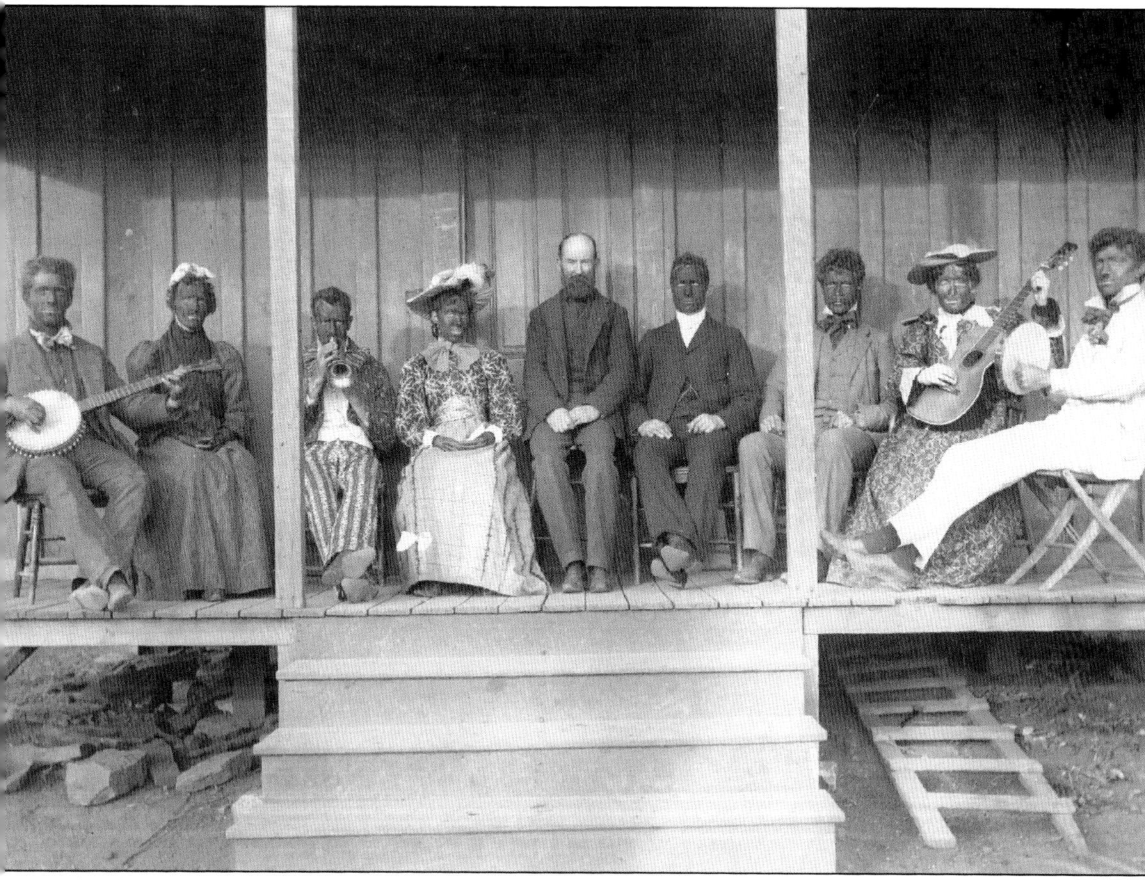

Like the Knox family, other African American families who moved to Lake County often settled in one of the urban centers like Lakeport. For instance, the only three African American children enrolled in public school in the county in 1876–1877 attended schools in Lakeport and Kelseyville (then known as Uncle Sam). The same trend persisted in 1879–1880 and 1899–1900. For generations, there were rumors of an enclave of the Ku Klux Klan located in rural southern Lake County. When rumors spread that the Stuparich Resort near Middletown had been sold to an African American social organization in 1928, the resort mysteriously burned to the ground. Even into the 1990s, some people believed this to have been the work of the Klan. Pictured here are the musicians of the all-white Negro Minstrel Band, posing on the porch of the Oat Hill Schoolhouse in the late 1880s. Although never segregated, some Lake County schools would have proved difficult for African American children to attend.

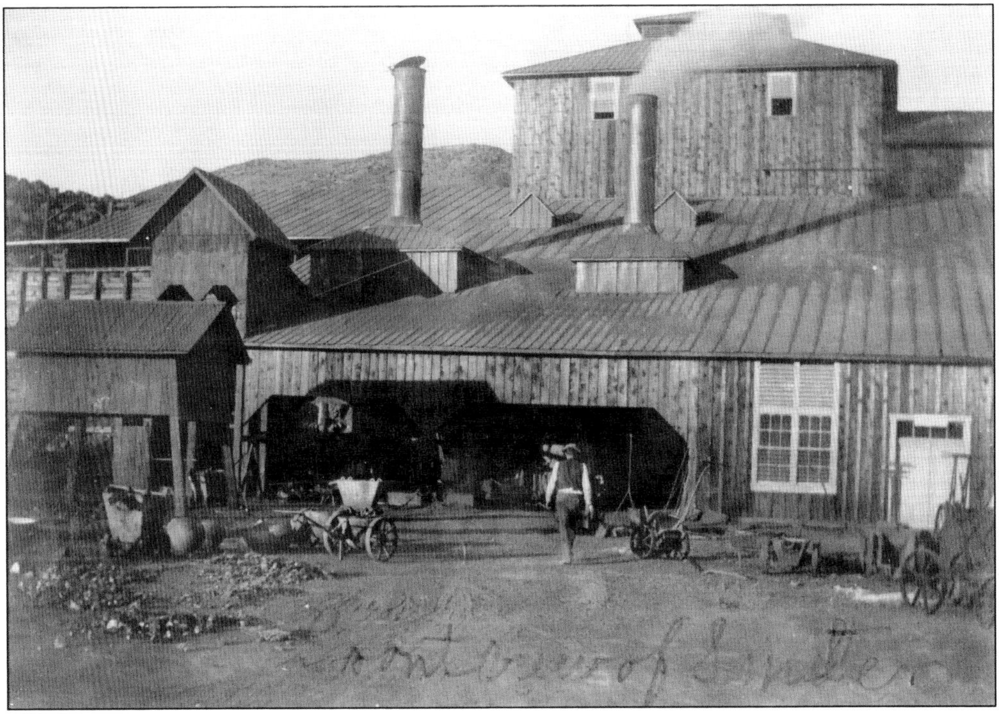

Starting in the late 1860s and continuing throughout the 19th century, a relatively significant population of Chinese worked as laborers and miners in Lake County. This was primarily centered on the Great Western Mine, which employed upwards of several hundred Chinese workers at any one time. The smelter of the Great Western is pictured above, and the road to the mine is pictured below. The fact that many of these Chinese laborers were unmarried men might help to explain why even the census records indicate nearly no Chinese children living in Lake County. At any rate, given the vicious anti-Chinese bent in California at the time, it is unlikely that even if there had been children, they would have been tolerated in Lake County's white schools.

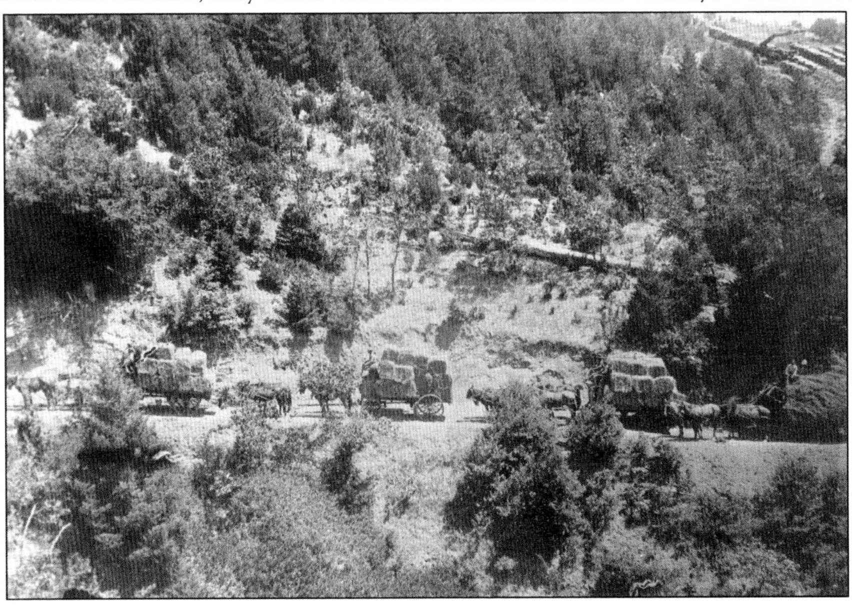

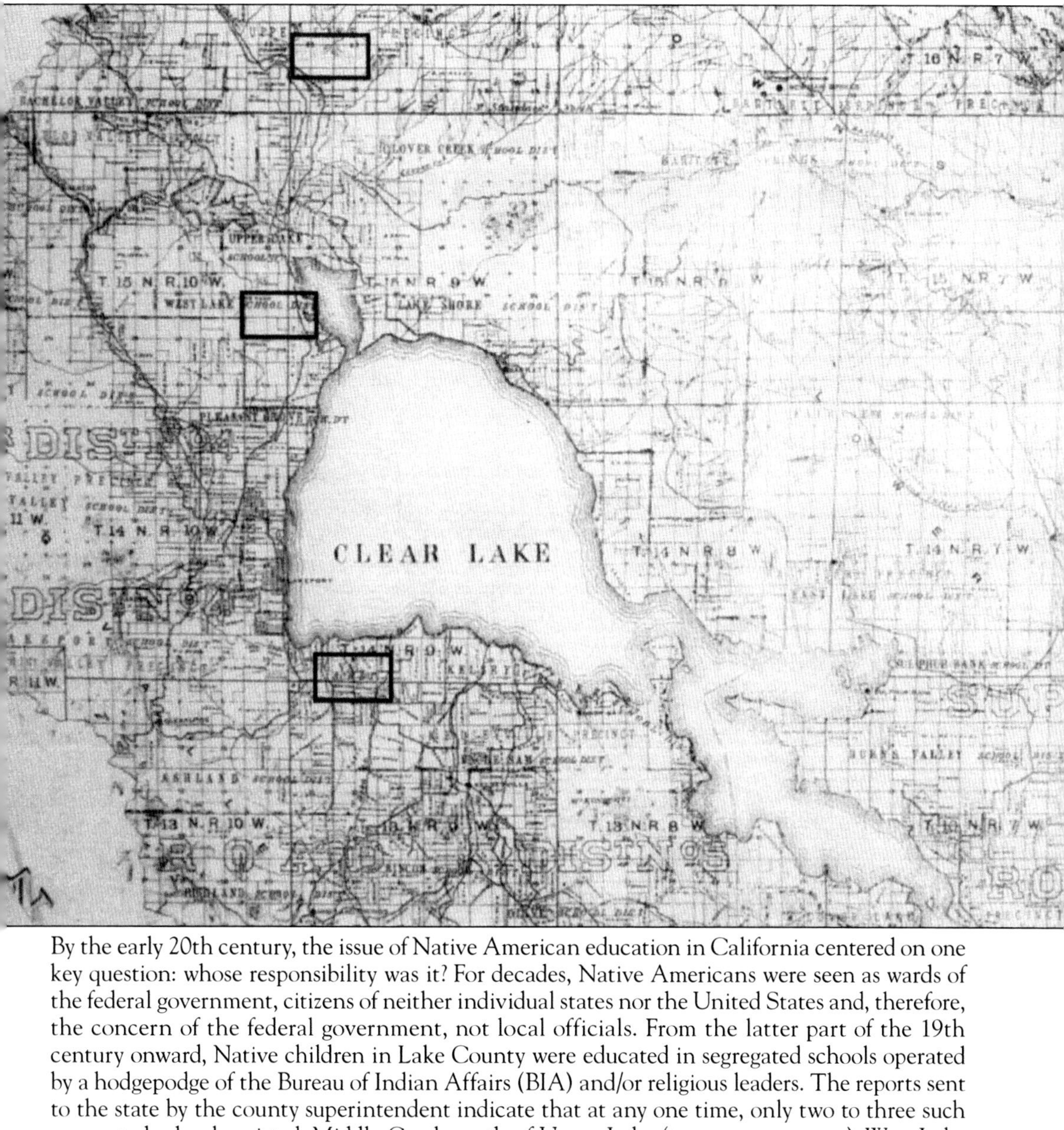

By the early 20th century, the issue of Native American education in California centered on one key question: whose responsibility was it? For decades, Native Americans were seen as wards of the federal government, citizens of neither individual states nor the United States and, therefore, the concern of the federal government, not local officials. From the latter part of the 19th century onward, Native children in Lake County were educated in segregated schools operated by a hodgepodge of the Bureau of Indian Affairs (BIA) and/or religious leaders. The reports sent to the state by the county superintendent indicate that at any one time, only two to three such segregated schools existed: Middle Creek north of Upper Lake (top square on map), West Lake north of Lakeport (middle square on map), and Big Valley north of Kelseyville (bottom square on map). Stories still told within families also suggest that many young children were sent to one of several BIA-operated boarding schools in the state.

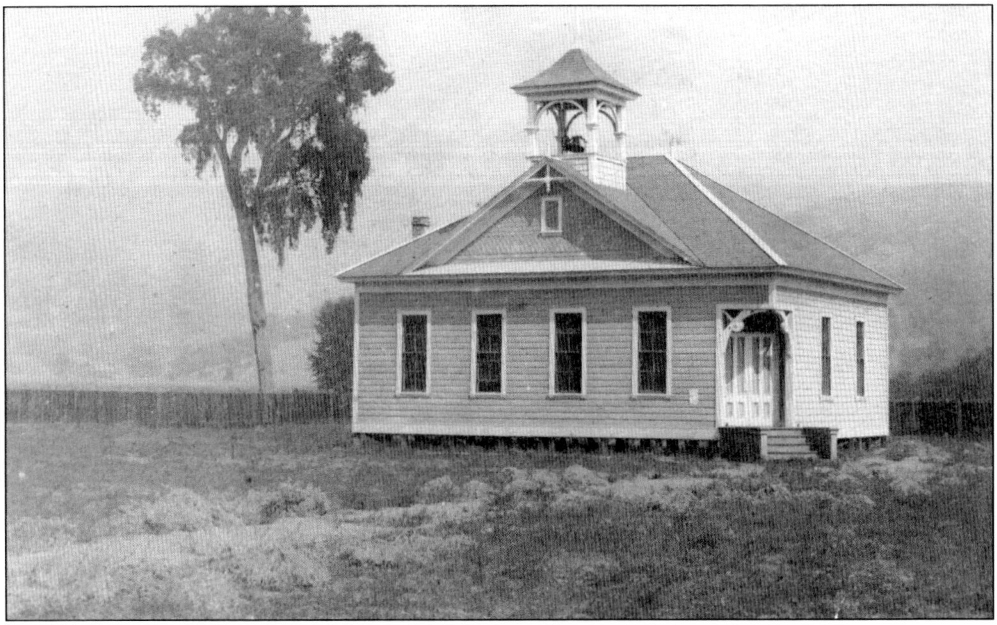

With their children being inadequately educated in a BIA-operated school since the 1910s, the parents of the Upper Lake tribe pushed for integration by suing the Middle Creek School District in 1923. Taking the middle ground, the judge ruled that the district (rather than the federal BIA) either had to build a separate school or integrate the students into the preexisting one. The district allowed the students to attend the white school, but they were taught in a separate room by a different teacher (schoolhouse pictured above). This remained the situation until 1925–1926, when the Middle Creek School District was dissolved and integrated into the Upper Lake Union District, Native and white children alike. Pictured below is the entry into the county court records of the lawsuit. (Below, photograph by author.)

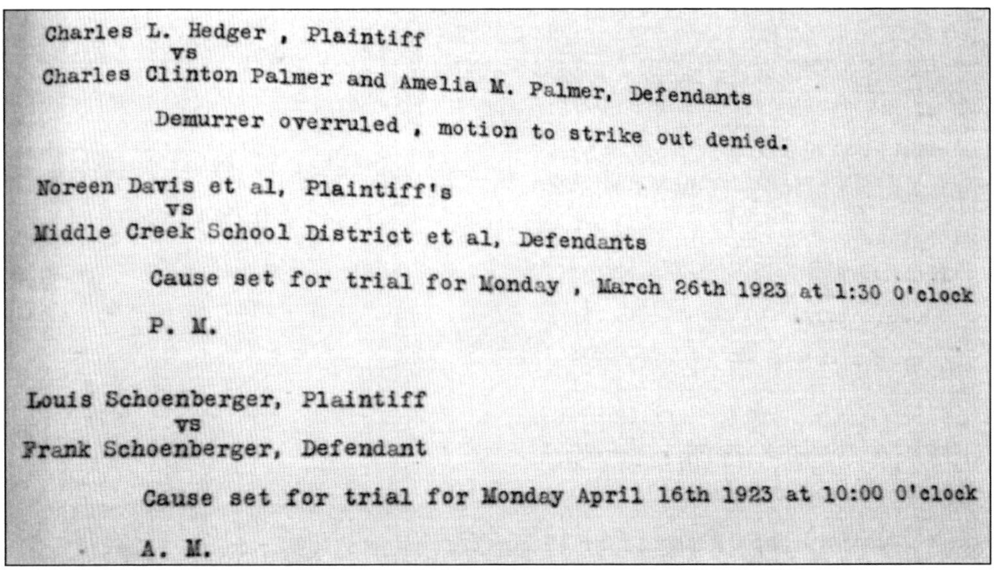

Charles L. Hedger , Plaintiff
vs
Charles Clinton Palmer and Amelia M. Palmer, Defendants

Demurrer overruled , motion to strike out denied.

Noreen Davis et al, Plaintiff's
vs
Middle Creek School District et al, Defendants

Cause set for trial for Monday , March 26th 1923 at 1:30 O'clock P. M.

Louis Schoenberger, Plaintiff
vs
Frank Schoenberger, Defendant

Cause set for trial for Monday April 16th 1923 at 10:00 O'clock A. M.

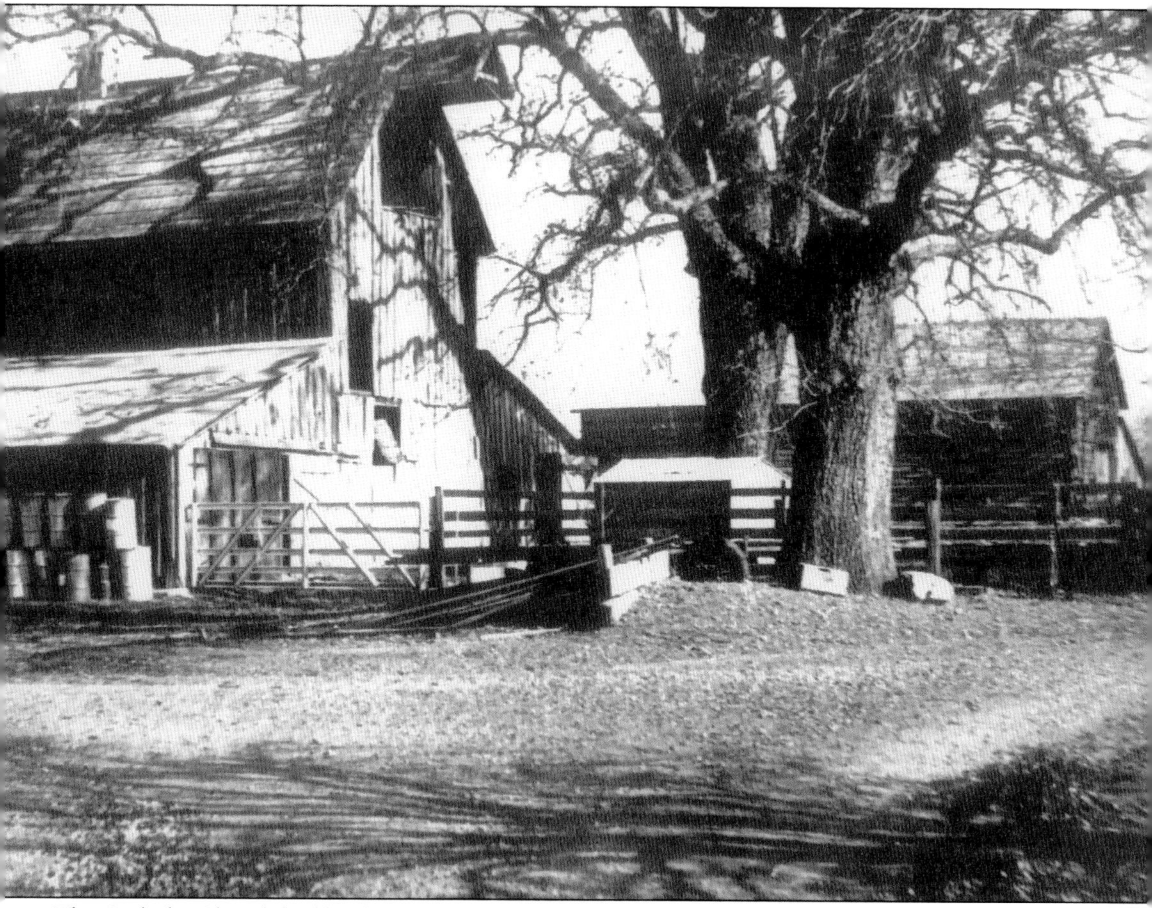

The Catholic Church had haphazardly operated St. Turibius Mission in Big Valley since the 1870s to serve the community of Pomo in that area. Rather than the federal government, the priests took it upon themselves to educate these Pomo children. Conditions, like at the BIA schools, were deplorable. The school and barn of the mission are pictured here. By the early 1920s, the Kelseyville Union School District started financially supporting a separate school when the mission largely ceased to exist. At the heart of segregation lay the racially charged biases towards Indians. According to the *Kelseyville Sun* in February 1923, "It has been generally understood that the objections to attendance of Indian children at the schools of the county . . . have not been racial, but more particularly from a sanitary point of view." Put plainly, Indians were considered dirty, and parents did not want their white children to get infected. Kelseyville finally integrated Native children into white schools in 1930–1931. The last segregated school in Lake County was the West Lake Indian School, which ceased operations in 1934.

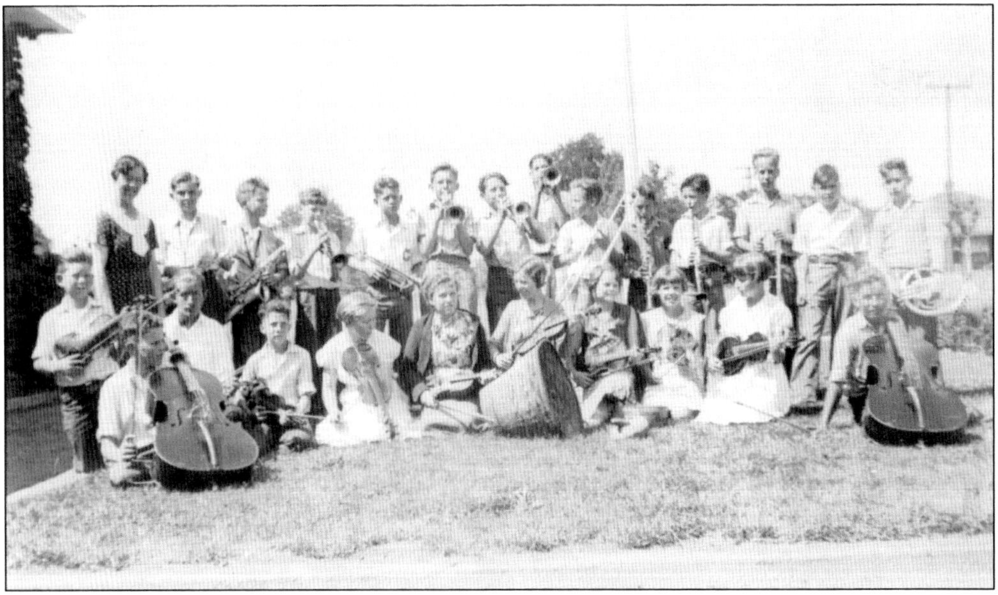

While at once wanting to keep Native American children at arm's length, during the first half of the 20th century, the white community in Lake County also embraced what it perceived as the romantic and noble culture of the Pomo. Pictured here is the all-white cast of the school play *Kabatin* in 1937 in Kelseyville. The name *Kabatin* is one of the names given to Clear Lake by the Pomo and was put to verse by the white R.S. Rodman: "When the Red Men first here came / They asked the Spirit for a name / Came the answer from within / Call these waters Kabatin." Even after the students were integrated, prejudice did not end overnight, and the challenges the first generation of integrated Native students faced can only be imagined.

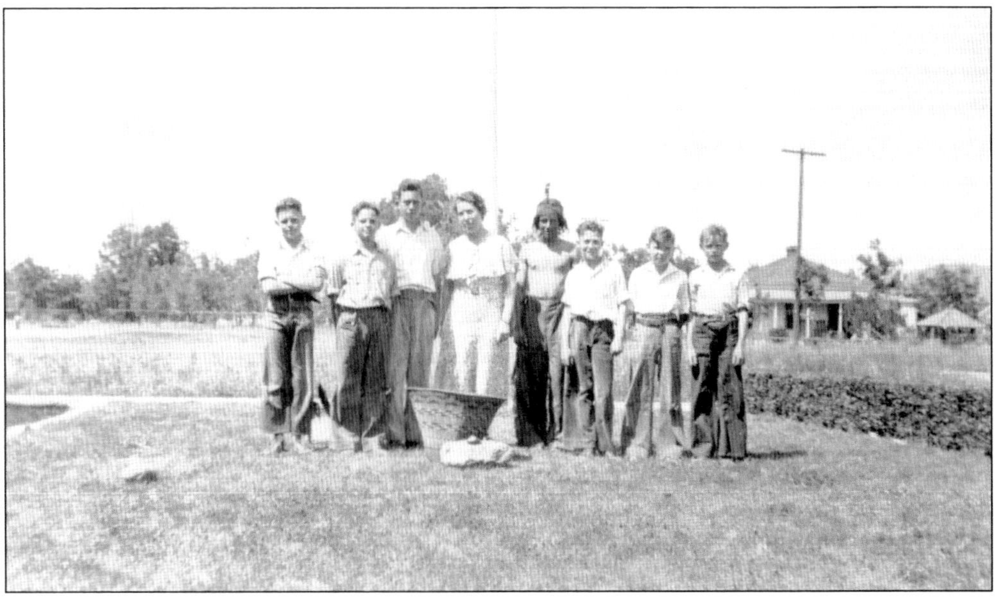

Eight

Lake County Schoolhouses
A History of Ruin and Renovation

The image of the "Little Red Schoolhouse" is now an icon of American culture. It does not matter that very few schools in rural America were ever painted red; in Lake County, schools were lead white, if they were painted at all. But the truth behind the color of the building and the stories associated with the schools themselves does not change the validity of the memories of those who attended and taught in them. Reminiscing at the ends of their lives, old-timers in Lake County could not finish a story without first relating one or two anecdotes about their time as students in county schoolhouses.

As the 20th century progressed and more one-room schools closed their doors in Lake County, former students looked back on their time in those cramped rooms with varying levels of nostalgia. For someone who found fault in the current school system, the myth of the one-room schoolhouse served as an exemplar of better education. For another person who longed for a perceived past when communities stuck together, the one-room schoolhouse became a symbol of a better time. For yet another person, that same one-room schoolhouse instead stood as an icon of exclusion and prejudice. The importance of the rural school in Lake County lay in the eyes of the beholder.

This diversity of opinion was reflected in the various fates of one-room schools in Lake County. The buildings themselves were among the first to be flagged for preservation during the 1960s and 1970s, when historic preservation swept the nation. Local historical groups and individual property owners recorded those schoolhouses still standing, their locations, and any stories that onetime students could recall. Despite such attention, on the whole, these buildings succumbed to thrifty landowners who reused them for other purposes, winter storms that ravaged their unprotected roofs, and the occasional wildfire that devoured all traces of a building. Only a few survive to this day.

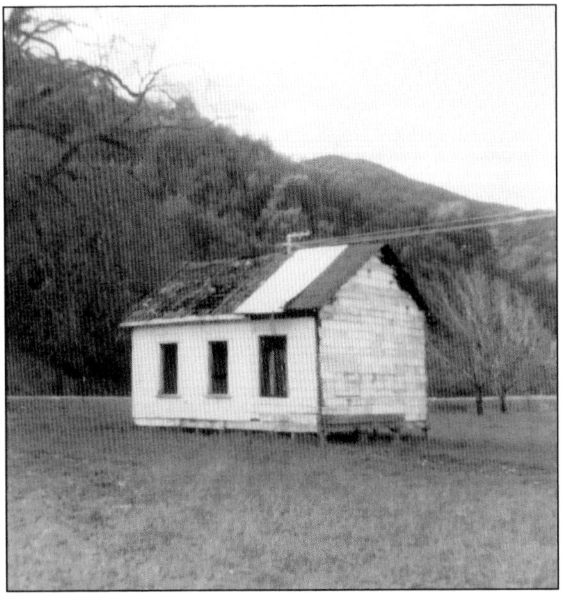

When a school district lapsed for the last time in the early 20th century, the schoolhouses themselves were either scrapped for wood or, as was more often the case, sold to a nearby landowner. The minutes of the Lake County Board of Supervisors are riddled with instances of these transactions. If the schoolhouse was of simple design, it could easily be used as a shed, barn, or extra living quarters. Pictured here is the abandoned Glen Eden Schoolhouse, which was still standing in the 1970s. A brass marker was installed at the site of the schoolhouse in 1972, identifying it to all passersby as an important historical remnant of Lake County's past. The marker was stolen, and the schoolhouse has since disappeared.

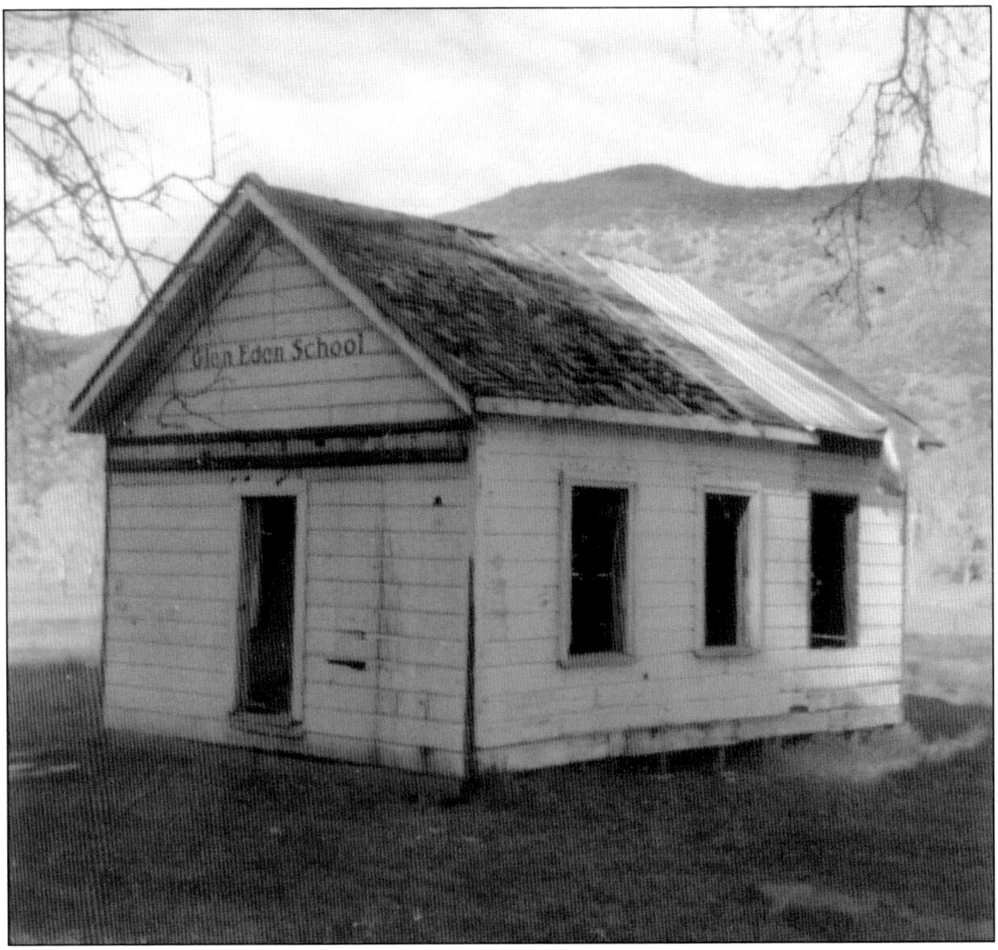

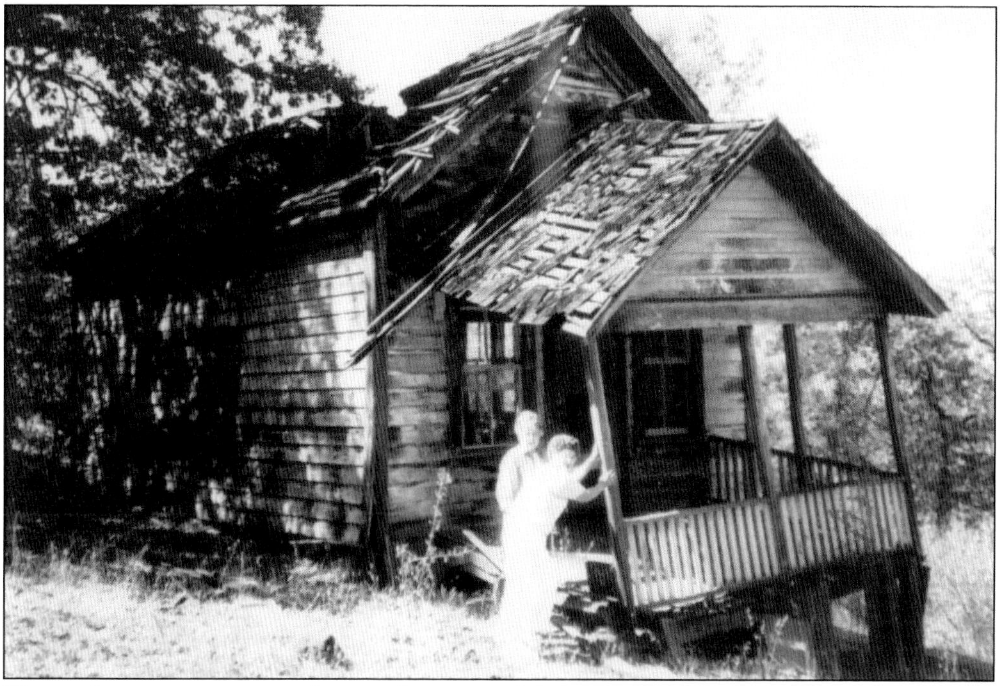

The push to preserve, or at the very least record, Lake County's historical schoolhouses was initiated by Henry Mauldin, the county's first official historian and a longtime resident. The placing of the brass marker at the Glen Eden schoolhouse was part of that attempt. When he was writing a brief history of school districts in Lake County in 1977, Mauldin traveled around the county to record the condition of those schools still standing. Pictured here are the remains of the Spruce Grove Schoolhouse and outbuildings, which had been moved a short distance from their original location by the landowner. With a leaky roof, a historic building has very little chance of surviving, and like the Glen Eden Schoolhouse, the Spruce Grove Schoolhouse succumbed to Mother Nature.

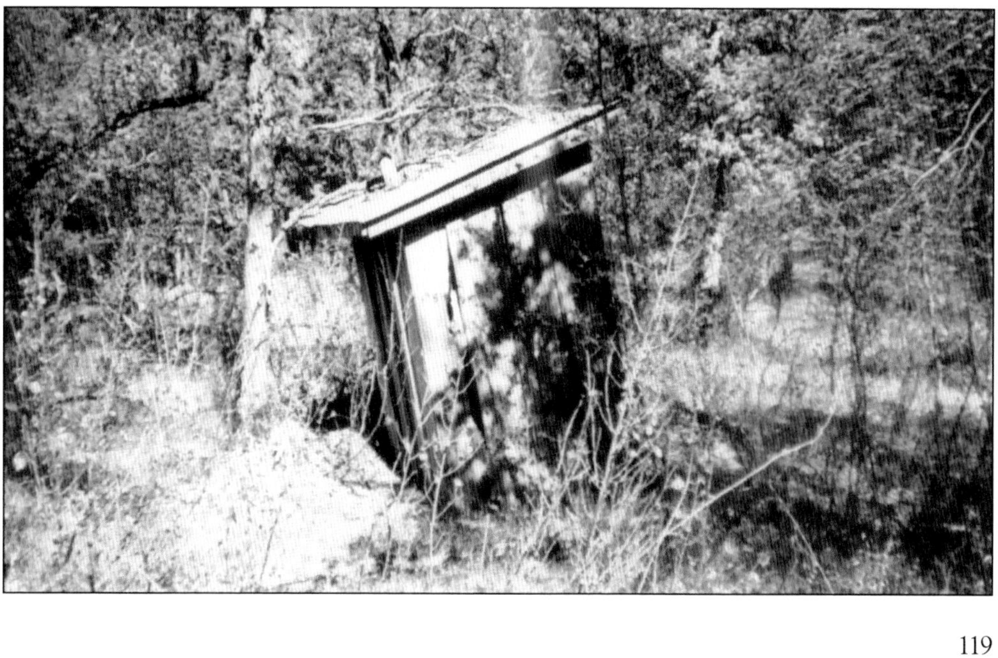

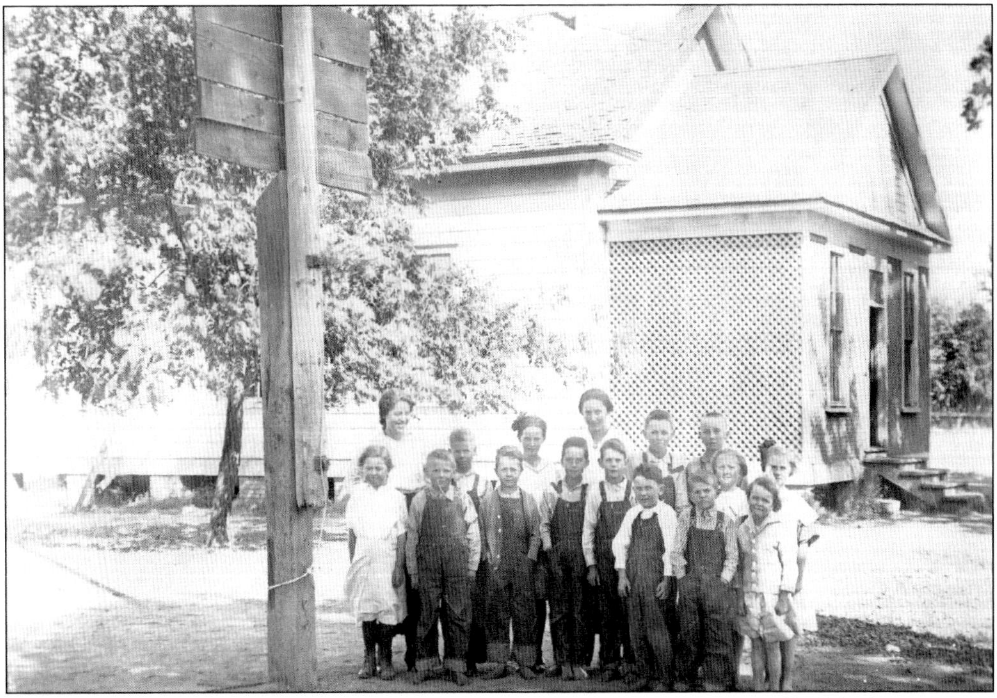

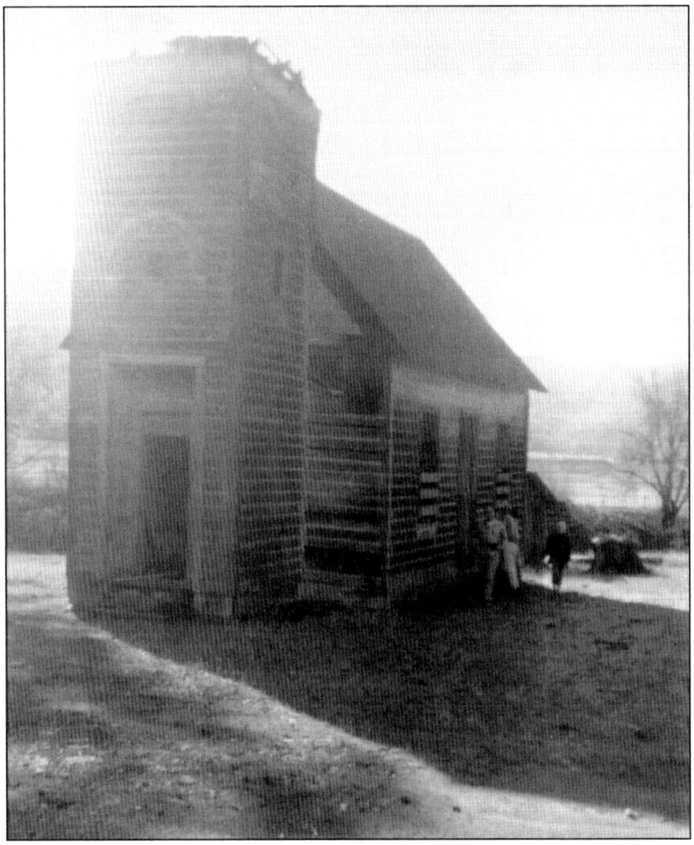

Not all of the historic schoolhouses in Lake County were left to rot by the property owners. In fact, several of them became houses. The Big Valley Schoolhouse (pictured above) remained on the property of the farmer in good repair for years. In addition to reuse, other landowners recognized the historical importance of the buildings now empty on their property. In the early 1990s, the owner of the property on which the last Long Valley Schoolhouse (pictured at left) stood began making plans to conserve the schoolhouse, although nothing ever came to fruition, and a fire eventually destroyed the building once and for all.

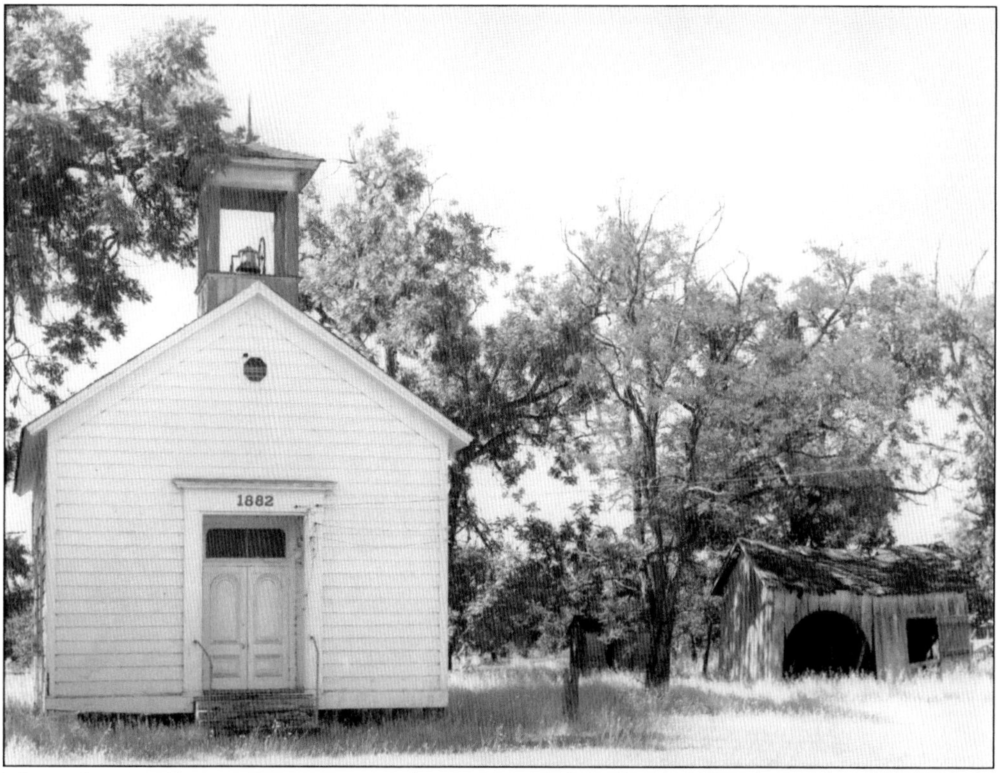

The only schoolhouse that remains today as it was left at the time of the district lapsing is the Kelsey Creek Schoolhouse near Kelseyville (pictured above). In the 1940s, an attempt was made to move the schoolhouse, but a group of citizens who wanted the building to stay where it was banded together and had the attempt stopped before it got off the ground. Over the years, people have ensured that it stayed standing by fixing the roof and keeping the grounds cleared. The Cobb Valley Schoolhouse (pictured below), which did not stop operating as a school until the 1970s, is now the clubhouse for a local chapter of the Lions Club.

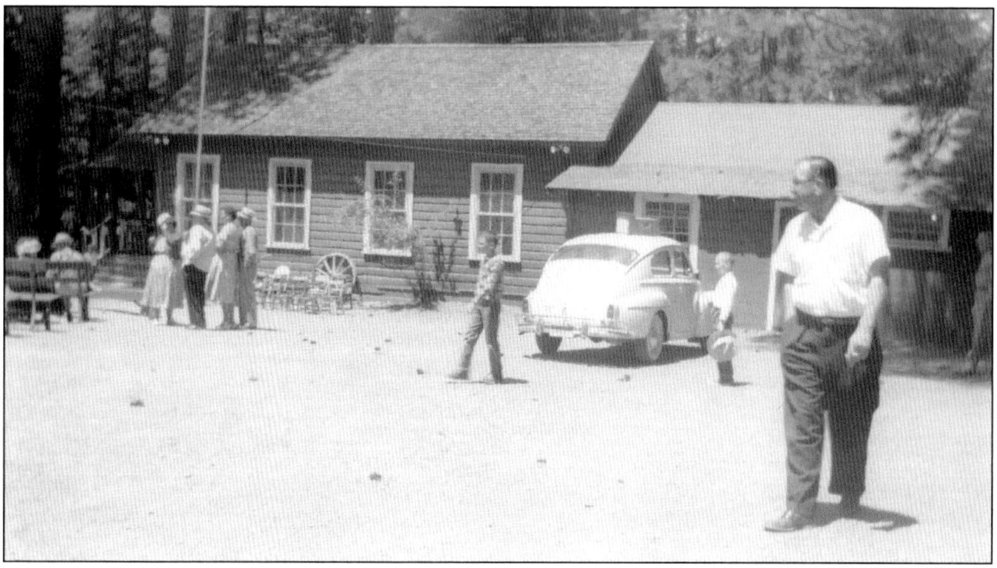

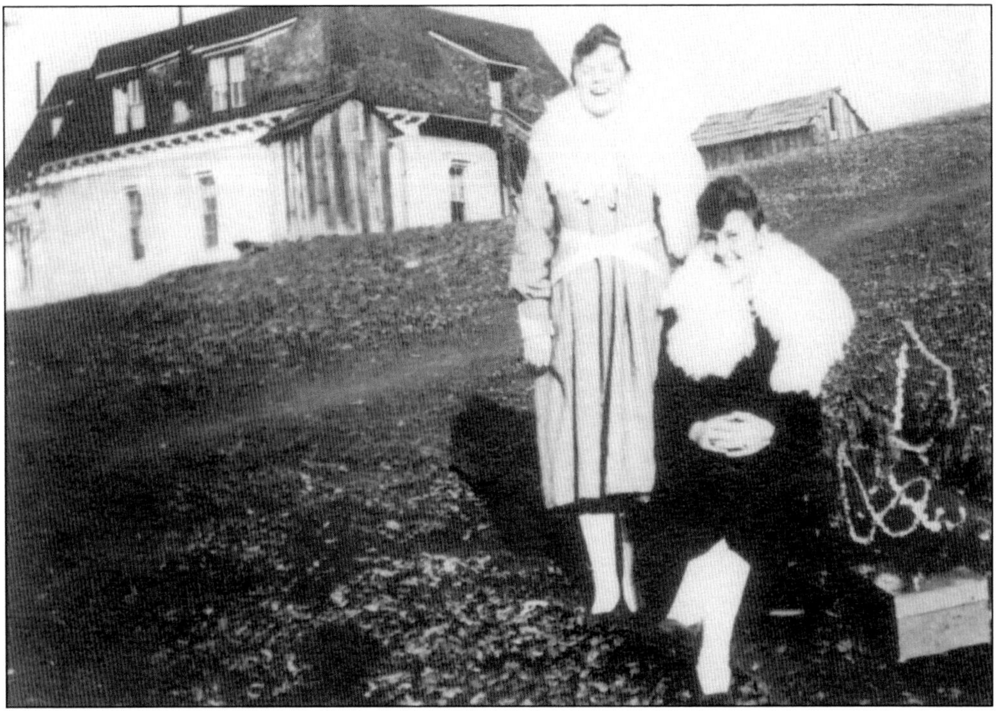

The Lower Lake Schoolhouse has the most unique post-school history of all the schools in Lake County. The building itself remained an important landmark in the town of Lower Lake. Pictured above, two young women (possibly former students) pose in front of the school. After ceasing to operate as a school in 1935, the building was sold and became a Masonic lodge. For the next 30 years, the Masons held brunches downstairs and their formal meetings upstairs. The school remained a lodge until the 1960s, when it was traded back to the county for another piece of property. The school remained largely vacant for some time. In the 1980s, it was briefly used to hold church services, which is when the picture below was taken.

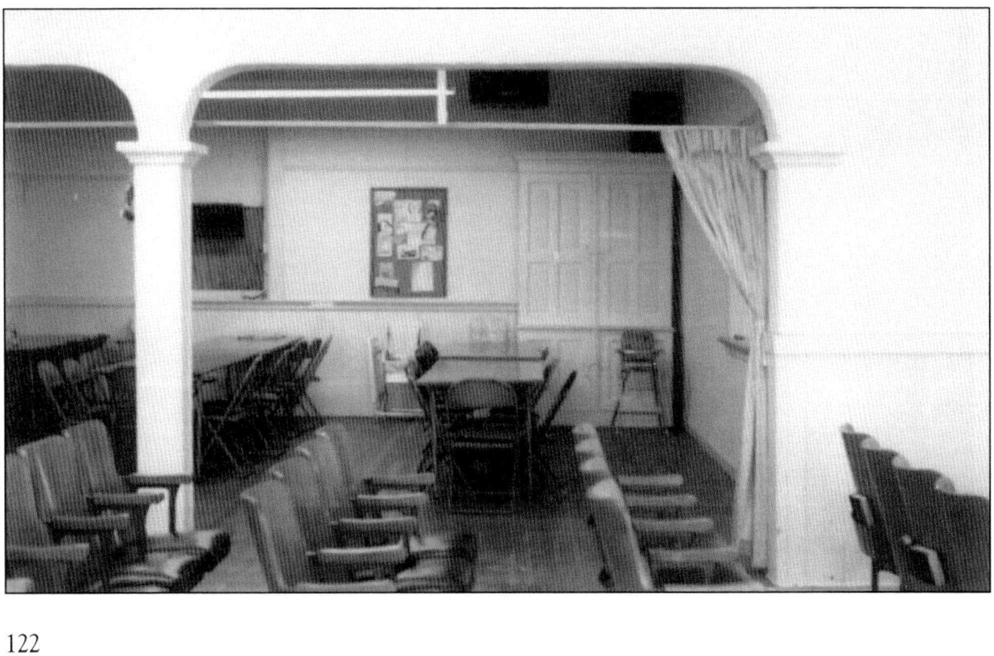

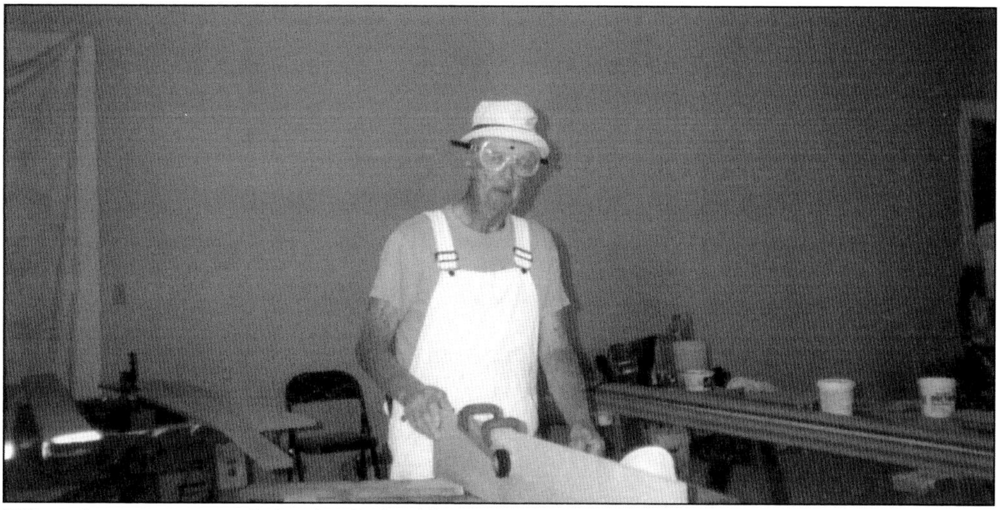

When the county intended to let the building be used by the local fire department for a controlled burning exercise in 1986, a group of concerned citizens formed the Lower Lake Historical School Preservation Committee (LLHSPC) to raise funds to renovate the school instead. After convincing the county that its mission was worthy, the LLHSPC raised enough money to begin renovations in the early 1990s. Pictured above is John Weaver, one of the founders of the LLHSPC. Below, each individual wood plank was removed from the auditorium upstairs to install new insulation and sheetrock. After this difficult task was accomplished, each board was meticulously put back in place.

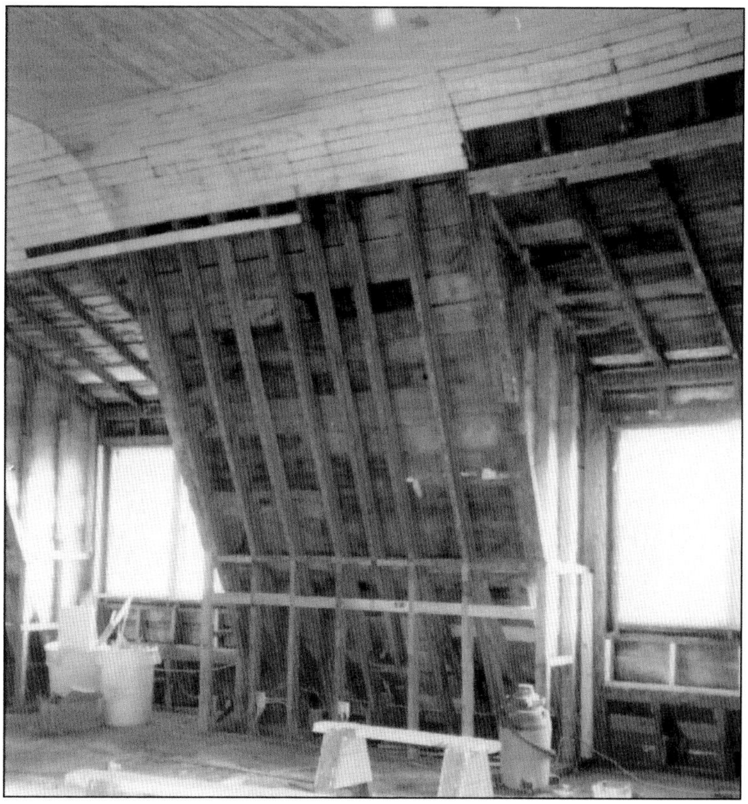

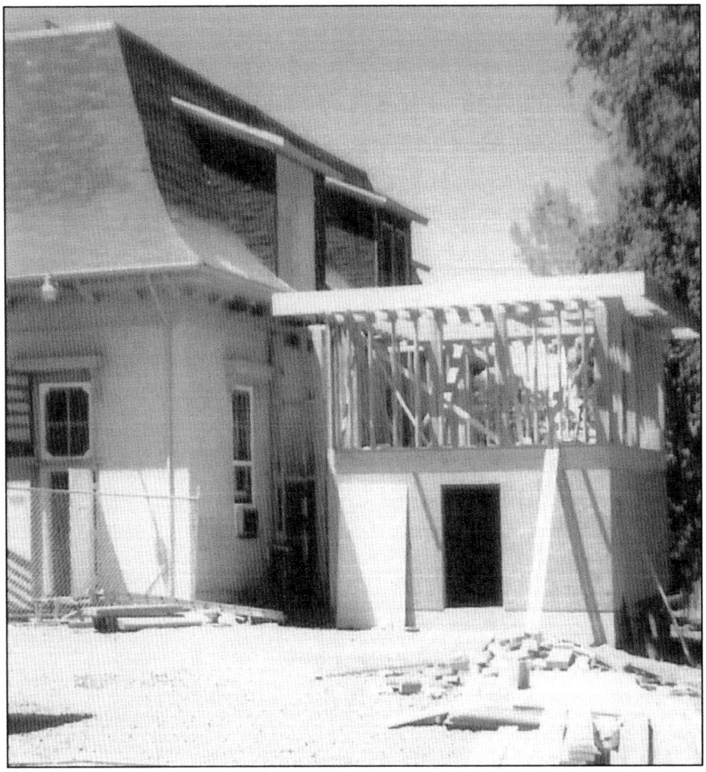

On October 21, 1993, a formal ceremony dedicated the building as the Lower Lake Historic Schoolhouse Museum, just one year after work had begun. By 1994, the second floor was renovated, and plans were put in place to make the auditorium ready once more for community events. Later, an addition to the building was made, which provided a storage room for the museum and restrooms for the auditorium (left). In 2006, plans were begun to replace the 1906 truncated bell tower with a replica of the original (below). This project was completed in 2007 with much fanfare.

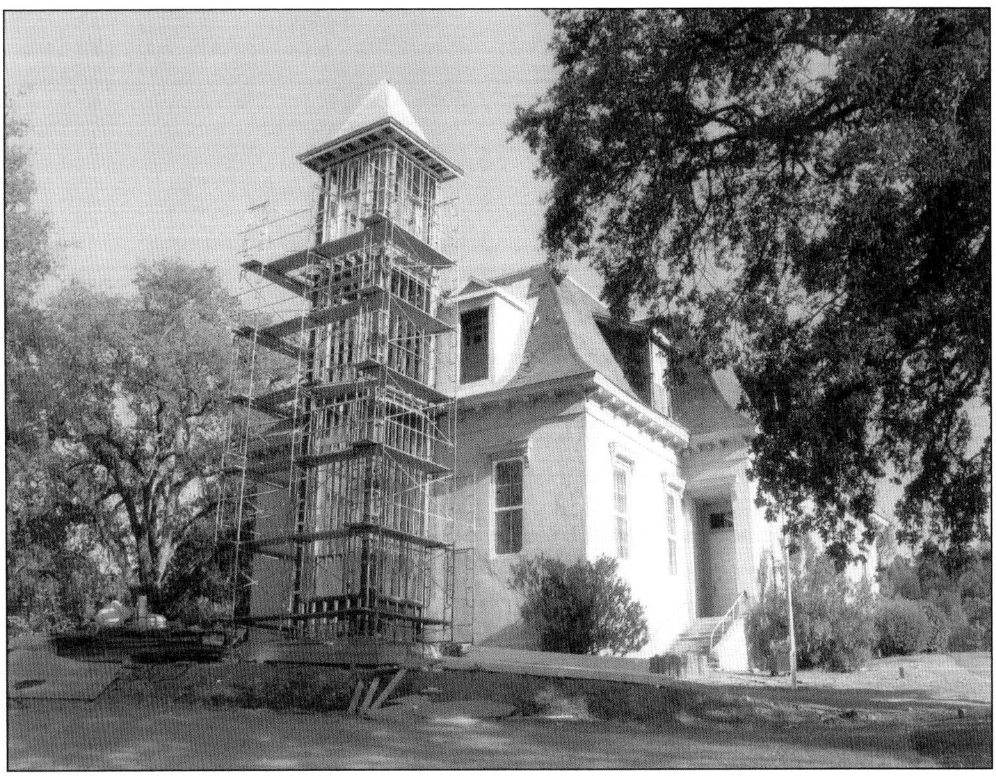

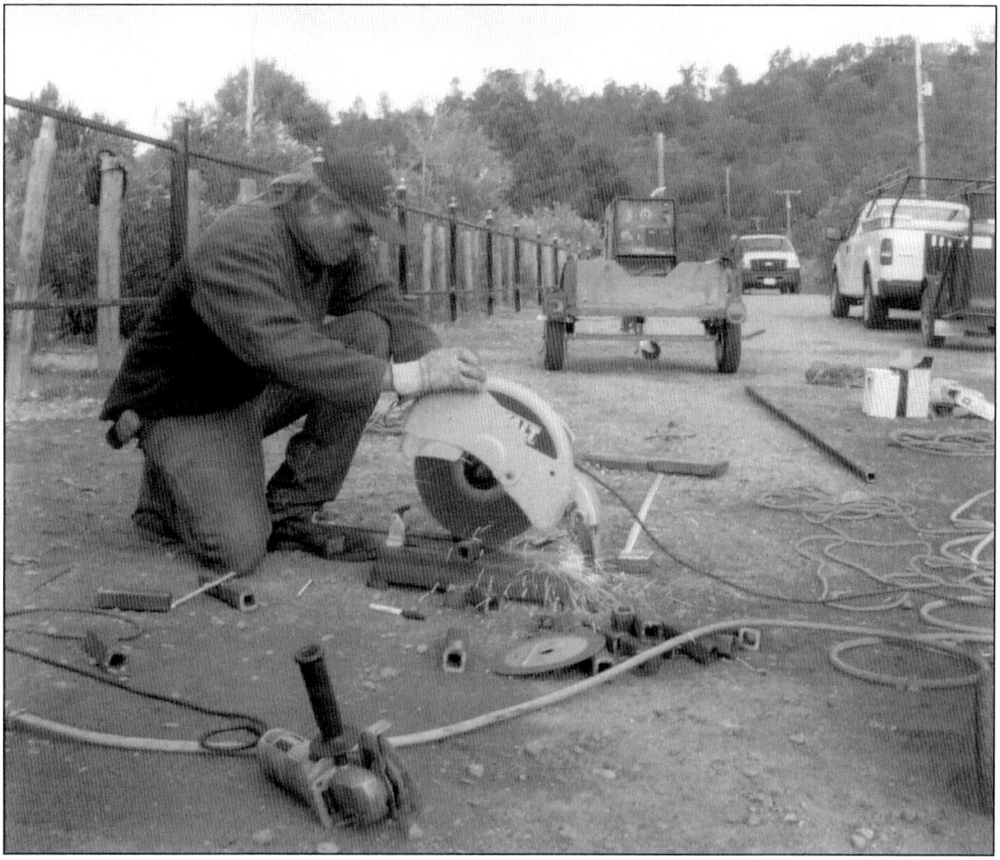

The building itself was not the only concern of the LLHSPC, which wanted the grounds to be landscaped to reflect the renewed importance of the structure to the community of Lower Lake. Additional landscape projects included the installation of a wrought iron fence around the property and a parking lot for visitors. As recently as 2015, the wood floors in the two large classrooms were restored to protect them from further wear from the thousands of people who visit the museum each year. School groups from around the county visit the museum to learn about the history of the area and get a feel for what it was like to go to school in early Lake County. The auditorium upstairs is regularly the venue for theatrical productions and a meeting space for community organizations—exactly as it had been used for decades when it was still a schoolhouse.

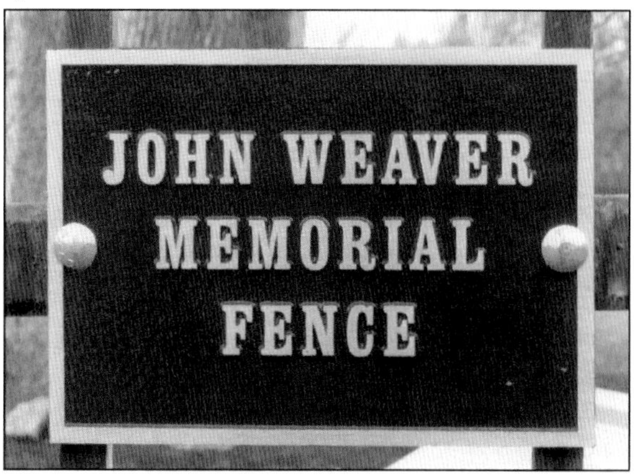

Bibliography

California Superintendent of Public Instruction. *Biennial Reports, 1860/61–1929/30*. Sacramento: State Printing Office.

Carpenter, Aurelius O. and Percy H. Millberry. *History of Mendocino and Lake Counties, California, with Biographical Sketches*. Los Angeles: Historic Record Co., 1914.

Gulliford, Andrew. *America's Country Schools*. Third Edition. Niwot: University Press of Colorado, 1996.

Hamilton, J.M. et al. *Lake County, California: Behold the Land Which was Hid of Old in the West*. Lower Lake, CA: Clear Lake Press, Lower Lake, 1888.

Lake County Board of Supervisors Minutes, 1867–1934. Books 1–9. Office of the Board of Supervisors, Lake County, California.

Mauldin, Henry. *A History of Lake County Schools*. Unpublished Report to Lake County Office of Education, 1977.

Palmer, Lyman L. *History of Napa and Lake County, California*. San Francisco: Slocum, Bowen & Company, 1881.

Swett, John. *Public Education in California: Its Origin and Development, with Personal Reminiscences of Half a Century*. New York: American Book Company, 1911.

Urban, Wayne J. and Jennings L. Wagoner Jr. *American Education: A History*. Fifth edition. New York: Routledge, 2014.

US Census Bureau. Fourteenth Census of the United States, 1920. Washington, DC: US Government Printing Office, 1923

———. Ninth Census of the United States, 1870. Washington, DC: US Government Printing Office, 1873.

———. Tenth Census of the United States, 1880. Washington, DC: US Government Printing Office, 1883.

———. Thirteenth Census of the United States, 1910. Washington, DC: US Government Printing Office, 1913.

———. Twelfth Census of the United States, 1900. Washington, DC: US Government Printing Office, 1903.

Weiler, Kathleen. *Country Schoolwomen: Teaching in Rural California 1850–1950*. Stanford, CA: Stanford University Press, 1998.

Wollenberg, Charles M. *All Deliberate Speed: Segregation and Exclusion in California Schools, 1855–1975*. Berkeley: University of California Press, 1978.

Zimmerman, Jonathan. *Small Wonder: The Little Red Schoolhouse in History and Memory*. New Haven, CT: Yale University Press, 2009.

Index of School Photographs